occupying

architecture

The term 'architect' is enshrined in law but 'architecture' has no legal protection. To counter this contradiction, architects resist two intrusions: one into the body of *their* profession, and the other into the body of *their* architecture. The former occurs when the work of an 'illegal' architect is recognised as architecture; the latter when the user occupies architecture. To repel these incursions many architects falsely maintain that architecture is merely a physical phenomenon with specific materials and dimensions – a building, but not any building: *their* building unoccupied. This book illustrates that architecture is not just a building: it is the relation between an object and its occupant.

There are two occupations of architecture: the activities of the architect and the actions of the user. The architect and the user both produce architecture – the former by design, the latter by use. But the terms 'architect' and 'user' are not mutually exclusive: they exist within each other. Just as the architect is a user as well as a creator, the user can be an (illegal) architect, occupying and making architecture through both use and design.

Occupying Architecture has three key aims: to investigate the relations between the architect and the user, to redefine the relations between the architect and architecture, and to challenge the separation of the architect from the user by a re-working of the terms themselves.

Beginning with the architect, the book proceeds to explore models for architectural practice that actively engage the issue of use, and concludes with an examination of the user. The authors draw on illustrations and examples from London, Las Vegas, Barcelona and elsewhere to discuss how and why architectural production and discourse ignores the user. The apparent contradictions between the 'producer' and the 'product' of architecture are highlighted before the activities of the architect and the actions of the user are explored.

Occupying Architecture focuses on the importance of the user in architecture, emphasising the cross-currents between design, theory and use, and the need for a wider cross-cultural approach to architecture. Proposing a complete re-working of the relations between design and experience to transform the practices of the architect, the authors call for the development of architecture within an expanded cultural and social practice. Architecture can be made of anything and by anyone.

Jonathan Hill is an architect, and a Lecturer in Architecture at The Bartlett School of Architecture, University College London. His work has been published and exhibited internationally; most recently 'The Death of the Architect' has been exhibited at the Bartlett in London and Haus der Architektur in Graz, Austria.

Cover illustration:

Jonathan Hill, *Exterior, The Institute of Illegal Architects*, 1996.

Model, Bradley Starkey. Photograph, Edward Woodman.

occupying
architecture

BETWEEN

THE ARCHITECT

AND THE

USER

Edited by

Jonathan Hill

London and New York

First published 1998
by Routledge
11 New Fetter Lane, London EC4P 4EE

Simultaneously published in the USA and Canada
by Routledge
29 West 35th Street, New York, NY 10001

Typeset in News Gothic by Keystroke, Jacaranda Lodge, Wolverhampton
Printed and bound in Great Britain by Bath Press Ltd

British Library Cataloguing in Publication Data
A catalogue record for this book is available from the British Library
Library of Congress Cataloguing in Publication Data
Occupying architecture : between the architect and the user / edited by
    Jonathan Hill.
        p.   cm.
    Includes index.
    1. Architecture—Human factors. 2. Architectural design.
    I. Hill, Jonathan, 1958–
    NA2542.4.I56 1998
    720′.108—dc21   97–34765
                                                           CIP

ISBN 0–415–16815–5 (hbk)
ISBN 0–415–16816–3 (pbk)

CONTENTS

contents

ILLUSTRATIONS

CONTRIBUTORS

Iain Borden is Sub-Dean of the Faculty of the Built Environment and Lecturer in Architectural History at the Bartlett, University College London, and a founding member of Strangely Familiar. He is co-editor of *Architecture and the Sites of History: Interpretations of Buildings and Cities*, 1995, *Strangely Familiar: Narratives of Architecture in the City*, 1996, *The Unknown City: Contesting Architecture and Social Space*, 1998, *Gender, Culture, Architecture: An Interdisciplinary Introduction*, 1998, *Framed: Architecture on Film, Film on Architecture*, 1998, and *InterSections: Architectural History and Critical Theory*, 1998.

Mark Cousins is the Director of General Studies at the Architectural Association. Educated at Oxford and the Warburg Institute, he was previously Head of Sociology at Thames Polytechnic. He has published widely on contemporary critical theory, including *Michel Foucault* with A. Hussain, and on the relation between psychoanalysis and the human sciences.

Paul Davies studied architecture at Bristol University and the Polytechnic of Central London. Presently he is Senior Lecturer at South Bank University and General Studies tutor at the Architectural Association. Writing about design for tourism has led him to lecture widely across Europe and the USA, usually about his favourite city, Las Vegas.

Fat is a cross disciplinary practice involved in the design and construction of architectural projects, research into art and architecture, the making of art, the design and organisation of exhibitions and events. The practice is made up of architects, artists, graphic designers and film makers and specialises in the curation of large scale urban art events. They are amongst the leading young practitioners in the fields of both architecture and fine art and have built widely in Britain and exhibited recently at the Venice Bienalle, the RIBA and the Architecture Foundation. Their work aims to blur the boundaries between architecture and fine art practice.

Ben Godber is a graduate of the Bartlett, University College London. He is presently working in architectural practice and pursuing research on London's sewers, sections of which were published in *The London Quarterly Literary Review* and *The Guardian*.

Jonathan Hill is an architect and graduate of the Architectural Association and the Bartlett, University College London, where he is a Lecturer, teaching history, theory and design. His work has been published and exhibited internationally. His most recent project, 'The Death of the Architect', has been exhibited at the Bartlett in London and Haus der Architektur in Graz, developed at Akademie Schloss Solitude in Stuttgart and published in *Architectural Design*, *The Architects' Journal*, *Building Design*, *HDA Dokumente zur Architektur* and *Quaderns*.

Lesley Naa Norle Lokko was born in Dundee, Scotland of Ghanaian–Scots parentage. She completed her primary and secondary school education in Ghana and studied languages and sociology in the UK and the United States. She received her BSc in Architecture at the Bartlett, University College London in 1992 and her Diploma at the same institution in 1995. Since then, she has been a faculty member of the Bartlett and the University of Greenwich. She has worked in practice with Elsie Owusu Architects, an all black women's practice in London and in Namibia and South Africa. She is the editor of the forthcoming anthology, *White Papers, Black Marks*, which looks at the relationship between race and architecture. Lesley is currently Assistant Professor at Iowa State University in the United States.

Muf Art and Architecture work as collaborative practice. The team have established an architectural notation which swells to absorb subject matter traditionally censored out of architecture. Currently Muf are the consultants to the London Boroughs of Hackney and Southwark implementing art and urban design projects which are embedded in the cultural and social fabric of the city. The team have taught since the late 1980s at the Architectural Association, the University of North London and Chelsea School of Art and Design, developing a body of theoretical work, which alongside built projects, has been published and exhibited internationally.

Jane Rendell is an architectural historian and designer. She is engaged in PhD research at Birkbeck College into gender and space in early nineteenth-century London. She is Senior Lecturer at Chelsea College of Art and Design. She is a founding member of the Strangely Familiar group and co-editor of *Strangely Familiar: Narratives of Architecture in the City*, 1996, *The Unknown City: Contesting Architecture and Social Space*, 1998, *Gender Culture Architecture: An Interdisciplinary Introduction*, 1998, and *Intersections*, a forthcoming book of essays on architectural history and critical theory.

Katerina Rüedi is Director of the School of Architecture at the University of Illinois at Chicago. She previously taught at Kingston University. With Duncan McCorquodale and Sarah Wigglesworth, Katerina was organiser of the *Desiring Practices* conference and exhibition at the RIBA and editor of the book of the same title.

Philip Tabor studied architecture at Cambridge, where his doctoral research was in computer-aided design, before becoming a partner in Edward Cullinan Architects. He is now Senior Lecturer at the Bartlett, UCL. Philip is also European editor of the *Journal of Architectural and Planning Research*, is on the editorial board of *Architectural Research Quarterly* and writes regularly for the *Architectural Review*.

Jeremy Till is a London based architect, teacher and writer. He has degrees in both philosophy and architecture and is presently Senior Lecturer at the Bartlett, University College London. As an architect, he collaborates with Sarah Wigglesworth Architects, including work on their widely published house/work project and a new building for the Siobhan Davies Dance Company. He has lectured worldwide, including as Visiting Professor at the Technical University, Vienna.

Carlos Villanueva Brandt was born in Venezuela and studied at the Architectural Association, where he teaches, running Diploma Unit 10 since 1986. Carlos has also been a Visiting Lecturer and Visiting Professor at the Royal College of Art. A founder member of Narrative Architecture Today (NATO), he has been in private (art and architecture) practice since 1984. He has published widely and exhibited work in Paris, Venice, Milan, Edinburgh, Boston, Tokyo and London. Carlos has produced architectural projects of varied sizes in locations ranging from Venezuela to Kazhakstan and built projects in London, Greece and Japan.

ACKNOWLEDGEMENTS

The idea of this book developed from my teaching activities at The Bartlett, University College London. Therefore, I particularly want to thank my teaching partners, Ganit Mayslits and Lesley Lokko, as well as the students who have contributed to the character of this book. Of the latter, I especially want to thank Carolyn Butterworth for her decision to lick the Barcelona Pavilion as it was one of those special moments when a student extended a project to the limits of its logic, confirming the highest hopes of her tutors, Ganit and myself. In addition, for their support and encouragement, I would like to thank Sarah Lloyd, Casey Mein, Valerie Rose, Eleanor Jackson and Sarah Amit at Routledge, Peter Cook, Adrian Forty, Christine Hawley and Duncan McCorquodale at The Bartlett, Xiaochun Ai at The Art Institute of Chicago and Roland Ritter at the Haus der Architektur Graz.

Jonathan Hill

introduction

Figure 1 *Joolz Pohl*, Clean Square, Dirt Square, *Place Georges Pompidou, 1993.*

One superior to the 'other'. No overlap. Nothing between them. The familiar opposition of contrasted but dependent terms that never meet. Even the slightest ambiguity subverts the hierarchy of prioritised term and diminished other.

1 H. Cixous, 'Sorties', in S. Sellers (ed.), *Hélène Cixous Reader*, London, Routledge, 1994, p. 41.

Bisexuality – that is to say the location within oneself of the presence of both sexes, evident and insistent in different ways according to the individual.[1]

Hélène Cixous

2 D. Haraway, *Simians, Cyborgs and Women*, London, Free Association Books, 1991, p. 150.

By the late twentieth century, our time, a mythic time, we are all chimeras, theorized and fabricated hybrids of machine and organism; in short we are cyborgs.[2]

Donna Haraway

In Haraway's scenario, we are cyborgs, a hybrid of technology and humanity. Whether attached to us physically, like the heart pacemaker, or perceptually, like the television, we are machine and human. Once we understand perspective, film or the net, the machine is in our minds even more than in our bodies. We cannot remove it, just as we cannot remove the technology of our human bodies: the heart, lungs, liver and brain.

3 For example, J. Baudrillard, 'The Ecstasy of Communication', in H. Foster (ed.), *Post-Modern Culture*, London, Pluto, 1985, pp. 126–36 and A. Perez-Gomez, *Architecture and the Crisis of Modern Science*, Cambridge, Mass., MIT Press, 1983.

Many of the arguments for the superficiality and emptiness of contemporary culture rely on the dominance of technology over humanity,[3] the flattening of thought

Jonathan Hill

to the empty abstraction of science. But if we are cyborgs, the machine is no longer negative, certainly no more or no less so than the human.

Haraway accepts the existence of the two terms, human and machine, but suggests that they are present in the same person, a cyborg. Her argument refers specifically to technology but it also offers a subtle revision of all dualisms. Rather than the hierarchical relations of binary oppositions, Haraway proposes a system of mutual dependencies.

In contemporary culture, the re-formulation of the subject and subject–object relations occurs at two levels, a cross-disciplinary one, such as Cixous on sexuality and Haraway on technology, and a disciplinary one, such as Roland Barthes on literature[4] and Dan Graham on art.[5]

The traditional art object in the gallery demands the physically distanced, passive contemplation of the viewer, for whom meaning is anchored to the artist. The reception of the artwork is isolated and internalised not collective and political. The viewer is absorbed and distanced at the same time. Whether successful or not, the repeated attacks on the autonomy of art have had a two fold agenda, first, to diminish the authority of the artist and the art institution and, second, to transfer some of that authority to the viewer. Consequently, in contemporary art, subject–object relations and the forms of perception particular to an activity are often the central focus of production as well as discourse.[6] The subject is recognised as an active, engaged participant, not a passive, empty vessel. Installation art is possibly the closest art form to architecture. Although neither a location inside or outside the gallery avoids the defining codes of the institution of art,[7] installation art constantly questions these boundaries, demanding a more critical and sensual relation between object and subject than the primarily visual one of the traditional artwork.[8]

It is highly noticeable that, while the authority of the 'author' and the activities of the 'reader' are discussed outside the architectural profession, they are absent inside the profession, which still maintains that the user[9] is a stable, centralised and passive subject, if of course he or she is acknowledged at all. Ironically, an architect's experience of architecture is more akin to the contemplation of the art object than the occupation of a building. Unfortunately, architects often choose to ignore this simple distinction. For architects, the classification of architecture as an art is a social and financial necessity. A plethora of cultural and social codes reinforce the superiority of art over the everyday, of contemplation over distraction. Architecture is, it appears, demeaned by its association with habit and the presence of the user is perceived as a direct threat to the authority of the architect.

4 R. Barthes, 'The Death of the Author', in *Image–Music–Text*, trans. S. Heath, London, Flamingo, 1977, pp. 142–8.

5 B. Willis (ed.), *Rock My Religion / Dan Graham*, Cambridge, Mass., MIT Press, 1993.

6 For example, the work of Hans Haacke or Jenny Holzer.

7 Peter Bürger distinguishes between the art institution, namely the gallery, and the institution of art, which includes all the codes, phenomena and objects that constitute the discipline. See P. Bürger, *Theory of the Avant-Garde*, trans. M. Shaw, Manchester, MUP, 1985, p. 25.

8 For example, Yves Klein's *Fire Wall* and *Fountain*, Museum Haus Lange, Krefeld, 1961.

9 The term 'user' is problematic because it can be coupled with pragmatism and rationality or drug addiction. However, it is a more appropriate term, for this book, than either the occupant, occupier or inhabitant because it also implies both positive action and the potential for misuse.

Jonathan Hill

Figure 2 *Bradley Starkey, White-hall, 1995.*

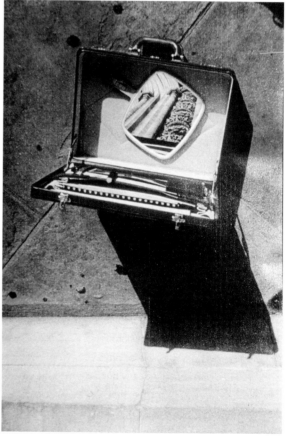

Figure 3 *Bradley Starkey, White-hall, 1995.*

Jonathan Hill

Habit is the ballast that chains the dog to his vomit.[10]

The dominant tendency fragments space and cuts it up into pieces. Specialisations divide space among them and act upon its truncated parts, setting up mental barriers and practico-social frontiers. Thus architects are assigned architectural space as their (private) property, economists come into possession of economic space, geographers get their own 'place in the sun', and so on.[11]

In architectural discourse, the experience of architecture is the experience of the architect, who lays claim to both the production and reception of architecture. The term 'architect' is enshrined in law. Now who is this designed to protect? Seemingly the architect as much as the user. Professionals protect their territories by deriding incursions from 'outside' as ignorant or mistaken, implying there is a truthful and correct interpretation of a fixed body of knowledge, to which they alone have access. For the purpose of economic and social self-protection, the architectural profession provides the products and practices of its members with an iconic status and cultural value, in order to suggest that only the work of architects deserves the title 'architecture'. Consequently, architects attempt to prevent two intrusions, one into the body of *their* profession, the other into the body of *their* architecture. The former occurs when the work of an 'illegal' architect is recognised as architecture. The latter occurs when the user occupies architecture. For the architect, the illegal architect and the user are analogous to dirt. They are matter out of place.[12]

the urge to make separations, between clean and dirty, ordered and disordered, 'us and them', that is to expel and abject, is encouraged in western cultures, creating feelings of anxiety because such separations can never be finally achieved.[13]

Unlike the law or medicine, architecture is not a strong, coherent discipline with internal self-validating codes that safely protect its members and exclude 'ignorant' outsiders. As Mark Cousins suggests in this book, architecture is a 'weak' discipline, not weak in a pejorative sense, but weak in contrast to a self-validating discipline. The weakness of the discipline of architecture is deeply threatening to the architectural profession. To repel the intrusions of the illegal architect and the user, architects assume that architecture is a physical phenomenon with specific materials and dimensions, a building but not any building, *their* building *unoccupied*. However, a more appropriate definition, and one that threatens the profession, is that architecture is not just a building. It is, primarily, a particular relation between a subject and an object, in which the former occupies the latter, which is not necessarily a building, but can be

10 S. Beckett, quoted in B. Massumi, *A User's Guide to Capitalism and Schizophrenia*, Cambridge, Mass., MIT Press, 1992, p. 47.

11 H. Lefebvre, *The Production of Space*, trans. D. Nicholson-Smith, Oxford, Blackwell, 1991, p. 89.

12 M. Douglas, *Purity and Danger*, London, Routledge, 1966, p. 2.

13 D. Sibley, *Geographies of Exclusion*, London, Routledge, 1995, p. 8.

Jonathan Hill

14 'Architecture has always represented the prototype of a work of art the reception of which is consummated by a collectivity in a state of distraction.' W. Benjamin, 'The Work of Art in the Age of Mechanical Reproduction', in H. Adrendt (ed.), *Illuminations*, trans. H. Zohn, New York, Schoken Books, 1968, p. 239.

15 S. Allen, 'Dazed and Confused', *Assemblage* 27, 1995, p. 48.

16 G. Deleuze and F. Guattari, *A Thousand Plateaus*, trans. B. Massumi, London, Athlone Press, 1988, p. 3.

17 In concentrating on the architect and user, it is not our aim to deny the role of others involved in the production of architecture, such as the client and builder, but simply to say that they are not the focus of this book.

a space, text, artwork or any other phenomenon that displays, or refers to, the subject–object relations particular to architecture.

Architecture is experienced in a state of distraction[14] but not a state of unawareness. It is a particular type of awareness that enables a person to perform, at the same time, a series of complex activities that move in and out of focus from a conscious to an unconscious level.[15] In architecture, habit, memory and experience are coupled with the sensual disembodiment of twentieth-century forms of communication to form a complex compound of spatial and temporal layers. Someone talks to you, caresses your back, while you listen to the phone, read the fax and peer out of the window. Architecture is experienced collectively and individually, each facet of a person reacting to a building and other people in distinct and maybe conflicting ways.

The two of us wrote Anti-Oedipus *together. Since each of us was several, there was already quite a crowd.*[16]

Occupying Architecture has three specific aims. First, to present a detailed investigation of the relations between the architect and the user, between design and experience.[17] The contributors discuss how, and why, architectural discourse and production ignores the user. More importantly, they focus on what is being ignored. How is architecture occupied and how is this different to the reception of other social and cultural phenomena? The second aim of the book is to redefine the relations between the architect and architecture. The denial of the user is compounded by an apparent contradiction between the 'producer' and the 'product' of architecture. The term 'architect' is enshrined in law. Fortunately, the word 'architecture' has no such legal protection. There are two related sides to this argument. Architects can transform their forms of authorship and production once they do not fear the creativity and unpredictability of use. Architecture is a far larger category than the work of architects, who are just one group of producers among many. The third aim of *Occupying Architecture* is to challenge the separation of the architect from the user by a re-working of the terms themselves. There are two occupations of architecture: the activities of the architect and the actions of the user. The architect and user both produce architecture, the former by design, the latter by use. As architecture is experienced, it is made by the user as much as the architect. Neither are the two terms mutually exclusive. They exist within each other. Just as the architect is also a user, the user can be an illegal architect.

Occupying Architecture starts with those chapters that focus mostly on the architect and ends with those that concentrate on the user. Texts in the centre of the book discuss the architect and user to an equal degree. However, its structure is circular as well as linear because, in the later chapters, the user is also an illegal architect.

The language used by architects and architectural historians has two obvious aims, to talk precisely about architecture and to exclude outsiders from the conversation. One of the purposes of this book is to dislocate architecture from the narrow confines of professionalism and to site it within an expanded social and cultural field. Another intention is to ensure that a wide audience is involved in the discussion. All these factors lead to an apparent contradiction that is both crucial and positive. The contributors are critical of the profession of architecture but work in schools of architecture that produce architects[18] because they realise that territory is power and work to change architecture from *within*.[19]

The chapters in *Occupying Architecture* are divided into three groups. The first, with texts by Mark Cousins and Katerina Rüedi, focuses on the formulation of the architect. The second, with chapters by Jeremy Till, Lesley Naa Norle Lokko, Fat, Carlos Villanueva Brandt, Muf and Jonathan Hill, re-assesses architectural practice in terms of the user. In the third group, with texts by Paul Davies, Ben Godber, Iain Borden, Philip Tabor and Jane Rendell, the user is the focus.

The first chapter is appropriately titled 'Building an Architect'. Beginning with an analysis of architectural education, Mark Cousins draws parallels between the present day and Vitruvius' woefully inadequate and fragmentary description of what an architect should know. Consequently, Cousins describes architecture as a 'weak' discipline, in which the boundary between inside and outside is confused. In contrast, the interior of a strong discipline is precise and visible, its boundaries equally certain; decisions are made only in reference to what is already inside the discipline. Cousins distinguishes a strong discipline, such as one of the natural sciences, which is purely concerned with objects, from other types of knowledge, such as architecture, in which the effect of an object on a subject is of fundamental importance. In conclusion he addresses the issue of architectural desire and suggests that architecture cannot be taught unless 'we think about what teaching is in terms other than simply the transmission of forms of knowledge, and until we open it to the question of the unconscious'.

In the second chapter, Katerina Rüedi discusses the acquisition of (an architect's) commodity value through the accumulation of cultural capital, a term devised by Pierre Bourdieu. As Rüedi states, 'cultural capital refers to the cultural status a particular person acquires, which has a direct or indirect bearing on their financial and political status'. Cultural capital is affected by gender, class and race, which can help or hinder its acquisition. Rüedi discusses the contract between state and profession through which the latter acquires embodied cultural capital indivisible from its 'owner'. Therefore, it is appropriate that the author of the text is also its subject. Rüedi's chapter

18 All the contributors teach, or have taught, in London. The particular conditions within the city have fuelled the development of an architectural culture which is unique and ripe for dissemination. In London, as in any big city, influences are local, national and international. In addition, the city easily absorbs both North American and European cultural influences. The contributors have pursued the majority of their architectural careers in a period of political and economic fluctuation and their discussion of architecture is never purely academic.

19 The avant-gardist denial of the institution of architecture collapsed on the myth of anti-institutionalism and resulted in either the withering away of radical practice or the incorporation of its de-politicised husk within an expanded institution. In excepting the original principles of avant-gardism, so many of the radical projects produced in recent years have concentrated on the minor. However, marginality is insufficient, and the role of the outsider is self-fulfilling. Institutions should be formed or re-formed not destroyed. They are essential to the advocacy of change.

Jonathan Hill

consists of her Curriculum Vitae, heavily footnoted and analysed. As Rüedi states, 'A Curriculum Vitae is the principal means of setting out commodity value.' It is therefore with subtle irony that the author expands her cultural value while questioning it. Rüedi details the moments of conscious and unconscious acquisition of (her) cultural capital in education and the profession. The Curriculum Vitae, and the profession of the architect, are shown to be the opposite of innocent and unbiased.

Lesley Naa Norle Lokko, Jeremy Till, Fat, Carlos Villanueva Brandt, Muf and Jonathan Hill question the familiar practices of the architect. Each offers a model for architectural practice in which the significance of the user is recognised and valued. The latter four focus on specific architectural projects while the former speak conceptually about practice.

It is well known that western discourse is founded on a series of dualisms, each with a 'superior' and 'inferior' component that define each other. The occupant of architecture, the inferior to the superior architect, is notably absent from architectural discourse. If the user appears at all it is obliquely in the discussion of other issues, which have themselves, until recently, been marginalised. A number of the suppressed terms, such as sexuality, are now acknowledged in architectural theory if not practice. Possibly the most notable absence of all is the issue of race, both of the architect and the user. But as Lesley Naa Norle Lokko states, 'despite protestations to the contrary, race has been architecture's subject matter all the time'. Lokko shows how the assumption that the makers and users of architecture have historically been positioned as white has affected its production and occupation. 'ResponseAbility', the title of her chapter, is appropriated from a quote by the writer Toni Morrison, from whom Lokko gains a number of insights that shift our understanding of architecture and race. In particular, Lokko states that the activities of making are not all that distinct from those of using and posits blackness as a seductive and creative architectural force.

The supporters of community architecture claim that in conventional architectural production the architect is a distant but biased expert wilfully ignorant of the desires and needs of the user. However, Jeremy Till argues that community architecture produces the disenfranchisement of both the architect and the user. As Gillian Rose states 'it is the architect who is demoted; the people do not accede to power'.[20] For Till, community architecture is founded on a series of dualisms, in which neither the prioritised or marginalised term nor the oppositional structure itself is questioned. Although the hierarchy of terms may differ, Till recognises that the architect and the user are equally reliant on the same dialectical structure. Consequently, he proposes that they relinquish the mythical purity of their communities and enter into a critical but constructive collaboration that is invigorated by the dreams and practicalities of both activities.

20 G. Rose, 'Athens and Jerusalem: A Tale of Three Cities', *Social and Legal Studies*, 1994, vol. 3, p. 336.

'Contaminating Contemplation' is written collaboratively by Fat (Fashion Architecture Taste), a group of artists and architects. The structure of the group is reflected in the text, in which the central narrative is interspersed by commentaries from individual members. In architectural discourse, the building is usually discussed as a work of art, an object of contemplation not use. This is the source of intense internal conflict for both the architect and the user because each is asked to perform a series of contradictory roles. The fusing of art and life is a familiar theme and, ironically, despite its anti-elitist credentials, it is usually located firmly in the realm of 'high' culture. Somewhat unfashionably, Fat argue that the esoteric and by definition exclusive debates about art and architecture do have a continuing relevance and value. The text describes a number of art strategies which take the 'viewer' beyond the act of contemplation into engagement with the terms that define 'high' culture. The chapter concludes with a discussion of parallel strategies within architecture, a discipline which presents a very different set of parameters.

Carlos Villanueva Brandt counters the traditional claim of the architect to be an objective depersonalised expert. Instead, he proposes a model for architectural production in which the architect is an active agent in direct action on a physical site at a range of scales, from the local to the strategic. In Brandt's concept of 'space within', the architect literally *uses* the site. Informed by the strategies of the Situationist International, 'space within' consists not only of constructed situations, but of precise combinations of situations and/or architectural structures. This process recognises the complexity of a site, the interweaving within it of the social, political and material and offers a direct but fluid relationship between the architect and the user.

The chapter by Muf Art and Architecture refers to a single project, the proposed improvements to the urban environment of Southwark Street in London. As Muf state: 'On first view the street seems neither more or less deserving of improvement than any other.' Southwark Street is immediately to the south of the former Bankside Power Station, the site of the new Tate Gallery of Modern Art, the principal collection of contemporary art in Britain. As a consequence of the arrival of the Tate, the previously rather ignored but centrally located Southwark Street is changing. But, as is often the case, the desires and needs of the existing residents, the Tate, and the new inhabitants it attracts only occasionally overlap. Muf's strategy is to establish a 'shared ground', which is both physical, social and a model for architectural practice. In contrast to the didactic design methodology of the stereotypical architect, Muf instigate a two-way process of negotiation and proposition which makes space for other forms of knowledge to influence the design process, for example the expertise that comes with living somewhere for twenty years or the experiences of a child. The chapter is divided into two elements. The first is a transcript of statements by local residents in '100

Jonathan Hill

Desires for Southwark Street', a video produced by the authors. The second is a record of Muf's activities and proposals.

Jonathan Hill begins with an analysis of the means by which the architectural profession excludes the user from architectural discourse and design, with particular emphasis given to the photograph. Artistic and literary production has to a considerable extent been transformed by the revisions in artist–viewer and author–reader relations but the influence of these ideas on architectural production is slight. In part, this is because they are consciously marginalised as they represent a threat to the authority of the architect. Consequently, the architectural profession employs a restrictive visual and verbal language that 'empties' architecture of its inhabitants. The text suggests that the traditional language of architectural production and discourse can be dismantled and recast to include, and respond to, the signs of inhabitation. In conclusion the chapter suggests that the 'illegal' architect, who questions and subverts the conventions, codes and 'laws' of architecture, is most likely to value the user and transform architectural practice.

In the chapters by Paul Davies, Ben Godber, Iain Borden, Philip Tabor and Jane Rendell, the professional architect is a marginal figure. The user is given prominence and is also the 'architect'.

Paul Davies identifies the architectural profession's fixation with necessity and its denial of luxury and waste as a fundamental error that ignores the mechanisms of desire and pleasure essential to use. Las Vegas is discussed as a landscape of luxury, in which the thronging crowds are not hapless exploited victims but active participants at the gaming tables and in the risky stratagems for growth in the western capitalist economy. In Las Vegas, the user is, at least in part, an energetic, discriminating consumer with purchasing power and a proactive role in the development of architecture. However, both the user and architect are usurped by a more powerful figure. The user is, after all, massaged by Las Vegas into losing money while the architect is sidelined by a means of procurement antithetical to the profession. In combining creative finance, design and use, Davies identifies the focus of Las Vegas in a new 'medici', the moneyed patron personified in the figure of Steve Wynn of Mirage Resorts. At Shadow Creek, the private golf course constructed as a sumptuous oasis in the barren Mojave desert as a site for the negotiation of power, Wynn is the principal 'architect', client and user.

Ben Godber establishes a precise definition and understanding of the relationship between the 'author' and the 'reader' within the discipline and practice of architecture, through an investigation of Mies van der Rohe's German Pavilion for the Barcelona Exposition of 1929 and The Downing Street Joint Declaration published in December 1993 by the British and Irish governments. Only the former is a conventional work of architecture but the authors of both objects of study are described as architects. Two pairs of photographic images, one pair depicting some of the immediate consequences of the Downing Street Declaration and the other depicting the Barcelona Pavilion, are the focus of the study. One image in each of the pairs is typical of an author's representation and the other is typical of a reader's representation. Godber formulates a third entity between the perceived binary opposition of didactic, prescriptive author *within* the institution and passive, receptive reader *without*. He argues that this third entity, the knowing, subverting reader, is best able to posit a challenging and provocative understanding of architecture and is, therefore, most deserving of the status of the architect.

Architecture is made by design and by use. The former is widely accepted and is presumed to be the domain of the architect. The latter, less recognised and valued, is the realm of the user. Iain Borden focuses on two architectures, both generated by skateboarding, 'one closer to the conventional territory of architecture as the activity of the conceptualisation, design and production of built spaces, and the other closer to the territory of the user and the activity of experiencing and creating space through bodily processes'. Borden theorises skateboarding as a body-centric architecture, in intimate contact with the formulation and projection of the self. The skateboarder creates architecture through design and use. The two terms of the architect–user dualism are no longer in opposition but are present within each other.

Home is the one place, the one architecture, that is perceived to be truly personal. Home always belongs to *someone*. Philip Tabor defines 'home' as a metaphor for not only a threatened society but also a threatened individual selfhood. The 'safety' of the home is really the sign of its opposite, a certain nervousness, a fear of the tangible or intangible dangers inside and outside. The home of home is seventeenth-century Netherlands, where the sea represented the threat of the outside. Tabor identifies a contemporary parallel in the telematic assault on identity. He chronicles the responses to the invasions of home and concludes that the electronic 'invasion' is benign if it is perceived not as an informational overload but as equivalent to a sublime light entering the domestic interior. Tabor's chapter can also be read as an allegory. The user is the architect of the home and just as territorial as the 'real' architect protecting *his* home, the profession.

The house is supposedly a stable vessel for the personal identity of its occupant(s), a home for, and mirror to, the self. But the concept of home is also a response to insecurity and the fear of change. The home must appear to be stable because social norms and personal identity are actually shifting and slippery. Jane Rendell's chapter focuses on the transformations to a single house in London, by the

Jonathan Hill

author and its other unexpected occupants, in which the fear of change is subverted to become the fear of stability and the only constant is change. The distinct activities, and propriety, of designing, making and using are compounded and confused in a very particular form of do-it-yourself, where 'form follows everything but function' and the illegal users of the house are also its illegal architects.

Figure 4 *Jonathan Hill,*
Occupied Territories, *1994.*

Mark Cousins 1

building an architect

I am not an architect and during the five years that I have been teaching full time at the Architectural Association I have watched architects and I have listened to them, and you have no idea what a strange experience that is. So in this text I want to try to formulate some of that strangeness. It is a strangeness that is compounded by the fact that I run the General Studies programme, which provides the historical, cultural and theoretical elements of an architectural education not directly addressed in the design units at the AA. I think that I am now even more unclear than I was five years ago as to what an architect should know. But perhaps as we progress we will see that the very idea of what an architect should know is an intrinsically complicated issue. It is not a question of taking one side or another in a set of arguments.

Let us try to give this some kind of architectural authority by looking at the chapter 'The Education of an Architect' in the first book of Vitruvius' *The Ten Books of Architecture*, in which he discusses not what the practice of architecture is, but the education of an architect, which, in a way, is an odd place to start. Let me quote: 'The architect should be equipped with knowledge of many branches of study and varied kinds of learning, for it is by his judgement that all work done by the other arts is put to the test.'[1] This knowledge Vitruvius calls not the combination of theory and practice, but the child of practice and theory:

> Practice is the continuous and regular exercise of employment where manual work is done with any necessary material according to the design of a drawing. Theory, on the other hand, is the ability to demonstrate and to explain the productions of dexterity on the principles of proportion.[2]

Vitruvius then divides the topic. He says, in everything, but particularly in architecture you may look at a subject-matter from two points of view. Either the thing itself, what he calls the 'thing signified',[3] or what gives the thing significance which is, for him, the more dignified part of the relation. Famously he gives a list of what the architect should be able to do:

> Let him be educated [not educated in something, just educated] . . . skilful with the pencil, instructed in geometry, know much history, have followed the philosophers with attention, understand music, have some knowledge of medicine, know the opinions of the jurists, and be acquainted with astronomy and the theory of the heavens.[4]

Now, it is not just that this seems an odd list. I do not mean that one can not reconstruct it historically. There is something curiously missing: there is no architecture.

1 Vitruvius, 'The Education of an Architect, The First Book', *The Ten Books of Architecture*, trans. Morris Hicky Morgan, London, Dover, 1960, p. 5.

2 ibid.

3 ibid.

4 ibid. pp. 5–6.

Mark Cousins

Let us now go through the way in which he glosses each section. 'Let him be educated.' Vitruvius gives an extraordinary reason why the architect should be educated, which I have no doubt was true for the author, and in a curious way may be quite true of architects, or some architects, at the moment. Architects should be educated on the grounds that they should be able to write treatises such that they will be remembered. There is not the slightest suggestion in Vitruvius' work that an architect would be remembered for his building. It is not even clear that, in Vitruvius' mind, there is an architect to a building, in the sense that we would say that it is designed by a specific person. But, according to Vitruvius, if you wish to be remembered as an architect you should be able to write an eloquent treatise which guarantees your memory. As always in antiquity, to be remembered is perhaps one of the strongest motives.

'Skilful with the pencil, instructed in geometry.' All he really says about this is that it would enable the architect, as if it were an optional extra, to make plans. And, actually he says in the same breath, arithmetic is also quite useful as this enables you to charge the client the correct amount. It is not given any great emphasis. Why should the architect be well versed in history? His knowledge of history should be able to entertain visitors to his building such that he would be able both to make and explain ornamentation: that is the story of this, this is in memory of that. Why should the architect study philosophy? Because 'it makes an architect high-minded and not self-assuming, but rather renders him courteous, just, and honest without avariciousness'.[5] **5** ibid. p. 8. That is not quite my experience of the world of architectural theory. The reason for understanding music is that one should know something of harmony because this is indispensable to building ballistic machines, and also extremely useful in a proper knowledge of acoustics. The whole question of medicine is useful only so that the architect will be able to site buildings in a healthy place. Knowledge of the work of the great jurists comes down, he says, essentially to drawing up contracts. It is really getting ridiculous by the time Vitruvius reaches astronomy. Here, he says, it would be helpful to know the theory of the sundial.

It does seem to me that this is one of the most ludicrous chapters of a famous book ever written. But the question I want to ask is – why? There are really two features of the chapter. One is the absolute absence not only of architecture, but of a concern for what architecture is or might be. Second, the assumption that architecture is an intrinsically weak discipline. If architecture is anything to Vitruvius here, it is a combination of other knowledges. After all, no one in Vitruvius' time would remotely imagine writing a text on philosophy, or medicine, or the law in the same manner. All these texts would be written with grandeur, spending, perhaps, many pages defining the object of the practice and its relation to the practice. In contrast, Vitruvius can offer

Mark Cousins

only a practical rag bag of things that an architect should know, that in no way elaborate the theory or the practice of architecture.

Actually, I do not think that the teaching of architecture, or rather the formulation of architecture as something like a teachable subject, is all that different at a formal level now. If you ask people what ought to be on the curricula of architectural education, it is extraordinary how quickly bits get plugged in and drop off. It is remarkable, for example at the AA, the way in which suddenly all the books on deconstruction are not taken out of the library and you cannot find any book on contemporary biology for weeks. You wonder what sort of a subject it is where people were passionately reading the texts of Jacques Derrida in the late 1980s and really quite abstruse stuff about shoals of fish in the mid-1990s? I think Vitruvius, in some ways, has some of the same problems.

It is clear that Vitruvius' text, unlike a text on law or perhaps a text on medicine, is quite unable to close the gap between talking about architecture as an organised, formal, academic knowledge and what actually happens. There are other disciplines, unlike law and unlike medicine, which remain, perhaps, constitutively secret. We might also, sociologically, think that it is in those forms of knowledge that remain not just a secret but somehow secretive, that, as a necessary consequence, there is an enormous gap between the popular expectation of, for example, what an architect is, what an architect does, and what architectural design is. I think it is quite difficult to find a topic as exemplary as architectural design in disconfirming the popular view of it, of disconfirming a public fantasy of what it is presumed to be, and what architects think they are doing, and maybe do not know what they are doing, as they do it.

I am suggesting that there may be, what we might call, 'weak disciplines' which does not of course make them weak. It means that the public, visible part of the curriculum, which it might, in practical terms, be necessary to know, none-the-less does very little to define the nature of the practice. As a consequence there emerges an almost unbridgeable gulf between the popular conception of what happens and what actually happens. It is not just a question of information either. It is not possible to explain simply architectural design. If an architect tried to explain what he or she does, they would find it almost like trying to tell a dream. If asked 'Well, what is it you actually do when you are designing?' an architect might start, as one can when telling a dream, and then suddenly get to the point when you think no, that is not it, that is not it at all, that is not quite what I meant; and you realise the other person is by now completely baffled. It is around this area that I would like to think in the following pages.

Maybe there is something between, what I am calling, a 'weak discipline', which I do not think is weak institutionally, but is weak in the way I have tried to identify, and in contrast with other disciplines. There are various components to this. The first one could specify in formal and philosophical terms, if we ask the question – is architecture a knowledge? I do not mean knowledge of architecture, but is architecture a knowledge? Is architecture a specific kind of appropriation and representation of objects? I think the answer is, kind of, yes and no. In terms of the philosophy of science, if you asked somebody at University College London, on the scale of dignified forms of knowledge, where did architecture come? I think they would first of all question what you meant. What do you mean, is architecture a knowledge? Most philosophers of science are used to interrogating a practice for its content and knowledge according to the question – to what extent does it conform to solid and truthful knowledge? An example would be the sorts of propositions which you would find in the natural sciences, especially in physics. It is still the case that, in the philosophy of science, physics continues to maintain a certain regnant dignity.

Now, it is obvious that architecture is not, and could not be, a knowledge of that kind. It cannot pretend to be scientific knowledge. It does not make propositions of that kind. Now, we do not want to go too far in to the philosophy of science, but one of the problems of the philosophy of science is that it often assumes that propositions that are not scientific are somehow basically flawed and inadequate. This seems to me an extremely foolish way of treating human discourses. I certainly think there is a difference between the discourses of the natural sciences and those that are not. Perhaps one very brief, simple way of characterising the difference is that the discourses of the natural sciences are purely concerned with objects. That is to say they are concerned with certain types of objects specified in and by a knowledge, such as physics or biology, and the relationships between objects in that discursive field.

No other object other than an object enters these discourses. There are, however, other types of knowledge where the definition of the object of knowledge includes the subject. In these types of knowledge you could either say that there is a subject as well as an object, or that there is an object of which the subject is a part. Clearly the discourse of art is of this kind because, fundamental to it, is the effect of an object on a subject. It also makes very little philosophical sense to treat architecture as a purely physical object because architecture is the effect of that object on a subject. And here, I think in terms of the notion of occupation, the subject of architecture is the subject who experiences architecture. Otherwise you have only a theory of the creation of architecture. Architecture is too important to be left to a theory of its creation.

Amongst the humanities it is perfectly possible to produce, and to defend, a rigorous conception of the object of the practice of architecture as the effects of objects upon a subject, without trying to claim this as scientific knowledge. It is a knowledge, but it is a knowledge of a particular kind. It is a knowledge of an object but only when it is represented in, and by, and for the subject. Now, in a way, what I

6 I. Kant, *The Critique of Judgement*, Oxford, OUP, 1952. Original German edition 1790.

have said is not very different from the problem as Kant saw it in *The Critique of Judgement*.[6] He is concerned to specify the relation (and I do not want to join him, but for him it is a relation of aesthetic pleasure) and he does it in such a way that it is both rigorous and distinct from, what we might call, the natural sciences and their way of posing the issue of knowledge. The problem with the Kantian discussion of art and of architecture is that there is only one condition on which you can accede to it. Kant says that in order to be within aesthetic pleasure you must approach the object in a mental state which he calls that of being disinterested – of having stripped away your appetite. As he says, for example with respect to a painting, there are various things you might want to do with it. You might want to own it, you might like it because it reminds you of someone you knew. All sorts of relations, associations and appetites will be brought to the object but none of these count in terms of the subject's relation to the art object or the architectural object. Only when they are stripped away in a mode of contemplation, of disinterestedness, can you call this the purified state of the subject's relation to the object.

Many of Kant's arguments in *The Critique of Judgement* are quite defensible and quite useful, but unfortunately the central one clearly will not do, especially in the twentieth century – the idea that one's fundamental relation to an object is of disinterest. On the contrary, it seems to me that, almost by definition, we have to treat our relation to the art or the architectural object as one of desire. I do not wish simply to use the word for the sake of using it. I want to use it because I hope it will illuminate something.

What on earth would it mean to talk about architectural desire? Let us try to answer that by asking about the origin of desire in general. Let me try to get through this quite quickly. Think of a baby. Let us imagine the relation between a mother and baby in the first months of life, in the period that Winnicott used to call primary maternal preoccupation, in which, before the baby could ever experience a need, the mother had got there first. The relation between the mother and baby can be an entirely happy, fluent circuit of need and satisfaction. Or rather, if we put that in logical terms, the need is never represented because it is immediately satisfied. This is a sort of just-so story of desire, I am not trying to talk about how empirically awful life is for mothers and babies. One day, however, there is a catastrophe, a necessary and constitutive catastrophe. The baby has a need and it is not satisfied. Total catastrophe strikes the baby at this point. The baby is expelled from somewhere and is precipitated into a completely other zone. A zone in which the baby has to spend the rest of his or her life. Let us call this zone the 'zone of representation'. Why call it representation? According to Freud, the first thing that the baby will do, on not getting a feed, is the easiest thing, which is to hallucinate a feed. You hallucinate what you need. The trouble is that hallucinations do not contain milk. So the baby is caught from now on in a circuit not of need and satisfaction, but of desire which is based on a lack, towards an object which in fact will not really satisfy. It is an economy of non-satisfaction.

From this point on human beings set out on a destiny of non-satisfaction. And they think that they desire objects, but those objects are not only themselves, they are always substitutions for something else which has been lost. Indeed that something that has been lost is the very dimension which supports the apparatus of desire. Let us call that dimension the lost object. It is important to recognise that the lost object is not a thing. You cannot find it, although people waste their lives looking for it because it is the dimension, the condition, under which desire for objects in general arose. It never was a thing. It only was a thing in retrospect once you have been expelled. None-the-less the whole relationship between objects in the world is now shadowed by the wish for the lost object. So much so that you might almost say that the desire that we have is shadowed, even though we can specify very clearly that the desire is for this thing or that person, by a doppelganger desire which states 'if I get that I will have everything'. Everything will be all right. For example, you lose your keys and the experience of losing your keys is so awful, and you so wish to find them, that you actually begin to think – if only I had my keys everything would be all right. Only when you find your keys do you realise that it is not much better at all. Finding the keys did not put everything right. This example is a minor daily occurrence in the adventures of the lost object.

What I am trying to talk about here, in a way that Kant was quite unable to, is that our relations to objects take place within a world of desire and representations, which is shadowed all the way by the world of the lost object. It is in this sense that some of our fundamental relations with objects show themselves. Freud says, for example, that no one has ever found an object, they have only refound it. Every desire for a repre-sentation, every desire for an object, including every desire to make an object at an unconscious level, is also a desire to refind in the new object the object which is lost.

Infants are confused and fairly stricken by this. Parents try to console them and cheer them up and they do so in a way that only makes the problem worse because what they say in effect is, 'Look, I know it's dreadful, you have lost that, you have had to enter the world of representation and desire but however awful it is, now you are here you can have anything you want.' And in effect the infant says, 'Anything? You mean really anything?' 'Absolutely. I know it is awful for you but God knows you are owed some compensation.' At which point, as Freud states, in effect what the baby says is 'OK, I'll have mummy' or daddy as the case may be. And the parents are then provoked by the child, who is maybe three or four years old, to say, 'Sorry, that was something else we forgot to tell you. They are off limits for a start.' In terms of this brief history of child development, the infant is now so completely baffled that he or she

Mark Cousins

spends the next five years worrying about model planes or wanting a pony. It is all just too awful to consider until they are re-awoken by their hormones a bit later. They would just rather forget the whole lot. And indeed every eight-year-old just wants to avoid any mention of sex – kissing is silly, the whole thing is revolting. The catastrophic effects of this, I want to suggest, are very real and mark us all for the rest of our lives, as we walk about as ex-children. That is to say, we repeat those same relations and it should come as no surprise to us that we do this in architecture as well.

Let us think for a moment, then, what it would be to want to make something. Making something will always have a paradoxical component to it. On the one hand it will be full of the strong urge to make something that is outside and beyond that economy, and at the same time to recapture the lost object. Something of these pressures is at work when we are confronted with a new and very strong art or architectural object, in which the object seems at once completely new and, to some extent, you wonder where it has been up until now. It is as if the strong object always gets there in the nick of time. But your relation to it as an object is caught between both recognising its extreme novelty, because I think there cannot be anything better psychologically than the production of new objects but nothing more difficult than the production of new objects, and at the same time an unconscious recognition that the newness is itself related to the domain of the lost object. And so an experience is carved out in which you cannot really tell whether the novelty or the antiquity of the experience is the one which predominates. Indeed, if one pushed this further, one might ask the question, in respect to making something, what is it that is missing?

Those knowledges which I called 'weak knowledges' contain real and indeed the most valuable knowledge but do not measure up to the way the philosophy of science characterises truthful utterances. And there is a further category which Freud movingly speaks about. It is what he calls theories of impossible professions. What is it to imagine an impossible profession? Now, obviously the model, for Freud, is the practice of psychoanalysis itself. That is to say, when he is put to the test and says, 'Well, what would the education of an analyst look like?', he is reduced to producing a kind of list of things: 'Well, you had better know something about classical mythology because somebody might dream like that.' Or 'You had better know about medicine because you do not want to be treating someone for paranoia when, in fact, they have got a brain tumour.' This is remarkably similar to Vitruvius' rather inconsequential list because what is at stake is the practice of psychoanalysis and indeed the practice of any 'weak discipline' is authorised not by the formal knowledge but by the subjective and ultimately unconscious relations to that knowledge. I am trying to put this in as formal a way as I can so that it does not just sound mystical. It is not mystical at all. It is real and it is absolutely intelligible.

So the question of making something, whether the object being made is an interpretation or a piece of architecture, cannot come about from the elements of the practice, because the elements of the practice are weak. They neither authorise nor constitute the practice as such. Contrast this, for a moment, with, for example, the practice of law where you can see the relations go exactly the other way. Law is such a strong discipline that you have to hide from it when you practice. You have to hide from it in the sense that it does not matter what your feelings are about your client, the law says you have to defend them. So you place yourself subjectively in another space other than where you are. You are able to divide yourself and that is part of the element of practice.

For any practice concerned with the unconscious process of making an object for a subject there is always something already missing because the question of the lost object actually enters into the practice. It certainly does not in the law. It certainly does not in physics. But the question of the lost object always enters into any human practice which, paradoxically, is concerned to produce something new. What one is trying to sketch here, in place of Kant's notion of disinterestedness, is a certain kind of complicated relationship between loss and fabrication. Therefore, it makes perfect sense to begin a process of creation with an investigation of loss, of the shadow, for which the object does not yet quite exist. That is one reason why I suggest that architecture cannot be taught in the way that the natural sciences can be taught. Architecture cannot be taught unless, and until, we think about what teaching is in terms other than simply the transmission of forms of knowledge, and until we open it to the question of the unconscious.

This text is based on a lecture delivered at the Bartlett School of Architecture, University College London, in April 1996. The lecture was given without notes and appears as a transcription by Jonathan Hill and Keith Papa.

Mark Cousins

curriculum[1] vitae[2]

THE ARCHITECT'S CULTURAL CAPITAL:[3] EDUCATIONAL PRACTICES AND FINANCIAL INVESTMENTS[4]

Name	Katerina[5] Rüedi[6]
Maiden Name	Kyselkova[7]
Date of Birth	07.02.1957[8]
Marital Status	Married[9]
Place of Birth	Brno,[10] Czech Republic
Nationality	British[11]
Languages	English,[12] German,[13] Czech, Italian[14] and French, some Russian
Skills	User of Sonata CAD, AutoCAD, Pagemaker & Microsoft Word[15]
	Holder of British Driving Licence[16]
Memberships	
	Architects Registration Board[17]
	Architectural Association[18]
	Royal Institute of British Architects[19]
	Society of Architectural Historians of Great Britain[20]
	Chicago Architecture Club[21]
	Chicago Women in Architecture[22]

EDUCATION[23] AND QUALIFICATIONS[24]

SECONDARY EDUCATION

1968–9 **Experimentální Gymnasium,[25] Ostrava, Czechoslovakia**

Classes in Czech Language, Mathematics, Geography, History, Latin, German, English[26]

1969–75 **Hampstead School, London, UK[27]**

Classes in home economics, French, woodwork, metalwork and

1973 9 O'Levels in: English Language, English Literature, Mathematics, Integrated Science A, Integrated Science B, History, Latin, Art

1 CSE Grade 1 in: Typewriting and Office Practice

RSA in: Typewriting and Office Practice[28]

1974 **Christianeum, Hamburg, Germany[29]**

Visiting Student. Classes in Mathematics and Physics

1975 **Hampstead School, London, UK**

5 A'Levels in: Biology, Chemistry, Physics, Maths, Art

TERTIARY EDUCATION[30]

1975–8   **Duncan of Jordanstone College of Art/University of Dundee, Dundee, UK**[31]

Courses taken: Design, construction, technology, structures, environmental services, history, design method, professional practice[32]

1976 Armitstead Prize[33]

1977 Flexel Prize[34]

1978 B.Sc.(Arch), Gordon Matthewson Student of the Year Award,[35] RIBA I

1980–3   **The Architectural Association, London, UK**[36]

AA Diploma With Honours

AA Thesis (Allegory and Simulation in Contemporary Montage) Pass with Distinction

Neff Award (Second Prize)

RIBA II

1983–4   **Kingston Polytechnic, London, UK**[37]

RIBA III

1984   **Architects Registration Council of the United Kingdom/Architects Registration Board**[38]

Registration as architect: ARCUK number 51637F

1988–90   **Bartlett School of Architecture, UCL, London, UK**[39]

M.Sc. in History of Modern Architecture and Thesis

'Guardians of Sleep: Architectural Education and the Culture of Simulation' Pass with Distinction

1992–   **Bartlett School of Architecture, UCL, London, UK**[40]

Ph.D. Research

'Bauhaus Dreamhouse: Architectural Education in the Age of Mass Media'

1992   **Royal Institute of British Architects**[41]

Registration as Chartered Architect: Corporate membership number 0562726I[42]

Katerina Rüedi

FOOTNOTES

1   This article is an amended and extended version of a text that first appeared in *Underground*, published by students and staff at the Kingston University School of Architecture in 1997. The author wishes to thank the editor, Shahed Saleem, for his agreement to develop the format further and wishes to make clear that Shahed Saleem should not be associated with any views expressed in this text. The text has been written by the author based on her own lived experience. Statistical information regarding the parentage of black members of the RIBA comes from the Society of Black Architects.

PROLOGUE

2   Architects are producers of architectural commodities (designs). They are also commodities in themselves. A Curriculum Vitae is the principal means of setting out commodity value; it is the 'come hither' of the architect.

3   The acquisition of architects' commodity value takes place through the judicious acquisition and reproduction of her cultural capital. Cultural capital is a concept first introduced by the French anthropologist and sociologist Pierre Bourdieu. Bourdieu introduces and develops the concept of symbolic and cultural capital in *Outline of A Theory of Practice* (1977) and *Distinction, A Social Critique of the Judgement of Taste* (1984). Crudely, cultural capital refers to the cultural status a particular person acquires, which has a direct or indirect bearing on their financial and political status. The acquisition of cultural capital begins in the cradle, within the family, and is consolidated 'in company' acquired through education, marriage, occupational allegiances and friendships. Cultural capital, just like economic capital, can be invested, speculated, lost and won.

Cultural capital is primarily used to accumulate social privilege. It is a system of symbolic social relations between signs that become signs of relations between human beings. Cultural capital is a fetish; it confers mythical and 'natural' commodity value on unequal and constructed social relations, which include architectural social relations. It is not freely available or reproducible but is restricted by class, race and gender boundaries. Being white, middle-class, well-read and socially adept is a form of cultural capital and helps in furthering a conventionally successful architectural career.

4   The purpose of this essay is to recognize and relate the acquisition and reproduction of cultural capital within education to economic capital, class, gender and race,

Katerina Rüedi

26

and to focus on key moments of financial support (private and public) which enabled the subject to bypass some of the restrictions of her class and gender.

THE SUBJECT

5   A non-Anglo-Saxon female name, indicating the subject is of Eastern European (Slavic or Greek) origin, a Caucasian.

6   A Swiss-German surname, indicating that the subject may be Germanic by marriage. Adopted by the subject by deed poll in gratitude to her step-father, a professional ice-hockey player and mechanical engineer.

7   A Slavic surname, taking the female form of the name of the father, indicating that the gender of the subject is female. The subject's father was an architect and a son of an architect. The subject's grandfather carries high cultural value in her country of origin as a modernist architect of note.

   The subject's mother, whose name bears no influence on that of the subject, was a single parent, a journalist, housekeeper, designer, illustrator and is now a painter. She has been a refugee, has lived in seven European countries, changed residences too numerously to recount and speaks six languages.

8   The subject was born into the period of the post-Second World War social contract in Europe. State investment in the education and welfare of its citizens allowed her to have access to free schooling and medicine.

9   The subject's husband is a male Caucasian architect, who runs his own practice, which he inherited from his father who is an architect. He is also a professional teacher and a director of a degree course at a school of architecture.

10 The subject's birthplace is a well-known centre of high quality modern buildings, some designed and built by the subject's grandfather.

11 Prior to acquiring British citizenship, the subject experienced harassment from immigration officials in other European countries.

12 English is not the subject's mother tongue. At the age of eighteen she decided to speak in the middle-class London accent used by the majority of figures of cultural significance in the nation.

Katerina Rüedi

13 The subject learnt German from her grandmother, who was a couturier of German–Jewish parentage.

14 The subject's mother and step-father live in Italy, commonly accepted as one of the centres of European culture in an area with no non-Caucasian inhabitants. The area is distinguished by its modern art and high gastronomic reputation for both food and wine.

15 The subject's computer training was provided free by the school of architecture where she taught. The subject's computer equipment was paid for by her husband's architectural practice, where she is an associate. The financial investment represented in this computer equipment and training is equivalent to 15 per cent of her annual salary.

16 The subject comes from a non-driving family. She was strongly encouraged to learn to drive by her first architectural employer. This single skill has greatly increased her personal safety and mobility.

17 State legitimation of professional cultural capital is essential to professional practitioners. During the era of state power, many professions in Britain and the rest of Europe have sought state support. The state has enacted legislation defining and protecting the professional's title and in many cases safeguarded major areas of work. In Britain the welfare state has sustained the legal profession and stimulated the expansion of the profession of medicine, architecture and engineering. It has also funded and validated much of professional education. Within education, the profession/ state alliance has led to mutual compromises as professions tried to limit entry by social classes newly enfranchised by state expansion of education. Consequently, in contrast to non-professional education, standards of admission and certification in professional education have generally been higher, attrition rates greater and the education process longer.

The cultural and economic capital of the professions relies on ensuring scarcity through monopoly. In order to grant the right to monopoly, the state (and the public that supports its power) needs guarantees that professionals will not abuse their knowledge. To be granted the social right to restrictive practices, the professional has had to fulfil an unspoken social contract. The state confers cultural capital on professionals to seal a state/profession alliance because (Dingwall and Lewis, 1983, p. 5) professional knowledge, by lying close to potential sources of social conflict, both represents and threatens state interests:

The professions are licensed to carry out some of the most dangerous tasks of our society – to intervene in our bodies, to intercede for our prospects of future salvation, to regulate the conflict of rights and obligations between social interests. Yet in order to do this, they must acquire guilty knowledge – the priest is an expert on sin, the doctor on disease, the lawyer on crime – and the ability to look at these matters in comparative and, hence, relative terms. This is the mystery of the professions. Their privileged status is an inducement to maintain their loyalty in concealing the darker sides of their society and in refraining from exploiting their knowledge for evil purposes.

Dingwall and Lewis believe that this function – the professions' resolution of potential social conflict – explains their close historical proximity to the agents of political power.

Architecture is no exception. Architecture symbolically represents the laws of property on which economic and social order rests. It also acts as one of the most public and invisible means of displacing social conflict through symbolic representation and the ordering of spatial behaviour. Just as doctors or lawyers have not willingly produced the sick individual or the guilty convict, architects have not, at least consciously, built symbolic and spatial nightmares.

Most professionals do not sell tangible goods but sell their knowledge. This turns their knowledge into a commodity – cultural capital. However, to maintain scarcity, that knowledge cannot be freely reproducible, through text or imagery. Instead, it must become indivisible from the expert – a special type of personal property. Professional knowledge has to become embodied cultural capital. This makes professional work, like other labour, into a fictitious commodity. For its value to be maintained, it cannot be reproduced independently of its owner. Its owners, as well as the knowledge itself, have to be produced as commodities. Such production takes place within education. The education of the professional therefore has to ensure that the professional is homogeneous, 'kind and safe'.

18 A private school of architecture and club for architects. The school is accredited and has an international reputation for independent study and innovation. It has a long tradition of famous teachers and alumni and forms an international network of contacts for its members. No figures exist for the ethnic origin of members of the Association.

19 The main professional body for British architects, which accredits architectural education and defines the nature of professional architectural knowledge in line with the European Directive. It is not the legal registration body for British architects. See note 41 for figures regarding ethnic origin of members.

Katerina Rüedi

20 A club for architectural historians. No figures exist for class, gender or ethnic origin of architectural historians. The annual membership fee is the lowest of the clubs that the subject belongs to.

21 A club for architects, where the subject has been invited to lecture and exhibit work. Figures for class, gender and ethnic origin are not available.

22 A club for women architects, which provides mentorship to students and support to members. In the United States, as in the UK, 35 per cent of entering students are female but only 10 per cent of practising professional architects are female. Long office hours, not conducive to family life, are taken for granted by the majority of architectural employers.

23 Education, according to Bourdieu, reproduces existing structures of the owner-ship of cultural capital. Students invest in its acquisition and reproduction; those that already have some cultural capital (offspring of the cultured classes such as art, music, literary and other professionals) before entering architectural education, not only retain it, but tend to 'increase' their investment.

The reproduction of cultural capital through education parallels the production, reproduction and consumption of the modern architectural profession. The architect's cultural capital is often beyond her own making. Clients, users, legislative bodies and the media all contribute to the architect's commodity value. To ensure that the archi-tect remains 'kind and safe' (ethical and competent), these groups have demanded and legitimised specific and homogeneous traits which have conferred guaranteed commodity value on the architectural profession as a whole.

This situation is changing. Architects can now practise in a wide range of areas of expertise, not all of them legitimised by the profession, but many of them actively encouraged by broader economic developments. Architects are writing academic texts and novels, making films, designing publications, constructing installations, advising users, writing briefs, developing property, marketing building components, working in construction companies, retraining as engineers and so on. However, the profession in the UK still has a lower percentage membership of women than medicine or law and minority representation is extremely low.

24 Cultural capital can take a number of forms: institutionalised, objectified, social and embodied. Institutionalised cultural capital consists of educational qualifications. Objectified cultural capital consists of possession of valued cultural artefacts; social cultural capital consists of access to privileged social networks – whether made

Katerina Rüedi

possible through education or the family; embodied cultural capital consists of the physical attributes and behaviour of the person who possesses it. It is a class of signs acquired unconsciously by architects and confers traits signifying the symbolic value of their 'owners'.

Bourdieu argues that education is a key site within which embodied cultural capital attaches to the body. In *Outline of a Theory of Practice* Bourdieu introduces the concept of the 'habitus' as a mechanism for the production and reproduction of embodied cultural capital (Bourdieu, 1977, pp. 72–95). For Bourdieu the habitus regulates the production of practices and the reproduction of cultural capital 'without in any way being the product of obedience to rules' and 'without being the product of the orchestrating action of a conductor' (Bourdieu, 1977, p. 72). The habitus is:

> the product of the work of inculcation and appropriation necessary in order for those products of collective history, the objective structures (e.g. of language, economy, etc.) to succeed in reproducing themselves more or less completely, in the form of durable dispositions, in the organisms (which one can, if one wishes, call individuals) lastingly subjected to the same conditionings, and hence placed in the same material conditions of existence.
>
> Bourdieu, 1977, p. 85

It is 'history turned into nature' (Bourdieu, 1977, p. 78). The habitus is, however, represented in individual bodies. Bourdieu describes how the tasks of the habitus include the classification of the body:

> In a class society, all the products of a given agent, by an essential overdetermination, speak inseparably and simultaneously of his class – or, more precisely, his position in the social structure and his rising or falling trajectory – and of his (or her) body – or, more precisely, all the properties, always socially qualified, of which he or she is the bearer – sexual properties of course, but also physical properties, praised, like strength or beauty, or stigmatised.
>
> Bourdieu, 1977, p. 87

The habitus reproduces embodied cultural capital to form a corporate identity for a specific social group. It gives collective symbolic value to body language, skin colour, gender, clothing, manner of speech, accent and other factors that constitute a shared identity:

> If all societies and, significantly, all the 'totalitarian' institutions . . . that seek to produce a new man through a process of 'deculturation' and 'reculturation' set such store on the

Katerina Rüedi

seeming most insignificant details of dress, bearing, physical or verbal manners, the reason is that, treating the body as memory, they entrust to it in abbreviated and practical, i.e. mnemonic, form the fundamental principles of the arbitrary content of culture. The principles em-bodied [sic] in this way are placed beyond the grasp of consciousness, and hence cannot be touched by voluntary, deliberate transformation, cannot even be made explicit; nothing seems more ineffable, more incommunicable, more inimitable, and, therefore, more precious, than the values given body, made body by the transubstantiation achieved by the hidden persuasion of an implicit pedagogy, capable of instilling a whole cosmology, an ethic, a metaphysic, a political philosophy, through injunctions as insignificant as 'stand up straight' or 'don't hold your knife in your left hand'.

Bourdieu, 1977, p. 94

25 The subject entered secondary education during the cultural thaw of the 'Prague Spring' and experienced three months of liberal education. These changes were reversed a year later. This was the subject's first and most formative exposure to the relationship between broader political change and educational reform.

26 The subject encountered subjects previously dismissed as 'bourgeois' – Latin and foreign languages – for the first time.

27 Upon arrival in the UK, the subject attended a trendy comprehensive school, with a mixture of children of (Caucasian) left-wing intellectuals and local workers. She obtained a liberal education in a politically active environment which did not focus solely on academic achievement. The subject experienced no gender discrimination there. The majority of students in the remedial English class, that she attended as a foreigner, were black.

28 The subject's typing qualification made her attractive to her first architectural employer, a one-man practice, whose principal was frustrated after years of typing his own letters. This, in addition to state financial aid to architectural employees in a deep recession, allowed the subject to enter practice when she might not otherwise have been able to do so.

29 One of two well-known elite secondary schools in the city, where the subject's uncle, now a university professor, taught.

30 The subject's tertiary education was acquired in two very different sets of circumstances. As a child of a low income single parent she attended undergraduate education with full state support for fees and maintainance. Had state support not been available, the subject would not have been able to attend tertiary education. The subject was funded by her stepfather to attend graduate education at an international private school.

31 A regional school focusing on professional competence. A significant number of students were of local origin. The majority were not aware of, or did not feel empowered to criticise the narrow teaching focus of the school, partly because criticism could deprive them of the credentials they sought. The school's teachers at the time were all male Caucasians. The subject's entering class of forty included three women and two minority students. The subject is the only one of her three female friends who has pursued a full-time architectural career. The school at the time claimed, in a review of schools conducted by *The Architects' Journal*, that its students were 'marketable products'.

32 The characteristic features of a profession, according to Geison (1983, p. 4) are:

1   formal technical training
2   intellectual skills
3   an institutionalised setting that certifies quality and competence
4   demonstrable skills in the pragmatic application of this formal training
5   institutional mechanisms ensuring that knowledge will be used in a socially responsible role.

The categories of formal technical training, demonstrable pragmatic skills, intellectual ability and social responsibility fulfil the social contract that professional knowledge be both useful and impartial. It thus ceases to be dangerous knowledge. Standardised examinations and certification maintain its homogeneity and scarcity. Together they provide a minimum standard by which the newly qualified professional gains the necessary state protection.

The architectural profession in Britain has effected these features, with greater or lesser degrees of success, by incorporating them into the education and certification processes. The first four desired characteristics of the professional define major areas of the architectural curriculum such as constructional knowledge, history and theory of architecture, professional studies and practical experience. They form the main part of the architect's cultural capital. However, because their knowledge is reproducible,

Katerina Rüedi

these features do not constitute embodied cultural capital. Reproducibility through the education process and thence text makes these professional attributes available to competing occupational groups, who have, of course, made use of them. If these were the only types of professional architectural knowledge, the monopoly of the architect could not be maintained.

However, the value of the professions also rests on the elevation of certain traits to a 'natural' status beyond conscious learning. This has transformed cultural capital into its embodied form and has, until recently, raised the exchange value of professionals above that of their competitors. Larson affirms that professional competence is indeed attained unconsciously and consciously:

> effects [of professional education] are measured in the non-physical constraint of accepted definitions, or internalised moral and epistemological norms. It is in one sense impersonal, for it makes the most general knowledge claims; yet it is also deeply personal, in that the individual who internalises the general and special discourses of his or her own culture experiences them as natural expressions or extensions of his or her own will and reason.
>
> Haskell, 1984, pp. 35–6

The terms 'natural' and 'will' are important because they place areas of professional expertise beyond conscious cultural influence. This resembles Bourdieu's concept of embodied cultural capital, where culturally produced collective traits are incorporated into individual behaviour and appearance. The illusion of individual and professional autonomy comes from the 'naturalisation' of such socially determined professional knowledge into personal will.

Impartiality and social responsibility, as qualities of behaviour rather than types of knowledge, form the first two features of the architect's embodied cultural capital. Termed ethics, they are acquired through exposure to respected forms of behaviour in both education and practice, and are symbolised in the professional Code of Conduct. The most important feature of embodied cultural capital, however, is the possession of design talent. Design has, since the foundation of the architectural profession, distinguished the architect from other members of the construction industry and formed the symbolic tool for the quasi-mysterious integration of technical, intellectual, practical and social knowledge. The acquisition of design talent today continues to operate largely beyond consciousness. Most architects regard design talent as natural (you either have it or you don't) and therefore as a quality that cannot be taught. It thus escapes examination as embodied cultural capital – a cultural construct (with a socio-economic lineage) and a commodity (with a market value), produced and reproduced

Katerina Rüedi

unconsciously. In its transmission of the embodied cultural capital of design talent and responsible social traits, architectural education relies on the mechanisms that produce and reproduce the profession as a dreaming collective.

33 During the first year of the undergraduate course one of the minority students left, after continuously being called 'banana'. The other stayed on, by laughing off his name 'Chink' for the next two years. All three women students were propositioned by a teacher within a week of arrival.

34 The subject gained this prize at the end of the second year, without understanding why. Flexel was, at that time, a ceiling heating product and she assumed that the award of the Flexel prize was therefore associated with good performance in a technical area. She was sure she did not have technical ability – the main focus of the school – because this was made repeatedly clear to her in reviews. Motto: 'If you cannot detail it, don't design it.'

35 The subject graduated with the highest award of the school, named after a (Caucasian) architect and planner. When presented with the prize (a crystal ball), she was advised by the Head of School 'to throw it at your husband when you are married'.

36 The school had a high proportion of foreign students at the time the subject studied there. The subject experienced no gender or race discrimination there; the majority of her friends were not British. The school encouraged a high level of individual responsibility, independent study and innovation, sometimes well beyond the bound-aries of the traditional professional model. The subject graduated with the highest award of the school. She met the editor of this book there. Four of the five referees that supported her last application for employment are ex-students or teachers of the school. All of the visiting professors at her current school are ex-teachers of the Association.

The Architectural Association is a private school with fees set in the region of £9,000 per annum. Fees for British architecture students at other British schools are in the region of £3,000 per annum and are usually paid by the state. Fees for overseas students at other British schools of architecture are in the region of £5,000 to £9,000 per annum and are normally paid by the student. Scholarships are available at the Architectural Association for talented students with limited financial means but at present these cannot support the majority of the student body. The relative autonomy to pursue a self-determined critical course of study therefore has a high relative international economic value, and still higher relative local one.

Katerina Rüedi

37   The subject passed her final professional examination at this school, by interview with the father (a Caucasian architect) of a subsequent female teaching colleague (an architect). The subject experienced no gender discrimination at this school. However, when she subsequently taught at the school, a significantly high number of students she taught who failed their studies were of non-Caucasian origin. This experience prompted the research and previous publication of material in this text.

38   The legal registration body for British architects, which deals with breaches in professional discipline and has powers to accept and remove architects from its register. Its board has recently changed to consist of 50 per cent lay members, in line with state and public demands for greater accountability for the professions. The subject's most recent employer (a Caucasian architect) was, until recently, a member of the board of this organisation.

39   The subject graduated with the highest award of the school. Her teachers were male Caucasians and were supportive of architectural criticism based on class and gender.

40   The subject is undertaking doctoral research in the institution where she has also taught. She is contributing essays to books edited by two (male Caucasian) architecture lecturers at the school and one (male Caucasian) architecture lecturer at the school has in turn contributed essays to a book which she edited. The subject's publication record is important to her cultural capital; promotions within architectural education are increasingly measured on research and publication performance.

41   A club for architects, where the subject has been invited to lecture and sit on committees. In 1995, out of 19,710 members, 41 called themselves of black origin.

EPILOGUE

42   The acquisition of embodied cultural capital remains outside consciousness because its purpose is not to produce the dominant culture but, rather, to unconsciously reproduce it, through the differentiated encoding of social and cultural class. Embodied cultural capital is therefore the most difficult type of cultural capital to acquire by those who are not consciously aware of it. This aspect of educational and professional success is normally publicly acknowledged by professionals, educators and students.

Katerina Rüedi

BIBLIOGRAPHY

Bourdieu, P., *Outline of a Theory of Practice*, New York, Cambridge University Press, 1971.

——, *Distinction, A Social Critique of the Judgement of Taste*, London, Routledge and Kegan Paul, 1986.

Dingwall, R. and Lewis, P. (eds), *The Sociology of the Professions: Lawyers, Doctors and Others*, London, Macmillan Press, 1983.

Geison, G. (ed.), *Professions and Professional Ideologies in America*, Chapel Hill, University of North Carolina Press, 1983.

Haskell, T. L. (ed.), *The Authority of Experts*, Bloomington, Indiana University Press, 1984.

Larson, M. S., *The Rise of Professionalism: A Sociological Analysis*, Berkeley, University of California Press, 1977.

——, *Behind the Postmodern Facade: Architectural Change in Late Twentieth Century America*, London, University of California Press, 1993.

Katerina Rüedi

ResponseAbility

THE ABILITY TO PROVOKE OR

PROVIDE RESPONSE

*Dull unwashed windows of eyes
and buildings of industry. What
industry do I practice? A slick
coloured boy, 12 miles from his
home. I practice no industry.
I am no longer a credit
to my race. I read a little,
scratch agains silence slow spring
afternoons.*[1]

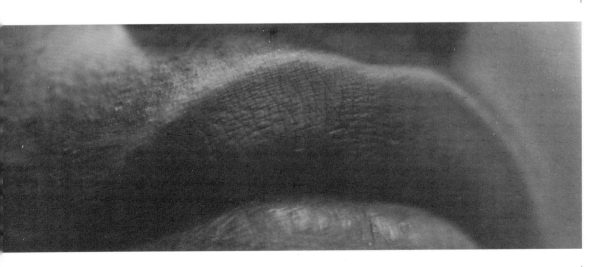

1 L. Jones, 'A Poem Some People Will Have to Understand', quoted in
G. Tate, *Flyboy in the Buttermilk*, New York, Fireside, 1992, p. 232.

INTRODUCTION

Race and architecture: two highly overworked and ill-understood terms. It is widely understood (implicitly *and* explicitly) that the makers and users of Architecture have historically and culturally been positioned as white. Scant attention has been paid to the racial identity of the makers and users of architecture and what impact the *mythical* identity of the white, male and 'universal' architect has had on the discipline. This chapter proposes to re-examine the terms 'architect' and 'user'; to open up this racialised discourse and to alter the terms of reference and expose a hidden richness in the ways in which we perceive and use space. At a time when the boundaries, binaries and hierarchies of architecture are under continued attack, it is now possible to re-examine a number of the 'taken-for-granted' terms. Jonathan Hill has asked us to re-think the relationship between architect and user but as he himself has already pointed out, 'the terms space, site, form, architect and user are themselves historical and ideological, not universal and neutral'.[2]

2 J. Hill, 'Between Six and a Million', *Defining the Urban Condition: Accelerating Change in the Geography of Power*, Washington DC, ACSA Press, 1995, pp. 179–81.

> *[Making] and [using] are not all that distinct for the [architect]. Both exercises require being alert and ready for unaccountable beauty, for the intricateness or simple elegance of the [architect's] imagination, for the world that the imagination evokes. Both require being mindful of the places where imagination sabotages itself, locks its own gates, pollutes its vision. [Making] and [using] mean being aware of the [architect's] notions of risk and safety, the serene achievement of, or sweaty fight for, meaning and response-ability.*[3]

3 T. Morrison, *Playing in the Dark: Whiteness & the Literary Imagination*, Cambridge, Mass., Harvard University Press, 1992, p. preface xiii.

In her 1992 essay, *Playing in the Dark*, novelist Toni Morrison spoke of writing and reading, not of making and using, and of the writer, not the architect. The substitutions are mine. Her essay offers an unusual insight into how racial formations lie at the heart of the American literary endeavour and how the construct of blackness both permitted *and* necessitated a counter-construction of whiteness. It is unusual for a number of reasons, but primarily because she focuses attention on a subject that has traditionally been shrouded in silence. What, she asks, is 'blackness' for? Whom does it serve? What are the effects of 'blackness' – both on perpetrator *and* victim? Uncovering a (literal) black hole in the history of the American novel, she examines the ways in which 'blackness' is constructed and hidden, submerged and exposed. The strategies she uses for uncovering this presence are worth expanding on, not least because the relationship between writer and reader is a crucial one in understanding the emerging discourse between architect and user.

Lesley Naa Norle Lokko

Marie Cardinal's *The Words To Say It* is a simple illustration of 'how each of us reads, becomes engaged in and *watches* what is read, all at the same time'.[4] Ostensibly the story of one woman's battle and eventual triumph over her 'madness', it is an autobiographical novel that contains a number of submerged racial narratives. Morrison's fascination with the unearthing of those narratives is triggered by the following passage by Cardinal:

4 ibid., p. preface xii.

My first anxiety attack occurred during a Louis Armstrong concert. I was nineteen or twenty. Armstrong was going to improvise with his trumpet, to build a whole composition in which each note would be important and would contain within itself the essence of the whole. I was not disappointed: the atmosphere warmed up very fast. The scaffolding and flying buttresses of the jazz instruments supported Armstrong's trumpet, creating spaces which were adequate enough for it to climb higher, establish itself and take off again. The sounds of the trumpet sometimes piled up together, fusing a new musical base, a sort of matrix which gave birth to one precise, unique note, tracing a sound whose path was almost painful, so absolutely necessary had its equilibrium and duration become; it tore at the nerves of those who followed it. My heart began to accelerate, becoming more important than the music, shaking the bars of my ribcage, compressing my lungs so the air could no longer enter them. Gripped by panic at the idea of dying there in the middle of spasms, stomping feet and the crowd howling, I ran into the street like someone possessed.[5]

5 ibid., p. preface viii.

The imagery that works as a catalyst for her (Cardinal's) anxiety attack is particularly powerful.

What on earth was Louie playing that night? What was there in his music that drove this sensitive young girl hyperventilating into the street? [What] ignited her strong apprehension of death, as well as this curious flight from the genius of improvisation, sublime order, poise and the illusion of permanence . . . one precise, unique note, tracing a sound whose path was almost painful, so absolutely necessary had its equilibrium and duration become; it tore at the nerves of those [other than Armstrong, apparently] who followed it. These are wonderful tropes for the illness that was breaking up Cardinal's life. Would an Edith Piaf concert or a Dvorak composition have had the same effect? What solicited my attention was whether the cultural associations of jazz were as important to Cardinal's 'possession' as were its intellectual foundations.[6]

6 ibid., pp. preface ix–x.

The observation shows how 'blackness' gives the writer a new source of imagery – 'like water, flight, war, birth, religion and so on, [the imagery] that make[s] up the writer's kit'.[7] For the black writer (maker), this imagery is problematic. Unlike Cardinal, who was a colonialist, a *pied-noir*, a Frenchwoman born and raised in Algeria, Morrison does not

7 ibid., p. preface xii.

. . . have quite the same access to these traditionally useful constructs of blackness: neither blackness nor 'people of colour' stimulates in me notions of excessive, limitless love, anarchy or routine dread. I cannot rely on these metaphorical shortcuts because I am a black writer struggling with and through a language that can powerfully evoke and enforce hidden signs of racial superiority, cultural hegemony and dismissive 'othering' of people and language which are by no means marginal, or [are] already and completely known and knowable in my work. My vulnerability would lie in

romanticising blackness, rather than demonising it; vilifying whiteness, rather than reifying it. The kind of work I have always wanted to do requires me to learn how to manoeuvre ways to free up the language from its sometimes sinister, frequently lazy, almost always predictable employment of racially informed and determined chains.[8]

8 ibid., p. preface xii–xiii.

Importantly and unusually, blackness is shown here to be a seductive *and* creative force – Morrison's agenda in *Playing in the Dark* is to expose the effect of this creativity on the literary imagination – *and its product.*

Morrison's observations are persuasive. Turning away from literature and the literary landscape back towards architecture, her essay – and my substitutions – open up a series of questions which directly address the identity of the architect and the nature of his [sic] practice. It would be an oversimplification to understand this chapter as one that seeks solely to attribute blame: that would simply construct a crude, binary opposition of the guilty and the innocent. What is more interesting, and what this chapter aims to do, is to look at how far the criteria by which guilt and innocence (and thereby response-ability) are determined have been historically constituted. Implicit too in this chapter is the awkward position of critical liminality: in one sense and particularly in *this* sense, to be critical is to be outside – outside, yes, but not marginal. Spatially, this is a limited and complex position. At this point, language – which is often much more adept at dodging the awful 'either/or' conundrum than architecture – which tends to be quite fixed about it – gets bogged down. So I must reckon with a different position, a different language . . . one which acknowledges the outside condition but does not deny it. In other words, I am writing out of the same cultural situation I am trying to examine and must be *aware* of this fact, not crushed by it. Although others have written extensively and in greater detail about the history and complexity of race, this chapter will focus selectively on certain aspects of that scholarship to support its argument. It is not intended to read as an exhaustive account of the etymology of the term but rather as an argument for the evidence of racial *thinking* in a discipline that, traditionally, has held itself 'above' such concerns. This chapter takes the view that, despite protestations to the contrary, race has been its [architecture's] subject matter all the time.

Lesley Naa Norle Lokko

'TO UNDERSTAND THE HOUSE-NEGRO, YOU GOTTA GO BACK. WAY BACK.'

You were called Bimbircocak
And all was well that way
You have become Victor–Émile–Louis–Henri–Joseph
Which
So far as I recall
Does not reflect your kinship with
Rockefeller[9]

9 Y. Ouologuem, 'À Mon Mari', quoted in K. A. Appiah, *In My Father's House: Africa in the Philosophy of Culture*, New York, Oxford University Press, 1992, p. 137.

Race, in its guise as an objective term of classification, has a number of peculiar inconsistencies. No case exists for the attribution of certain physical, moral or intellectual capabilities based on skin colour. 'The sense of difference defined in popular usages of the term "race" has both described and *inscribed* differences of language, belief system, artistic tradition and gene pool, as well as all sorts of supposedly natural attributes such as rhythm, athletic ability, usury, fidelity and so forth.'[10] When we speak of the black 'race' or the Aryan 'race', we are actually speaking in metaphor: biologically, no such 'thing' exists.

10 H. L. Gates Jr., in 'Introduction: Writing "Race" and the Difference It Makes', in H. L. Gates Jr (ed.) *"Race", Writing and Difference*, Chicago, The University of Chicago Press, 1985, p. 5.

'Racism' is the name given to a type of behaviour which consists in the display of contempt or aggressiveness toward other people on account of physical differences (other than sex) between them and oneself. It should be noted that this definition does not contain the word 'race', and this observation leads us to the first surprise in this area which contains many: whereas racism is a well-attested social phenomenon, 'race' itself does not exist![11]

11 T. Todorov, '"Race", Writing, and Culture', quoted in Gates, op. cit., p. 370.

So what is it?

Class- or *slave*-consciousness was certainly evident among the ancient Arab civilisations of the seventh and eighth centuries but although there is little evidence to support a singling-out of Africans from the general slave population, there is little doubt that, eventually, differences of colour began to matter. Freed slaves of white origin, from the Eurasian steppes, for example, would have assimilated into the general population – for black slaves, this was clearly more difficult. Already, the fusion of colour and class (essentially, what race is *about*) begins to surface. Blackness – in a place where whiteness counts – begins to matter. The image of the Moor in early Spanish literature shows us that between the conquest of Granada in 1492 and the expulsion of the Moors in 1609, powerful representations of the de-humanised 'other'

Lesley Naa Norle Lokko

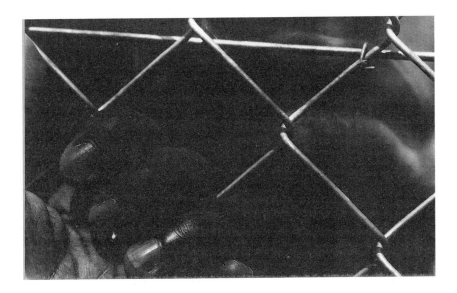

in ballads, dramas and novels are already in place. As a metaphor for 'darkness', the Moor is the catalyst for the Spanish (and later, European) obsession with *limpieza de sangre*, a theme that will run throughout European history, culminating not only in Auschwitz but, more recently, in Tuzla.

The year 1492 marked the beginning of a new era – lasting almost 500 years – in which Europe (a cultural, rather than geographical entity) shaped the modern world. On the seas, in agriculture, industry, politics, the rapid growth and expansion of urban centres, the half-dozen revolutions and, of course, the imperial project – Europe marked the globe in a way that no 'civilisation' had done before, or since. Racial *thinking* – pseudo-scientific ideas about race and difference – very quickly became the basis of an ideology that made the material exploitation of distant and different lands, peoples, customs, etc., a palatable, even *natural*, phenomenon. 'Neither imperialism nor colonialism is a simple act of accumulation and acquisition. Both are supported and even perhaps impelled by impressive ideological formations.'[12] By the seventeenth century, largely due to the importance of the slave trade in the economies of half-a-dozen European countries, race was widely understood as a trope of irreducible, absolute difference. The most obvious victims of racism are those whose identities were constructed within the colonial project: Africans, Asians and indigenous Americans but equally, those who were *displaced* by colonialism: West Indians, Africans and Asians in Britain, Arabs in France, etc. Although racism, to paraphrase Shohat and Stam, usually follows historical or concrete oppression, in general, 'the colonised were ridiculed as lacking in culture and history because colonialism, in the name of profit, was destroying

12 E. Said, *Culture & Imperialism*, London, Chatto & Windus, 1993, p. 8.

Lesley Naa Norle Lokko

13 E. Shohat and R. Stam (eds), *Unthinking Eurocentrism*, London, Routledge, 1994, p. 18.

the material basis of their culture and the archival memory of their history'.[13] At the height of their powers – in 1914 – European empires controlled more than half the globe: a staggering 72 million km^2 and almost 560 million people. The loose use of the term 'imperial' in everyday language points to a deep schism in the collective memories of Europeans and their subjects. The Chambers Dictionary defines 'imperial' as *'pertaining to, or of the nature of, an empire; sovereign, supreme; commanding, august; (of products, etc.) of superior quality'*. But 'empire' may also be defined in terms of brutal enslavement, institutional terrorism, cultural degradation and murder. Some 60 million Africans died during 500 years of the transatlantic slave trade – a number that has been quietly consigned to the small print of history. Quite literally, one man's empire is another man's hell.

Contemporary Eurocentric discourse, to which architecture is subject, is the residue of both colonialism and imperialism, two interdependent but differing phases of European history. Colonialism refers both to distant control (Indochine, Belgian Congo, Philippines) and to direct European settlement (Algeria, South Africa, Australia, the Americas, New Zealand). Interestingly, the words 'colonisation', 'culture' and 'cult' all stem from the Latin verb *colo* – (past participle: *cultus*, future participle: *culturus*). Occupying the land, agriculture, the telling of history and the affirmation of values are part of a constantly changing group of values and practices, etymologically linked.

The term 'diaspora' rises directly out of this history and the diasporic condition, which is of particular interest to me, has had a deep and lasting impact on the former slave-holding or colonial power(s). For slave-owning nations such as the United States, Brazil and the Caribbean, the insistent presence of diasporic blacks remains deeply problematic. Equally, for the former colonial powers, the demographic and cultural make-up of their urban centres has been irrevocably changed. In the delicate and biased balance of global power, societies which were once able to escape the harsh realities of colonial (and capital) expansion through enforced distancing practices (*apartheid*, immigration policies, even urban planning), now must stomach the by-products far closer to home.

14 C. West, *Keeping Faith: Philosophy and Race in America*, New York, Routledge, 1993, p. 16.

The black diasporan condition of New World servitude – in which they were viewed as mere commodities with production value, who had no proper legal status, social standing or public worth – can be characterised as, following Orlando Patterson, natal alienation [my italics]. This state of perpetual and inheritable domination that diasporan Africans had at birth produced the modern black diasporan problematic of invisibility and namelessness.[14]

Lesley Naa Norle Lokko

Invisibility and namelessness: two aspects of what Nadine Gordimer calls 'the old, admitted complicity in the slave trade or the price of raw materials'. Trapped by that complicity, like the Moor in the Text, the diasporan black presence will not be dispelled – the natives are coming 'home'. While direct colonial rule is no longer formally practised, the world remains hopelessly shackled to an indirect, abstract and economic form of rule: played out through the North/South divide, the G7, NATO, the IMF, World Bank and an unholy alliance of technology, information and 'culture' (Hollywood, UPI, Reuters, CNN, Internet, etc.). Global poverty is on the increase; burgeoning famine and paralysing debt are simply the backdrop for the opening up of resources for foreign (read: *colonial*) interests and internal (often brutal) political suppression. Again, as Shohat and Stam have already noted, there is a distinction to be made between '*colonial* discourse as the historical product of colonial institutions and *colonialist/imperialist* discourse as the linguistic/ideological [read: architectural] apparatus that justifies, contemporaneously or even retroactively, colonial/imperial practices' [my insertion].[15]

15 Shohat and Stam, op.cit., p. 18.

So the issue of *response-ability* remains neatly divided. Into the question come two very different histories: one, 'belonging' to the past but through which the present must be understood and the other, a contemporary condition that continues to threaten the supposed stability of the New World order. Where does one look for response-ability? In the past, in pre-colonial, Utopic Africa (or Asia, or the Americas) with its 'untainted' cultural practices, one of which is surely architecture? In the present, in contemporary New York–London–Paris (read: *Harlem–Hackney–Barbès*)? Or in the future, at some unknown synthesis (or perhaps departure) from both? The well-known Diasporic mantra states: *know from where you come: if you don't know where you've come from, how can you know where you are going?* Banister Fletcher's *The Tree of Architecture*[16] shows that, with regard to race, there *is* no way of knowing from where one comes – that history is wholly absent. There are a number of issues relevant to the aphorism above that are worth examining here, not only in terms of their historical worth but also in the way they permit – *force* – an altered perspective – and locate possible strategies for response.

16 *The Tree of Architecture* appears at the beginning of Banister Fletcher, *A History of Architecture on the Comparative Method*, London, Batsford, first published in 1896.

RESPONSE

So we came out possessed of what sufficed us, we thinking that we possessed all things, that we were wise, that there was nothing we did not know . . . we saw that, in fact, we black men came out without a single thing; we came out naked; we left

17 H. Callaway, *The Religious System of the amaZulu*, Cape Town, C. Struik, 1970.

18 C. Jencks, *Le Corbusier and the Tragic View of Architecture*, Cambridge, MA, Harvard University Press, 1973, p. 102

19 F. Fanon, 'The Fact of Blackness', in J. Donald and A. Rattavisi (eds), *'Race', Culture and Difference*, London, Open University Press (with Sage Publications), 1994, p. 233.

everything behind because we came out first. But as for white men . . . we saw that we came out in a hurry; but they waited for all things, that they might not leave any behind.[17]

Revd Henry Callaway

I look for primitive men not for their barbarity but for their wisdom.[18]

Le Corbusier

The men they took away knew how to build houses, govern empires, erect cities, cultivate fields, mine for metals, weave cotton, forge steel.[19]

Frantz Fanon

So now we come to the question of response and then very quickly to a number of basic questions. Response to what? What kind of response? A singular response? Or several? A built response? Or a metaphorical one? Or several? Or none of the above?

In 1971, Steve Biko addressed a number of black organisations in South Africa at a conference hosted by ASSECA (Association for the Educational and Cultural Development of the Africa People). His opening statement remains a powerful indictment of the nature of the relationship between race and culture. 'One of the most difficult things to do these days is to talk with any authority on anything to do with African culture. Somehow, Africans are not expected to have any deep understanding of their own culture, or even of themselves.'[20] His chapter in *I Write What I Like*, entitled 'Some African Cultural Concepts', is a deeply moving and nostalgic account of everyday, pre-colonial life.

20 S. Biko, *I Write What I Like*, Oxford, Heinemann, 1978, pp. 40–1.

> *We always place man first and hence all our action is usually joint community-oriented, rather than the individualism which is the hallmark of the capitalist approach. Attitudes of Africans to property again show just how unindividualistic the African is. As everybody here knows, African society had the village community as its basis. Africans always believed in having many villages with a controllable number of people in each, rather than the reverse. This obviously was a requirement to suit the needs of a community-based and man-centred society. Hence most things were jointly owned by the group, for instance, there was no such thing as individual land ownership. The land belonged to the people and was merely under the control of the local chief on behalf of the people. When the cattle went to graze, it was on an open veld and not on anybody's specific farm.*[21]

21 ibid., p. 43.

Lesley Naa Norle Lokko

Biko's suggestion that Africa's special contribution to the world – that of giving it a more human face – is yet to come will raise a chord with anyone who has spent time in Africa. Two further passages from this same chapter are worth quoting in full:

> The Westerner has an aggressive mentality. When he sees a problem, he will not rest until he has formulated some solution to it. He cannot live with contradictory ideas in his mind; he must settle for one or the other or else evolve a third idea in his mind which harmonises or reconciles the other two. And he is vigorously scientific in rejecting solutions for which there is no basis in logic. He draws a sharp line between the natural and the supernatural, the rational and the non-rational and more often than not, he dismisses the supernatural and the non-rational as superstition. . . .

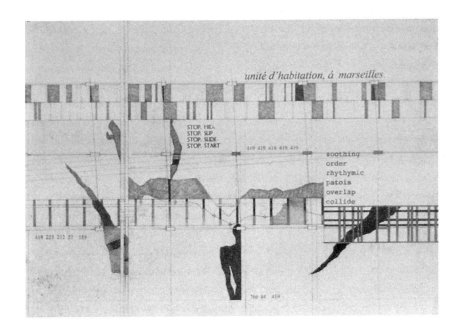

unité d'habitation, à marseilles.

> . . . Africans, being a pre-scientific people do not recognise any conceptual cleavage between the natural and the supernatural. They experience a situation, rather than face a problem. By this I mean they allow both the rational and non-rational elements to make an impact upon them and any action they may take could be described more as a response of the total personality to the situation than the result of some mental exercise.[22]

22 ibid., p. 44.

Lesley Naa Norle Lokko

It is of course true that the picture painted by Biko no longer exists. Modern-day Africa is as torn apart and fragmented by internal (African) disputes as anywhere else. But the account is nevertheless arresting and must be considered. And here I must tread carefully because it is instinct, not intellect (not mutually exclusive, but different) which drives the following points.

Biko's words invoke the same schism I spoke of earlier, when referring to the collective memories of Europeans and their subjects and the differing ways in which 'Empire' is perceived and remembered. On the one hand, there is an 'illegal' past, rendered obsolete by the colonial process, the terms 'Third World' and 'developing nation' and the unequal division of international labour. This discredited past is simply a reflection of the way in which Africans, through the missionary/colonial/imperial encounter, were taught to see their past as a 'wasteland of non-achievement',[23] a vision from which the continent and the Diaspora still suffers. And yet on the other hand, within the post-colonial world, there exists a growing and powerful opposition to this view – a desire to re-evoke and re-examine that past in order to conceive of strategies for coping with an uncertain and problematic future. Closing the gap between these two worlds requires the setting up of another, *essential* relationship between the past and the technological present, which is unlike any other. This relationship, if it is to succeed, (and here Gordimer says it so well) must 'be recognised as something distinct from the inherent threat of all-white culture'.[24] The technological age (to which the 'modern' tradition of architecture belongs – I am not simply speaking of modernism) cannot be denied – it is with us in Africa for ever. The tools of all-white culture – writing, reading, Architecture – should be recognised as '*independent* of that threat' (my italics)[25]. *Aware, not crushed.* For the contemporary black/African architect, there is an enormous force waiting to charge him – part of the Yeatsian drive 'to express a life that has never found expression'.[26] For the contemporary black/African architect, his 'commitment is the point at which inner and outer worlds fuse; his purpose to master his art and his purpose to change the *nature* of art, create new norms and forms out of and for a people'[27] already in the process of re-creating themselves. As Malindi Neluheni (herself a black South African planner) questions in 'Apartheid Urban Design', 'design by whose standards?'[28]

The idea of stridently calling on architecture to make a response to this particular concern is a peculiar one, not least because architecture, generally speaking, is rather slow off the mark. One possible clue in the mystery of how to find a response is to look more closely at the nature of architecture itself: perhaps there is something there, hidden in the cultural, artistic, professional and legal codes in which the discipline cloaks itself. We are accustomed to speaking of architecture as an autonomous, distanced process – coupled with and yet curiously divorced from what we loosely term

23 Ngugi wa Thiong'o, *Decolonising the Mind: The Politics of Language in African Literature*, London and Nairobi, Heinemann, 1986.

24 N. Gordimer, *The Essential Gesture*, London, Jonathan Cape, 1988, p. 141.

25 ibid., p. 142.

26 ibid., p. 140.

27 ibid., p. 137.

28 M. Neluheni, 'Apartheid Urban Design', in L. Lokko (ed.), *White Papers, Black Marks*, Chichester, John Wiley & Sons, forthcoming.

Lesley Naa Norle Lokko

'society' (oh, there's a pressing need for a new word here, one that encompasses a whole *range* of issues: cultural, political, social, economic . . . a kind of 'cablinasian'[29] term). Neither fish nor fowl, architecture has always straddled an uneasy divide – small wonder it weighs so heavily. It has always been possible to reference architecture through a set of 'other' voices – philosophy, art history, feminist theory, etc. Its traditional 'voice' is the drawing/model/treatise/manifesto – discussion of this voice is often limited to traditional formal qualities, supposedly intrinsic to architectural form, such as quality of light, space, organisation, material, axialities, orders and so on. This reduction supports the classification of architecture as an object-driven exercise

– the building, in the end, is everything – and manages to side-step the question of context. But we know that the 'voice' is subject to the same hidden (or subtle) forces that Morrison pointed out earlier in the chapter. We know that techniques of representation, production, language and vision are historically and ideologically constituted. We know too that the product, the end-result, is appropriated and lived through and that this is beyond the architect's grasp. To go back to Morrison: 'Black slavery enriched the country's creative possibilities. For in that construction of blackness *and* enslavement could be found not only the *not-free*, but also, with the dramatic polarity created by skin colour, the projection of the *not-me*. The result was a playground for the imagination.'[30] How does one interrogate or enter the playground?

To enter into this aspect of relationship between race and architecture, it is necessary to enter through the back-door and not through the front. The 'voice' of form, of formal and spatial relations, is actually a highly complex, highly seductive whisper: its ability to cope with these questions in its present state is limited. But I would suggest that there are a number of interesting and unusual opportunities around this particular impasse. Vision, language, text, flesh – these are a few examples of the way in which we might re-think the subject of this relationship. Each suggests a history, a context and use – particularly appropriate in the question of 'maker/user'.

29 The term 'cablinasian' was coined by the US Golf champion, Tiger Woods, who is part African American, part Asian, part white and part Native American. The term is currently in popular usage.

30 Morrison, op. cit., p. 38.

Lesley Naa Norle Lokko

Sometimes it is the other way around. A white person is set down in our midst, but the contrast is just as sharp for me. For instance, when I sit in the drafty basement that is The New World Cabaret with a white person, my colour comes. We enter chatting about any little nothing that we have in common and are seated by the jazz waiters. In the abrupt way that jazz orchestras have, this one plunges into a number. It loses no time in circumlocations, but gets right down to business. It constricts the thorax and splits the heart with its tempo and narcotic harmonies. This orchestra grows rambunctious, rears on its hind legs and attacks the tonal veil with primitive fury, rending it, clawing it until it breaks through to the jungle beyond. I follow those heathen – follow them exultingly. I dance wildly inside myself; I yell within, I whoop; I shake my assegai above my head, I hurl it true to the mark yeeeeooww! I am in the jungle and living in the jungle way. My face is painted red and yellow and my body is painted blue. My pulse is throbbing like a war drum. I want to slaughter something – give pain, give death to what, I don't know. But the piece ends. The men of the orchestra wipe their lips and rest their fingers. I creep back slowly to the veneer we call civilisation with the last tone and find the white friend sitting motionless in his seat, smoking calmly.

'Good music they have here', he remarks, drumming the table with his fingertips/ Music. The great blobs of purple and red emotion have not touched him. He has only heard what I felt. He is far away and I see him but dimly across the ocean and the continent that have fallen between us. He is so pale with his whiteness then and I am so coloured.[31]

31 Z. N. Hurston, 'How It Feels to Be Coloured Me', in A. Walker (ed.), *I Love Myself When I Am Laughing and Then Again When I Am Looking Mean and Impressive: A Zora Neale Hurston Reader*, New York, Old Westbury, 1979, pp.152–5.

Vision, in the Western, Cartesian sense of the word is interesting for a number of reasons. The modern era has been dominated by the visual: beginning with the Renaissance and the scientific revolution, modernity has concerned itself primarily with the sense of sight, aided by the invention of the telescope and microscope – vision conquering things both near and far. Visuality, in relation to architecture, is particularly interesting because it is the medium through which architecture, by and large, is imagined and then experienced: the medium of choice of both maker and user. Where this medium intersects with race is also interesting and provides one of the first openings into this relationship.

The late medieval fascination with the metaphysical implications of light (light as divine *lux*, rather than perceived *lumen*) gave rise to the linear perspective, symbolising total harmony between mathematics and God's will. Light and dark have a permanent and symbolic place in Western thought – the medievalists often conceived of God in terms of light, and regarded it as the original metaphor for spiritual realities. European languages, in particular, are filled with references to the binary relationship of light and dark, good and evil, black and white. The casual and sloppy use of the terms black, dark, night, etc., subtly and implicitly fix that original relationship, even when the religious connotations have been eroded. But light and dark are also simple, fundamental qualities of the architectural experience: with the efforts of Brunelleschi and Alberti, the three-dimensional space of the world is translated onto a two-dimensional surface and light enters the body of architecture, chasing out the dark (bad).

Hal Foster, in *Vision and Visuality*, draws attention to the 'difference within the visual – between the mechanism of sight and its historical techniques, between the datum of vision and its discursive determinations – a difference, many differences, among how we see, how we are able, allowed or made to see and how we see this "unseeing" or the unseen'.[32] The three-dimensional, rationalised space of perspectival vision bequeathed the singular, static and fixated 'eye' to the modern world (and its architecture) and this again has radical implications for the racialised maker/user. If the black maker/user 'belongs' to a tradition that neither sees the world as a divine text, nor as a mathematically regulated spatio-temporal order which privileges only the dispassionate eye of the neutral and objective viewer, what alternative strategies for seeing (and thus making and using) are available? For the architect and user, engaged simultaneously as performer and interpreter, the terms 'making' and 'using' imply a shared world vision and an endlessly flexible language – what are the implications for the architect and user if the vision is no longer shared and the language intolerable?

> *Any number can provide a base for counting, though in most cultures the base has been five, ten or twenty, in correspondence with the groupings of fingers and toes. One of the curiosities of ethnology is the quaternary system of the Yuki Indians in California. They counted on the spaces between fingers.*[33]

The ideology that supported the imperial–colonial project was almost wholly reliant on a set of linguistic, physical and metaphorical binary groupings: *us/*them; *West/*East; *master/*slave; *white/*black – a set of convenient, if arbitrary, rules. Prior to Derrida's deconstructionist reading of philosophy, epistemological, ethical and logical systems were constructed on the basis of these conceptual oppositions. One of the terms in each set is privileged, the other debased and it is important to remember that most of the binaries organise knowledge in ways that are flattering to the Eurocentric imagination. Derrida's analysis of the denigrated and marginalised term within the binary relationship is interesting to anyone concerned with race: his readings suggest a binary relationship all of its own. Again, like Morrison, his analysis points to the fact that, rather than being *marginal*, blackness is absolutely central to the construction of whiteness – ain't no white without black, although the statement (historically speaking),

32 H. Foster (ed.), *Vision and Visuality*, Seattle, Bay Press, 1988, p. *preface ix.*

33 M. Gardner, *The Night is Large*, London, St. Martin's Press, 1996, p. 261.

Lesley Naa Norle Lokko

is not readily reversible. Contrary to the natural unities presented in the pairing of opposites, these pairings are actually the result of a process of overdeterminism: the constitution of an identity is always based on exclusion and the establishment of a violent hierarchy between the two resultant poles. Fanon understood this violence only too well. 'Decolonisation, which sets out to change the order of the world, is, obviously, a programme of complete disorder. [It] is the meeting of two forces, opposed to each other by their very nature . . . their first encounter was marked by violence and their existence together – that is to say the exploitation of the native by the settler – was carried on by dint of a great array of bayonets and cannon.'[34] The second act of colonialism is usually one of construction – the occupation and settlement of the land. Like colonialism and construction, perhaps decolonisation and deconstruction have more in common than was previously (if at all) suspected.

Stuart Hall's writings on the issue of identity provide an interesting model for architectural thought. Speaking of identities, he writes:

> Though they seem to evoke an origin in a historical past with which they continue to correspond, actually identities are about questions of using the resources of history, language and culture in the process of becoming, rather than being: not 'who we are' or 'where we came from' so much as what we might become, how we have been represented and how that bears on how we might represent ourselves. Identities are therefore constituted within, not outside representation.[35]

In the aftermath of the raw imperial endeavour, a new set of conditions comes into play: diverse, different and hybrid. The binaries have been replaced with a language that attempts to resist the old couplings in favour of a new set of spatio-social conditions. This is the space of a new experience, one that belongs solely to the contemporary, post-colonial world. The binaries of white/black, same/different might therefore be replaced by 'white *within* black' or vice versa, 'same *without* difference'. The possibilities for an architectural rendering (or multiple renderings) of the terms are myriad.

> The griot keeps the past alive in the minds and hearts of the group and, in the shaping of the recitation, the consensus of the group about its own identity evolves through time. The griot comments on the past in the light of the present and vice versa, communicating not in the disengaged, third person voice that has been the hallmark of conventional Western history, but in a manner fully engaged with the on-going drama of the group.[36]

Cheryl Chisholm

34 F. Fanon, *The Wretched of the Earth*, trans. C. Farrington, France, François Maspéro, 1961, p. 27.

35 S. Hall, 'Introduction', in S. Hall and P. du Gay (eds), *Questions of Cultural Identity*, London, Sage Publications, 1996, p. 4.

36 C. Chisholm, 'Voice of the Griot: African American Film & Video', in B. Abrash and C. Egan (eds), *Mediating History*, New York, New York University Press, 1992, p. 22.

Lesley Naa Norle Lokko

In other forms of cultural production, most notably music and film, practitioners have explored a wide range of alternative strategies for pursuing their art. Some of these strategies by-pass the formal conventions of music- and film-making in favour of modes of representation such as rap (analogous to the griot oral tradition of the Senegambian peoples of West Africa), jazz, carnival, the magical realist, the resistant postmodernist and the para-modernist (a more appropriate term, I feel). Jazz, in particular, has provided fertile ground for the African American architectural imagination. Araya Asgedom's essay, *The Unsounded Space*, establishes a fascinating relationship between jazz, repetition, Heidegger and structure. Asgedom shows how, in jazz improvisation, the past is brought forward to the present, 'not for its past material, but for its possibilities'.[37] Crucially, *convention* and *possibility* coincide at regular intervals during a given performance: if this occurrence is successful, if all the players retrieving past material and simultaneously improvising 'get it right', then this is what gives rise to an 'extraordinarily transcendental experience, where the players feel

37 A. Asgedom, 'The Unsounded Space', in Lokko, op. cit.

Lesley Naa Norle Lokko

38 ibid.

39 J. S. Mbiti, *African Religions and Philosophy*, Oxford, Heinemann, 1969, pp. 108–9.

40 Asgedom in Lokko, op. cit.

41 ibid.

42 ibid.

43 ibid.

in touch with the big picture and their moment of hearkening becomes timeless, peaceful yet energising and euphoric'.[38] This act takes us directly back to the African anti-Cartesianism of 'I am, because we are; and since we are, therefore I am'.[39] Asgedom goes on to link the dying wish of Socrates, 'to cultivate and make music',[40] to the work of Victor Zuckerkandl, the German philosopher of music. Zuckerkandl calls 'the order of auditory space'[41] the counterpart to 'visual–geometric–haptic space'[42] and Asgedom uses this pronouncement to raise a series of radical, provocative and complex questions about our understanding of the relationship between ourselves and the external world, in which architecture carries such weight. In societies where music and language are synonymous, there is an altogether more delicate, sophis- ticated relationship between the 'external world of things and objects and the interior of our bodies and selves'.[43] He cites Peter Eisenmann, who concludes his 1992 essay *Vision's Unfolding: Architecture in the Age of Electronic Media* with the following words:

44 ibid.

> Architecture will continue to stand up, to deal with gravity, to have 'four walls'. But these four walls no longer need to be expressive of the mechanical paradigm. Rather, they could deal with the possibility of these other discourses, the other affective senses of sound, touch and of that light within darkness.[44]

Bakhtin's reading of the carnival as an anti-Classical aesthetic that rejects formal harmony and unity in favour of the asymmetrical, the heterogeneous, the miscegenated is another powerful strategy worth considering. Demonstrating a kind of rebellious, vulgar beauty, the carnival favours what Rabelais termed a *grammatica jocosa* (playful grammar) which frees language (music, dance, form) from decorum and formality. The carnival rejects the idealised notion of beauty and exalts and exaggerates the grotesque, the base, the raw – carnival, essentially, is anti-grammatic. Again, this concept can be linked directly to race – to the diasporic experience. Black musicians have always improvised, turning the throw-away, cast-off detritus (washboards, tubs, oil drums, steel pans) into dynamic, energising musicality. Jazz musicians have always

45 A. Jaffa, '69' in G. Dent (ed.), *Black Popular Culture*, Seattle, Bay Press, 1992, p. 266.

> . . . stretched the capabilities of European instruments by playing the trumpet 'higher' than it was supposed to go, by hitting two keys, mis-hitting keys (like Monk did), flubbing notes to fight the equipment. In such cases, the violation of aesthetic etiquette and decorum goes hand in hand with an implicit critique of conventional and political hierarchies.[45]

Lesley Naa Norle Lokko

The architectural equivalent of treating 'notes as indeterminate, inherently unstable sonic frequencies rather than . . . fixed phenomena'[46] is a critique that strikes right at the heart of the discipline. Irrationality, disorder, instability? Architecture, as we know, is not in the business of providing these things. At a lecture I gave recently, Ian Hall (a musician of African descent and no relation to Stuart) told the audience that at some point in the seventeenth century, someone 'sat down' and tried to re-create the lost art of Greek drama. What he came up with instead is what we now call opera. His question, which remains an interesting and provocative thought, was whether, by consciously putting together the terms race and architecture, one could come up with something entirely new – again, neither race nor architecture *exactly* (whatever is understood by those terms) but some unforeseen combination, subliminally new.

[46] ibid., pp. 249–54.

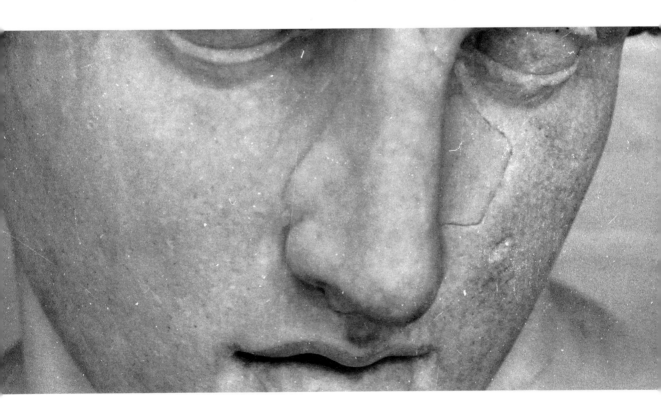

Lesley Naa Norle Lokko

ABILITY

47 D. P. Amory, 'Watching the Table Disappear: Identity and Politics in Africa and the Academy', paper given at the African Studies Association, 1990, quoted in Shohat and Stam, op. cit., p. 345.

Doesn't it seem funny that at the very point when women and people of colour are ready to sit down at the bargaining table with the white boys, that the table disappears? That is, suddenly there are no grounds for claims to truth and knowledge anymore and here we are, standing in the conference room making all sorts of claims to knowledge and truth but suddenly without a table upon which to put our papers and coffee cups, let alone to bang our fists.[47]

48 E. Fox-Genovese, 'The Claims of a Common Culture: Gender, Race, Class and the Canon', *Salmagundi*, No. 72, Fall 1986, p. 121, quoted in Shohat and Stam, op. cit., p. 345.

Surely it is no coincidence . . . that the Western white male elite proclaimed the death of the subject at precisely the moment at which it might have had to share that status with the women and peoples of other races and classes who were beginning to challenge its supremacy?[48]

This chapter has struggled with a number of different and divergent threads: first, to place architecture at the centre of an on-going debate about the place of race in contemporary society and at the same time, align this placement with the overthrow of the architect/user dualism, with which the book, as a whole, is preoccupied. I have tried to show the complexity (and indeed uncertainty) that accompanies such debate: in particular, the uncertainty surrounding where to place or offer oneself — maker? User? Past, present or future? Perhaps the categories, in this instance, are irrelevant and the 'answer' lies, as Asgedom suggests, in some synthesis of all three? Second, it has struggled to place what appears to be an unrelated discourse within contemporary architectural theory — showing the relationship between colonialism/racism/imperialism and visual theories, deconstruction theory, structuralism, 'the death of the author', post- and paramodernism, etc. Third, and finally, *Occupying Architecture* is interested in pushing the boundaries of architecture: materially, spatially, programmatically, formally. In understanding race as a creative, vibrant addition to that discourse, architecture stands ready to recognise difference, to acknowledge it, take it into account and, crucially, allow itself to be transformed. Identity, even *architectural* identity, is, as Hall has pointed out, a matter of 'becoming'. In the final analysis, architecture must surely display the ability to try.

Lesley Naa Norle Lokko

There is no forgetting how we could live if only we could find the way. We must continue to be tormented by the ideal. Its possibility must be there for peoples to attempt to put into practice, to begin over and over again, wherever it has failed, wherever in the world it has never been tried, or has failed. This is where your responsibility to the Third World meets mine. Without the [ability] to tramp towards that possibility, no relations of whites, of the West, with the West's formerly subject peoples can ever be free of the past, because the past, for them, was the jungle of Western capitalism, not the light the missionaries thought they brought with them.[49]

49 N. Gordimer, *The Essential Gesture*, London, Jonathan Cape, 1988, p. 284.

Lesley Naa Norle Lokko

Jeremy Till 4

architecture of the
impure community

Some time ago I was attending a constituency meeting of my local Labour party. In a comradely nod to the campaigning roots of the party, each meeting had a period devoted to 'political education'. The topic this time was community architecture. What I remember most of all was the anger of the speaker as he sustained a half-hour diatribe, eyes glaring, which laid all the sores of society at the feet of the architect. All the normal crimes – tower blocks, housing estates, white walls, balcony access, aesthetics over function – were recounted and then conflated with conservative and repressive political regimes. The story left the audience in no doubt as to the evil of architects and their implied association with political corruption. This was then juxtaposed with the benefits of community architecture in which the users were seen to have control over their environmental destiny in a truly democratic manner. The speaker ended by insisting that architects should be stripped of all their power and simply left with their pens, there to be pushed in directions instructed by the community. In effect, the only attribute left to the architect was to be the ability to draw lines without making splodges.

Everyone clapped. It was a classic story of good guy vs. bad guy, and the audience knew which side they were on. Pathetically I sat on my hands, revealing neither my profession nor my vocation. There was something so dogmatically oppositional in the structure of the talk that any responder would have been forced to take sides. This I was not prepared to do. Maybe it was the aggression in the air – I still remember those eyes – which meant I could not face further public humiliation. Maybe also I could feel more politically correct in my silent association. Maybe I had nagging doubts about my pens which always splodged. I snuck off guilty at not having defended my vocation and missed the raffle.

This essay is my response. It is a response that suggests that the issues at stake are more complex than suggested by the simple dualism that structures much discussion of community architecture, including that at the Labour party meeting. My argument is that the oppositional genesis of community architecture results in its marginalisation, and with it an associated political disempowerment. Before positing an alternative way out of this dilemma, I wish to examine some of the premises for community architecture and the way that these may paradoxically result in an environment divested of the strength which it is set up to have. I concentrate on a period, the 1980s, and a place, the United Kingdom, because this context gave rise to a view of community architecture which manifested in an exaggerated way some of the traits of the movement set in other times and places; it provides a model against which to test the wider claims of community architecture. My interest is to explore whether this model provides an alternative to normative practice and in particular whether it genuinely redefines the relationship between architect and user. My argument takes to task some of the theoretical claims made for the movement; in this it rides the waves of political incorrectness. This is intentional. Community architecture has protected itself with a soft layer of liberal rectitude which has pre-empted a sustained critique; my own behaviour at the Labour Party meeting is indicative of the problem.

THE MYTH OF COMMUNITY

The book on Community Architecture by Nick Wates and Charles Knevitt (a book which played a central role in promulgating the movement) opens with an apocalyptic description of the Broadwater Farm riots of 1985, when 'violence erupted' on a North London housing estate.

> As families and the elderly cowered in their homes, gangs of youths – armed with bricks, knives, bottles and petrol bombs – confronted hundreds of police armed with riot shields and batons. What had been thought of as a model housing estate on its completion only twelve years previously became, for several hours, a battleground.[1]

1 N. Wates and C. Knevitt, *Community Architecture*, London, Penguin, 1987, p. 15.

Against an architectural backdrop, the authors suggest that there was 'a possible link between social unrest and the degree of control that people have over their environment'.[2] The book then proceeds with a benign introduction to community architecture. The argument is never explicitly made, but the implication of this hysterical opening of social unrest is clear: traditional architecture, because of its remote and irresponsible genesis, is the cause of social breakdown; community architecture, with its engaged and democratic genesis, will overcome these ills. Central to this argument is the idea that community architecture will 'lead to more stable and self-sufficient communities, and to more contented and confident citizens and professionals'.[3]

2 ibid., p. 16.

3 ibid., p. 28.

The word 'community' is always suggestive but never fully defined, holding out the promise of containing the values of interaction, mutual support and communality. It is perhaps not surprising that the community architecture movement reached its peak in the 1980s, when the politics of Thatcher and Reagan made an assault on those very values. Whilst both politicians announced the dismantling of the centralised state, their policies achieved quite the opposite. At the same time their ideological stress on the economic right of the individual led to the atomisation of society. Caught between the imperious power of the state and competing demands of individuals, the idea of community becomes a natural and appealing response. However, as Richard Sennett points out the *idea* of community is often at odds with the reality of the social

Jeremy Till

4 R. Sennett, *The Uses of Disorder*, London, Penguin, 1971, pp. 32ff.

construction of community. The result is what he calls 'the myth of the purified community'[4] in which a group forms a theoretical community but never engages in it. Sennett notes that this is a general condition which:

> is bred out of the way that human beings learn at a certain point in their own development to lie to themselves, in order to avoid new experiences that might force them to endure the pain of perceiving the unexpected, the new, the otherness around them. Through this peculiar learning process 'belonging' to one another becomes a shared sense of what we think we ought to be like, as one social being, in order not to be hurt.[5]

5 ibid., p. 41., my italics.

The *word* 'community' thus does all the work on its own, avoiding the need for actual participation in the community. The result is that 'communally painful experiences, unknown social experiences full of possible surprise and challenge, can be avoided by the common consent of a community to believe they already know the meaning of these experiences and have drawn the lessons from them together'.[6] Any real collective intent to resist the domination of the state or the divisive forces of the competing individuals is dissipated because the myth of the community does not take into account its actual political and social construction. The philosopher Gillian Rose notes that this attitude to community 'separates each person into a private autonomous competitive person and a fantasy life community, a life of unbounded mutuality. A fantasy life which effectively destroys the remnant of political life.'[7] To some extent the political climate of the 1980s made a retreat into the *purified* idea of community understandable, particularly in the United Kingdom where the disempowering of local government cut off what could have been the only source of funding for the establishment of communities in the real, and not ideal, sense of the word.

6 ibid., p. 40.

7 G. Rose, 'Athens and Jerusalem: A Tale of Three Cities', *Social and Legal Studies*, 1994, vol. 3, p. 337.

In the case of community architecture, the authority of both state and architect is meant to be dissolved by the empowerment of users within a community. However, this dissolution is achieved by recourse to the idea of the purified community which will fictively, but in fact impotently, resist the impositions of both state and individual. The impotence of this condition is disguised under the illusion that community architecture stands for the architecture of community. Because it is designated community architecture and because it 'looks like' community architecture, it is meant to bring with it all the aspects of community. Community architecture contains visual and linguistic resonances which are there to persuade a social body of the presence of community, whilst in fact it may ignore the actual construction of that community and thereby allow the forces of both state and individual to reassert themselves unchallenged.

Jeremy Till

If community architecture genuinely embodied a community one would expect that it would result in a radical spatial reconfiguration, in particular that of the relationship of the public realm to the private. And yet the spatialisation of much community architecture bears an uncanny resemblance to suburban forms, which for Sennett represent the ultimate manifestation of the purified community, individuals claiming their own territory under a mythical feeling of collectivity.[8] The 'community' suggested is one which relies on suburban or anti-urban antecedents and one which effectively turns its back on the city as a container for collective life. It is a community which is defined by groups of a narrow social definition, at worst driven by self-interest, and is therefore exclusive and not inclusive, as a true public social community could be.

In its construction of a myth of purified community, community architecture suffers the same utopian tendencies as the modernist architecture that it was set up to overturn. Even though modernist architecture and community architecture are radically different in their means of production, they both bring with them idealised visions of society so that, as Gillian Rose notes, '(community architecture) elevated ostensibly to assuage the ravages of modernism ensures that the range of argument about architecture remains utopian', a comment that she precedes with the statement of a 'general law that one day's utopia becomes the following day's dystopia'.[9] Community architecture ostensibly (and in the worst cases sanctimoniously), set up as it was to address the social aspirations of the user, thus runs the risk of inevitable disappointment when those aspirations are scarred by conditions and events beyond the control of the social or architectural determinist. The result is that the hopes of the user are falsely raised, so that, as Rose notes, 'the imaginary liberation from "total" domination amounts to legitimation of a new architectural utopianism . . . (which) takes place at the wake of the disenfranchised people'.[10]

The utopian problem of both 1980s community architecture and modernist architectural practice results in a will to create pure forms for pure occupation. Both architectural models, however, suffer Rose's fate that today's utopia becomes tomorrow's dystopia — accident, dirt, politics, tension, selfishness, social structures — all these and more rush in to besmirch the purified ideal. The very perfection of these models' genesis makes this scarring inevitable. My response to this problem starts with a dialectical obviousness. Architecture, be it the community version or the 'traditional' version (by the end of this essay I yearn for these distinctions to be dissolved) must relinquish its delusion of purity and accept contingency and the reality of social construction. We should not talk of community architecture, but the architecture of the impure community. But where my argument has a dialectical genesis, it does not end up in an oppositional entrenchment — on the one hand celebrating the impure, the chaotic, on the other hand resignedly accepting defeat in

8 The same problem can be seen in the support that community architecture gives to the notion of defensible space. This approach, championed by Oscar Newman in the 1960s and 1970s relies on the demarcation of the individual's territory from the public realm as a means of defence from crime and violence. Public space, which in the idealised community stands for the space of collective life and discourse, is thus either completely lost or else effectively taken over by privatised space. O. Newman, *Defensible Space*, New York, Macmillan, 1972.

9 G. Rose, *Broken Middle*, Oxford, Blackwell, 1992, p. 300.

10 ibid.

Jeremy Till

the face of more powerful conditions beyond. Rather, with a critical acknowledgement of the forces of state, individual and community it is then able to act *intentionally*, starting with a critical awareness of actual conditions and moving forward in a productive manner by using the residual strength of spatial reconfiguration.

POLITICAL AMNESIA

There is something obscene about Wates and Knevitt's use of Broadwater Farm as an architectural nemesis and the subsequent redemptive status of community architecture. Their argument is one of architectural determinism inasmuch as the spatial structure of a housing estate is seen as the prime factor in causing social unrest, and that in response community architecture alone will create stable communities which 'can create employment . . . (and) help reduce crime, vandalism, mental stress, ill health and the potential for urban unrest'.[11]

To promote, say, balcony access over chronic unemployment as the cause for social unrest is symptomatic of a determinist approach to architecture in which the built form is argued to have a direct causal effect on social behaviour. Not only is this argument extraordinarily misinformed but is also extraordinarily dangerous. Misinformed because, in its focus on architecture alone, it conveniently overlooks the wider social and political structures that contribute to the production and inhabitation of the built environment; dangerous because of the political amnesia that it thereby induces. To blame the architect for society's disruption is to forget the political conditions which promote those disruptions, which is why the argument may be so convenient for conservative critics such as Alice Coleman in her book *Utopia on Trial*.[12]

In the same manner, many of the proponents of community architecture will champion its social benefits on the one hand, whilst underplaying its political intent on the other. This political amnesia is implied by Wates and Knevitt when they state that 'community architecture is not political in the party political sense of the word . . . it transcends traditional Left/Right politics'.[13] This curious claim for 1980s community architecture is very different from the 1960s radical architecture movement. Activists for the latter, such as Colin Ward, were explicitly political in their intent and saw the users' involvement in the production of their own environment as an overtly political act. Ward states that 'it would be foolish to suggest that it (tenant control) is not a political matter. It is political in the most profound sense: it is about the distribution of power in society.'[14] Wates and Knevitt are prepared to accept this political content in one breath, but then state in the next that community architecture 'is not rigidly pro- or anti-public or private ownership of land'[15] – a division that must surely be one of the key

[11] Wates and Knevitt, op. cit., p. 20.

[12] A. Coleman, *Utopia on Trial*, London, Hilary Shipman, 1985.

[13] Wates and Knevitt, op. cit., p. 21.

[14] C. Ward, *Tenants Take Over*, London, Architectural Press, 1974, p. 43.

[15] Wates and Knevitt, op. cit., p. 21.

Jeremy Till

political issues of the day. Such political ambivalence may be seen as part of a wider drift towards the politics of consensus, but it is in the end a dispiriting and dis-empowering stance to take. Just as with consensus politics, where a central position is taken so as to offend neither left or right, community architecture ends up confirming a status quo.

Probably the most powerful symbol of the *seemingly* apolitical nature of community architecture is Prince Charles. The future monarch must constitutionally stay within politically neutral territory; his loud and public association with community architecture supposedly provided that territory. However, his pronouncements on the subject often veered dangerously towards a political position, most famously in the 'Divided Britain' controversy. Following an interview with Rod Hackney, then the President of the RIBA, the *Manchester Evening News* revealed Prince Charles' fears for the nation. The story ran: 'The biggest fear of Prince Charles is that he will inherit the throne of a divided Britain.' Hackney was then quoted. 'He (Prince Charles) is very worried that when he becomes king there will be "no-go" areas in the inner cities, and that the (racial minorities) will be alienated from the rest of the country.'[16] The story, which cleverly managed to anger both the Queen and Margaret Thatcher, was never fully retracted. A political storm ensued, in which the connections between inner city decay, conservative rule and community architecture formed a heady, and never resolved, mixture. What is interesting is that the story was leaked (whether intentionally or not has never been revealed) through the foremost proponent of community architecture, Rod Hackney. The political implications of the movement managed vengefully to sneak out from behind the neutral mask that community architecture often presented to the world. In this light it might be argued that Prince Charles was using, whether knowingly or not, the political potential latent in community architecture – a potential that is largely suppressed through recourse to the consensual stance set up to quell the doubts of left and right. The political content of the Prince's pronouncements was almost completely ignored by the architectural profession who saved their rage for the responses to what they perceived to be the directly 'architectural' attacks (on style and personalities) that he had made – an outpouring of architectural grief which is indicative of the profession's unwillingness to face up to the political implications of their work.

As in its utopian tendencies, community architecture here again holds up a mirror to normal architecture. The two meld, dispiritingly caught in infinite reflec-tions, cut off from the world beyond. My suggestion is to twist the mirrors, to see these architectures partially reflecting themselves, but to see those visions disturbed and invigorated by the structures outside, and in particular political structures. I use the word political in the widest sense of the word to encompass aspects of class,

16 As quoted in Wates and Knevitt, op. cit., p. 42.

Jeremy Till

67

economics, gender and sustainability as well as more normative left/right definitions. It is here that community architecture (or rather my replacement, the architecture of the impure community) could be instructive, because its intentions and potentials are more overtly political than those of 'normal' architecture. But to realise the potential it is essential to abandon the consensual stance typified by Wates and Knevitt – a stance which amounts to little more than a betrayal of the rights of the user. Community architecture must take a stance towards left/right politics and explicitly move to the left away from the tendencies of the dominant social and economic structures, including privatised public space and individualised territories. It cannot afford to be neither 'rigidly pro- nor anti- public or private space' because that ownership is one of the central factors in constituting the space of the community. The community is manifested in the production of its space and architecture contributes a part (but not the whole) to the production. It is only by facing up to the political content of that production that the rights of the user can be realised. What an architecture of the impure community demands is a discussion which starts at the political and encompasses, amongst other aspects, the territories of gender, the relationship between domestic and work, the form of sustainability[17] or the spatiality of social demarcation. Only thus can architecture be aware of the tensions within the social construction of the impure community and from this awareness move to acting within and on those tensions with intent. In this way an architecture which stands for, looks like, an architecture of the purified community is replaced by architecture which reconfigures the space of the actual, impure community. This revision to the model of community architecture has a wider relevance because it points to a way of releasing the political content latent in the production of any architecture.

17 Some of the most interesting reconfigurations in the community housing movement are now being driven by issues of sustainability – most notably in the Co-Housing movement in the USA.

TASTEFUL TECHNIQUE

To a large extent the political content of architecture is suppressed by the discussions of style and technique which dominate so much architectural discourse. The example of community architecture is instructive here too. Wates and Knevitt's double negative (a sure sign of partial guilt) that 'community architecture is not in any sense anti-design'[18] scarcely disguises the fact that the rhetoric of the movement is elsewhere explicitly anti a certain type of design, namely modernism. To a large extent community architecture avoids a direct discussion of style through its focus on the process of collaborative design as opposed to the architectural product. However, despite this disavowal of style, it slips into the argument anyway.

18 Wates and Knevitt, op. cit., p. 21.

There is an underlying assumption that a certain vernacular will emerge effortlessly from the process of collaboration because that is what people most naturally relate to. Thus the Prince can conflate an argument about social use with one about style in his speech at Hampton Court which so enraged the architectural profession. 'What I believe is important about community architecture is that it has shown "ordinary" people that their views are worth having; that they need not be made guilty or ignorant if their natural preference is for the more "traditional" designs.'[19] The Prince's later association with a set of architects who propounded highly conservative stylistic values compounded the problem and forever associated community architecture with a certain type of regressive vernacular – a stylistic strait-jacketing which has hijacked a more productive discussion of the movement. We are thus caught within exactly the same limits of aesthetic terminology that afflict normal architectural debate – it is just that the labels have been changed. More fundamental and potentially redemptive aspects of the production of space are subsumed under a spurious aesthetic debate. The voice of the community is thereby emasculated, an emasculation which has been institutionalised in both the United Sates and the United Kingdom through community 'design' panels, whose token gestures of democratic involvement disguise their superficiality and eventual impotence.[20]

The depoliticisation of architecture, community and other, by recourse to aesthetics is further compounded by the emphasis on technique. Symptomatic of this is the naming of a parallel organisation, the Association of Community Technical Aid Centres (ACTAC). The intention was to challenge the word *architecture* in Community Architecture, which its founders saw bringing with it too much of the authority of the architect, and to replace this with the idea of 'community technical aid'. This title alone subscribes to the myth of political neutrality through recourse to technology; the aid provided to the community is simply of a 'technical' nature. This attitude to the architect (and here I have dissolved the distinction between types) as a technical facilitator is inevitable given the separation of architecture from the political sphere. It is a separation which has implicit dangers because, as Richard Bernstein notes, 'it lends support to the politically dangerous myth that there is a proper domain of social issues where social knowledge is appropriate (neutral expert knowledge) – a domain that is better left to the experts and social engineers and which is to be excluded from the political sphere'.[21] Architects can thus argue that they are involved in the bettering of society through technique and expertise alone, whereas in fact by the disavowal of the political they are betraying the potential empowerment of the user.

The claim of community architecture to have radically revised the relationship between the architect and user here looks fragile. The involvement of the user in the

[19] As quoted, ibid., p. 38.

[20] See for example, R. Wellington Quigley, 'Framing the Fit', in William Saunders (ed.), *Reflections on Architectural Practice*, New York, Princeton Architectural Press, 1996, p. 172. Quigley notes that with design review boards: 'Conflict is almost obligatory. Obviously, once a review board is in place, it has a responsibility to reject the architect's first design, no matter how skilled, since to accept it would be to imply impotence.'

[21] R. Bernstein, 'Rethinking the Social and Political', in *Philosophical Profiles*, Philadelphia, University of Philadelphia Press, p. 254.

Jeremy Till

design process is set in opposition to the system of normative practice in which the architect is assumed to dispense design down from on high against the wishes of the client. The idea of authoritative imposition is a myth that sustains the profession inasmuch as it sets architects apart from the amateur, but it is an idea that bears little resemblance to actual practice. With the possible exception of a small elite of firms, it is an accepted imperative for most architects to listen to and work with clients and end-users – not to do so would be commercial suicide. One of the defining features of recent practice has been the speed at which the relationship of architect to client has changed,[22] particularly in the commercial field. The perceived notion of the architect presenting a *fait accompli* to the client has been replaced by the architect bending to the demands and needs of the client and end users. In this light the difference between the commercial architect and the community architect is perhaps less than the ideologues of community architecture would have us believe, even if the criteria by which the eventual designs are judged 'better' are centred around economic criteria in one instance and social criteria in the other. In the commercial field the architect has to a large extent been marginalised into a limited role of producing surface aesthetic and technical efficiency – a fate which community architecture also suffers. It is how to overcome this marginalisation that I wish to address in the final section, with a particular emphasis on examining a new model of the relationship between architect and user.

RECONFIGURING POWER

I have thus far examined some of the claims made for community architecture; what is apparent from these is not that community architecture is radically different from conventional architecture, but in fact shares some of the same symptoms, from utopian illusion through political amnesia to an obsession with style and technique. This conclusion may be surprising given the way that community architecture was set up in opposition to many of the values and operations of conventional architecture. My argument is that community architecture, through its dialectic genesis, suffers from the fate of all binary argument, namely that it never succeeds in reformulating the original points of opposition, but is in fact caught within their ideological structure. The most explicit manifestation of this binary thinking comes in Wates and Knevitt's book with a chart entitled 'What Makes Community Architecture Different?'.[23] Two columns are formed, one entitled Conventional Architecture, the other Community Architecture, and an oppositional battle set up against a series of topics. For the 'Status of the User', we are given 'Users are passive recipients of an environment' for conventional

22 See R. Gutman, *Architectural Practice*, New York, Princeton Architectural Press, 1988.

23 Wates and Knevitt, op. cit., pp. 24–5.

architecture versus 'Users are – or are treated as – clients' for community architecture. The list continues in a simple binary way, sometimes using emotive language to make its point. Passive user/Active user. Remote, imperious expert/Enabling, companionable expert. Large scale/Small scale. Totalitarian/Pragmatic. Universal/Particular. Hieratic/Demotic. International/Regional. Repetitive/Personal. Top-down/Bottom-up.

I have already suggested that many of the attributes here associated to conventional architecture bear little resemblance to the actual configuration of practice, but relate to the myth and aura that is attached to the profession – a myth which the profession does little to shrug off because it seemingly sustains its authority. However, for the purpose of the ideologues of community architecture the clichéd myths form a polemical and convenient point for oppositional departure.[24] A number of problems arise from this determinedly oppositional stance. Much of the debate is conducted within the framework of conventional architecture, but that framework is never unravelled. In fact quite the opposite happens. Any binary opposition has an underlying hierarchy; in this case the weaker of the pair, community architecture, is marginalised into its own category, caught within its language and the received limits of the words 'architecture' and 'community'. Meanwhile the controlling architectural ideologies go unchallenged, or are even reinforced. Margaret Crawford identifies these trends in the formulation of the 1960s radical architects whose call 'for the apparently total social and professional transformation' in fact instituted 'an incomplete negation, which simply reversed the already fictional roles of the all powerful architect and the ideal client while accepting the ideological assumptions on which they were based'.[25] The point is that in the 1960s US version, the 1980s UK version and others in between, the movements deflect much of their energy into what they perceive to be the failings of the profession and conventional architecture, and in so doing miss the transformative potential of a different kind of practice.

The main thrust of community architecture's oppositional stance is to overturn the power relationship between architecture and user. The conventional architect is seen as the possessor of irresponsible power; in the community architecture model they must be divested of this power. Within this model there is, as Gillian Rose notes, 'a disqualification of critique and equivocation so that all power is either completely bad or completely good – total domination or holy community'.[26] For the ideologues of community architecture the power of the architect is completely bad, a situation exacerbated by the association of the architect with the powers of the state. The figure of the architect stands for both remote expertise and as a symbol of state coercion, a figure which finds its most potent visual and political form in the guise of modernism. Community architecture is there to resist this figure. Any act of interpretation or intent by the architect is now to be treated with suspicion as an act of imposition. The

24 The language used to describe the birth of community architecture raises the stakes still higher – it is the language of battle. Rod Hackney's election as president of the RIBA is the end of 'a civil war' with 'a decisive victory for community architecture', whilst later, despite the successes of community architecture, 'a constant state of guerrilla warfare existed'. Hackney himself encouraged this siege mentality through his directly confrontational politics within the RIBA.

25 M. Crawford, 'Can Architects be Socially Responsible?', in Diane Ghirardo (ed.), *Out of Site*, Seattle, Bay Press, 1991, p. 39. In fact Crawford cannot extricate herself from the dialectic that she has identified and the despairing answer to the question posed by the title of her essay is: probably not except on the margins of youth and individual. This bypassing of the transformative potential of the profession is criticised by Bruce Robbins, see note 27 below.

26 Rose, *Broken Middle*, op. cit., p. 303.

Jeremy Till

politically sensitive architect responds by accepting the unchallengeable right of the user to assert their own ends and becomes no more than a stylistic and technical facilitator. The result, as Rose eloquently puts it, is that 'it is the architect who is demoted; the people do not accede to power'.[27] What is set up as a productive collaboration may end as a disempowering of both parties. Rose argues that:

27 Rose, 'Athens', op. cit., p. 336.

> By renouncing knowledge as power . . . we have disqualified any possible investigation into the dynamics of the configuration and reconfiguration of power. The presentation of power as plural yet total and all-pervasive, and of opposition to power thus conceived as equally pluralistic, multiform and incessant . . . unwittingly participates in a restructuring of power which undermines the semi-autonomous institutions such as knowledge or architecture, which alleviate the pressure of the modern state on the individual. The plural but total way of conceiving power leaves the individual more not less exposed to the unmitigated power of the state.[28]

28 ibid., p. 337, emphasis in the original.

Within the context of community architecture the user is thus not only potentially disempowered but also exposed.

Within the normal model of community architecture, it is argued that, with the disavowal of knowledge, the act of collaboration alone is enough for the empowerment of the user. The failing of this approach is that it ignores the transformative potential latent within the use of any knowledge. The linking of power to knowledge has too often been identified only with the repressive tendencies of power. Foucault himself, the most insistent reader of the power/knowledge axis, resists this monolithic interpretation. Power, he says, 'needs to be considered as a productive network which runs through the whole social body, much more than as a negative instance whose function is repression'.[29] Against the argument that the only responsible architect is the one who bows to the demands of the user, I would posit that it is irresponsible for architects *not* to use their knowledge – but only if they have critically accepted the potential dominations and repressive structures that spatial formations might produce.

29 M. Foucault, *Power/Knowledge, Selected Interviews and Other Writings*, New York, Pantheon, 1980.

It is Rose's acknowledgement of architecture as a 'semi-autonomous' discipline with the potential to alleviate the pressures of the state that points to a way forward. The notion of the autonomy of architecture is an ideal which the profession has clung to in the desire for self legitimation. The establishment of a definable area of knowledge is seen as a prerequisite for any profession. The mistake is to identify this abstract knowledge with practical and actual autonomy – and yet the profession persistently defines itself as an enclosed unity. The fact that contradictions may arise (in stylistic battles, different technical approaches and so on) should not be seen as a threat to that unity but rather as a strengthening of it because those contradictions are always

Jeremy Till

defined by and limited to the terms set by professional authority. What follows from this abstracted notion of an architectural world set apart from the outside world is an indoctrinated separation between the architect on the one hand and the public on the other. To a large extent it is this distinction between architect and people which gives rise to the ire of the community architecture movement. However, as I have argued, the dogmatic dissolution of the boundary between the two has hardly served the people very well, resulting in an emasculated version of architecture reduced to the lowest common denominators of style and technique.

The problem lies in the fact that the autonomy of architecture and architects is no more than a fiction convenient for those both inside and outside the hallowed ground. Architects find it so much more cathartic to pick off one another than, say, an external profession such as surveying. Equally, it serves the opponents of architecture to define the profession as an inviolate authority. In both cases, the energy is misplaced. Bruce Robbins, a Professor of English (how often is it that professions have to look to outsiders to point to their weaknesses?) notes: 'Professions are not as isolated or as self-enclosed as they enjoy accusing themselves of being and better use would be made of their political energies by accusing more deserving, if less conveniently accessible targets.'[30] However, the point is not just to chase the easier targets but to use the energy in a more productive reformulation of practice.

All such talk of the autonomy of architecture is not just distracting but also misinformed. Not only is the epistemological definition of architecture much more fragile than its theorists would have us believe, but also every action of the architect is affected by contingent forces beyond their control. In addition it is clear that, as Robbins notes, 'cross border exchange between the public and the profession is happening all the time'.[31] The rigid classifications of architecture and the architect now appear spurious. Architecture is open to a much wider range of influences and possibilities than the monolithic professional view would have us believe; the community of architects is as impure as the community for which they are designing. The importance is to see this not as a sign of weakness, but as an opportunity for a more expansive definition of roles.

Architects are possessors of both specialised knowledge and conditioned, evolving, understanding as they move between the roles of expert and user – because we are all users in the end as well. It is an acknowledgement of this combination of knowledge and understanding that is central to any reformulation of practice which has the potential to empower the user. I have previously suggested the figure of architects as 'Angels with Dirty Faces'[32] – a figure which oscillates between retreat and engagement in the world; in the endless flux these angels dissolve the futile and static oppositions of dialectical thinking. Instead they are androgynous dreamers of worlds

30 B. Robbins, 'Pathetic Substitutes', in Saunders (ed.), op. cit., p. 177.

31 ibid.

32 J. Till, 'Angels with Dirty Faces', *Scroope*, University of Cambridge, vol. 7, 1995, pp. 14–19.

Jeremy Till

full of flaws and contingencies, at times hovering like light doves, at others returning to grounded messy experiences. With feet on the ground, these angels evade the delusions of utopia, but as sceptical optimists they never succumb to Tafurian despair in the face of other forces. The knowledge of such angels is constantly mediated by common experience and this, in its impurity and restlessness, is not seen as a threatening imposition but as a productive force of change.

If the architect is in this permanent state of tension, then so too can the user be. It should not be seen as a sign of weakness for users to identify with the figure of the architect. Both are torn between the separation of particular and universal, and both can be invigorated by the movement between angelic aspirations and dirty realism. It is through this shared movement that the 'problem' of users renouncing their rights to the architect is dismissed as no problem at all; instead a true collaborative enterprise opens up. Inevitably in this collaboration matters of aesthetic will be intro-duced (since that is one method by which the community can find their means of expression and aspirations). Inevitably too there will be matters of technique to be addressed, but there will need to be an acknowledgement that this is not a neutral act. More importantly, such collaboration will lead to discussions of spatial reconfiguration – because it is in space that the tension between dirty realism and angelic aspirations is manifested. I use the word spatial here not in its formal sense, but in its social sense – as a condition which is both the product of social practice, and the potential container and producer of social activities.[33] Such space is a condition that includes matters of taste and technique, but sets them in a broader cultural context. It is a condition which makes explicit issues of boundary, of social relationships, of formal hierarchies, of making visible the unseen powers beyond. In this way it is a condition which necessarily confronts the political nature of architecture and the production of space.

A collaboration between architect and user where they both take on the figure of 'Angels with Dirty Faces' not only leads to a politically charged architecture of the community, but also unravels the supposed autonomy of the profession. Both parties in the collaboration need to learn from each other; the potential user brings to the table matters of everyday life which are ignored in traditional architectural discourse. However, the acceptance of the everyday is not seen as a collapse of the lofty ideals of the profession but as the opening up to a productive realm in which both architect and user enact reciprocal transactions between the simple realities and the highest dreams. It is a movement which avoids the middle ground of muddy compromise, but occupies what Gillian Rose calls the Broken Middle – a place where users and architects alike 'confront themselves and each other as particular *and* as universal (and which) yields the dynamics always at stake in any comprehension of diremption – the articulation and reconfiguration of activity and passivity, norm and cognition, morality

33 See E. Soja, *Postmodern Geographies*, London, Verso, 1989, p. 20 and J. Till, 'Architecture in Space Time', in Clare Melhuish (ed.), *Architecture and Anthropology*, Architectural Design, London, Academy Editions, November 1996, pp. 9–14. Both arguments follow Henri Lefebvre.

Jeremy Till

and heteronomy'.[34] As we have seen, Rose uses community architecture as a key example of a false 'holy' middle – a place where the tensions inherent in any community are patched over in an ineffective attempt to create an idealised condition between individual and state. By going to the furthest shores of community architecture, I have attempted to illustrate this failed promise which denies the user an empowering and empowered role. My alternative occupies the less defined place of the broken middle in which both architects and users relinquish the impossible purity of their communities and open up to a critical engagement with the forces beyond. Together they create and recreate architectures of the impure community.

[34] Rose, *Broken Middle*, op. cit., p. 303.

Jeremy Till

contaminating

contemplation

1 H. Lefebvre, *The Production of Space*, trans. D. Nicholson-Smith, Oxford, Blackwell, 1991, p. 25.

The fact is that around 1910 a certain space was shattered. It was the space of common sense, of knowledge (savoir), of social practice, of political power, a space thither to enshrined in everyday discourse, just as in abstract thought, as the environment of and channel for communications; the space, too, of classical perspective and geometry, developed from the Renaissance onward on the basis of the Greek tradition (Euclid, logic) and bodied forth in Western art and philosophy, as in the form of the city and the town. . . . This was a truly crucial moment.[1]

Henri Lefebvre

2 W. Benjamin, 'The Work of Art in the Age of Mechanical Reproduction', in H. Arendt (ed.), *Illuminations*, trans. H. Zohn, New York, Schocken Books, 1968, pp. 239–40.

A man who concentrates before a work of art is absorbed by it . . . the distracted mass absorbs the work of art. Architecture has always represented the prototype of a work of art the reception of which is consummated by a collectivity in a state of distraction. . . . Buildings are appropriated in a twofold manner: by use and perception – or rather by touch and sight. Such appropriation cannot be understood in terms of the attentive tourist before a famous building. Tactile appropriation is accomplished not so much by attention as by habit. (Optical reception) occurs much less through rapt attention than by noticing the object in incidental fashion . . . the tasks which face the human apparatus of perception at the turning points of history cannot be solved . . . by contemplation alone.[2]

Walter Benjamin

Oh, how our democratic instincts bind us! How our art is diminished by a weakness for sentiment, by desire – desire to be without guilt. Not guilty and yet, not innocent. For the user is apparently an innocent and who would do harm to the innocent?

Then again, why accommodate the user? Why not laugh in the face of the user, he who is happy to see us go without our daily bread in the pursuit of endeavours which might enlighten him and yet, for which he has no stomach? Do we embrace the user merely because he supplies a dose of wholesome earthy goodness?

The user, like a child, prods the soft underbelly of architectural myth, asks many questions – questions that touch raw nerves, and raise to the surface difficult paradoxes and unpalatable truths. For the user contaminates space and yet is not willing, nor it seems able, to partake of the more esoteric debates about what he soils. Lurking within the question of the user is the ugly spectre of elitism and after all, in our democratic age, the age of inclusion, who can afford to be seen to be elitist?

A prevailing but useful myth would have it that space is the tool of the architect, that the architect is the manipulator of space. Admittedly, this myth has its basis in numerous conceits, not least the failure to offer a reasonable definition of 'space'[3] and the misplaced arrogance which excludes from this space that architects manipulate,

3 Lefebvre, op. cit., p. 42.

Fat

all other determinants outside of architectural space – the spaces of economics, geopolitics, bureaucracy – in other words, precisely those spaces over which architects constantly complain they have no control. Is it not ironic that the architect became a manipulator of space as such, that this space became the subject of architecture, precisely at the moment it was shattered and only after the contamination of its fragments with other things? Architects, perhaps with good reason, have always preferred to ignore the pollutants and concentrate only on the fragments, to pretend, in other words, that this rupture had not taken place.

Before this moment, the architect was a manipulator of substance or material. The very body of architecture was this substance onto which was inscribed patterns and representations which carried forth meanings which could be read and understood. In seeking to capture space as the unadulterated subject of architecture via the eradication of its pollutants, the contaminants which etched themselves onto the surface of things, of material, were also done away with, lest they should leak into space and thus undermine its purity.

But is not one compelled to ask – what precisely is this space that architects speak of? Is it no more than the gaps that lie between discretely placed objects? And thus, is it not similar in character to the inconvenient gaps that lie between hygienic kitchen objects and which are prone to the collection of filth?

Clues present themselves in the irony that the architect's perceived control over space as opposed to substance or material, an idea that sprang from an apparently liberative rupture within the visual and literary arts (made manifest in the works of Picasso, Proust and Joyce amongst others) coincided with an unprecedented if very partial shift in political power from the few to the many. This provided architecture with a new paradoxical problem – the user, a mythical figure who had previously enjoyed an apparent understanding of the codes and meanings inscribed on the manipulation of substance and material, but was at a loss to come to terms with a reduction of environmental meaning, which went hand in hand with a new emphasis on the manipulation of that existing between and moulded by, material and substance. This liberative rupture meant that space was to become pure, and was be articulated as such. Abstract, geometrical and compositional, shorn of decoration, space was to be universal and homogeneous – free from contamination.

> The types of buildings or 'spaces' that are considered part of the architectural cannon force a certain kind of appreciation of space – to contrast two examples, in the art gallery (as a prime 'architectural space') and the football pitch (as a 'non-architectural space') one finds very different conceptions of what space is, or what spatial experience might be. The art gallery is a passive, contemplative and abstract space, while the football pitch is active and dynamic, where spatial relationships ebb and flow and space is made legible (creating meanings which are experienced or seen – threat, danger, promise). Note how football commentators can articulate sophisticated spatial analysis and compare to the difficulties (and hence, the imprecise vagaries) architects have in describing the nature of their 'abstract' space.

However, at exactly the same moment, the user, excluded from the new space, was subject to a limited increase in democracy, just enough to become a potent force. Buildings would increasingly be commissioned by bodies representing the user rather than by elite individuals. Hence, at precisely the instant that architecture focuses on space and dispenses with common codes, the user – the reader and sharer of these codes – appears on the scene – truly, a man with no name in a territory chartered by others.

Hence we are confronted with two problems which go to the heart of architectural practice. The first of these assumes that the exclusion of the user from esoteric and therefore, exclusive and specialised debates about architecture, which influence the creation of the environment that the user inhabits on an everyday basis, is a political matter – an issue of power relations between those who create space on their own terms and those who are forced to inhabit it. The second problem is that attempts to address this issue, and which ally themselves to a politics of liberation, tend to locate themselves within a discourse of art, itself a highly specialised and exclusive language.

And what of use itself? Does not the fact of use bring forth serious questions which threaten to dislodge us from our rightful place? For architecture is peculiar, lest we forget, in that unlike other visual art forms, it exists not merely as an object of contemplation but is used.

Seeking a role as a purveyor of transcendental value, the discourse of architecture seeks to inoculate architecture by locating it firmly within the other of art. And yet, as an intrinsic element in the city, it is simultaneously sited within the everyday. On the one hand the user, a born amnesiac who suffers sufficient confusion, is required to take on the role of 'contemplator' and 'receptacle' of cultural value, on the other, he (she?) is expected to passively occupy architecture under the normative conditions of habitual existence – that is, to participate in the making of a space. For space implies both use and contemplation.

4 A. Loos, 'Architecture', in Y. Safran and W. Wang (eds), *The Architecture of Adolf Loos*, London, Arts Council, 1985, p. 108.

Adolf Loos once famously wrote,

> *Only a small part of architecture belongs to art: the tomb and the monument. Everything else that fulfills a function is to be excluded from the domain of art.*[4]

Has this dictum been borne out by the subsequent history of architectural discourse? Is not architecture nearly always spoken of in terms of art and in relation to other art forms? Are not spaces described and made subject to criticism as objects of contemplation?

In another more complex sense, Loos' statement fundamentally informs the

Fat

conception and perception of architecture to the present day. In the light of conventional readings of the statement and in the context of other Loosian maxims,[5] it
appears to betray more than a hint of puritanism. The distinct impression given is not
that architecture should be viewed as being outside of the arts, quite to the contrary.
Rather that use somehow pollutes, dirties the purity of art. In this sense, the statement
has a tragic dimension, illuminating the predicament of the architect who as an artist
has constantly to contend with the invasion of use.

Central to this question is the nature of art itself. What might be suggested by
Loos' statement is that art is as pure as the driven snow, an assertion which, as Loos
certainly understood, does not stand up to much critical analysis. And yet it is this
idealised view of art – as something belonging to a higher realm, something beyond
the everyday, something not to be contaminated by the existence of social relations –
that informs architecture's desire to be included within its realm, and hence, to be
understood as an object of contemplation. Whilst such a notion seems idealistic, to say
the least, it is the basis of the privileged position of aesthetic discourse within
architecture and the starting point for the exclusion of the user.

The most pronounced instances of these conditions are to be be found, ironically,
in the greatest purveyors of architectural information – the photograph, the drawing
and the magazine. The magazine presents an important alibi for architecture acting
under the premise of art. First, its wide dissemination allows the perception of architecture to be made available to a much wider proportion of the population than
would actually visit or in habit the buildings thereby reinforcing its apparent democratic
credentials. Second, and simultaneously, it forms the basis of the case for the defence
that architecture might be a form of art. In presenting architecture, via the drawing and
the photograph, as the object of contemplation, it allows architecture to appear free
from the contaminating presence of the occupier. Further still, this process informs
and reinforces the actual inhabitations and uses of buildings which become places
of pilgrimage, of contemplation. Thus art goes as far as to purify use – the empty
photograph exudes a kind of morality.

The word 'user' itself, has moral overtones. It connotes a mercenary practice in
human relations and carries undertones suggestive of drug use, and thus intensifies
the apparent existence of impurity inferred by the presence of the user. Hence the user
is subconsciously perceived as a reprehensible and contemptible character and is
treated as such. And, are not the desires and tastes of the user important determinants
in the debate which seeks to locate architecture within high culture and which disdains
the inclusion of mass or popular culture within its margins?

But surely, we architects, as souls of the most sensitive variety, have the
democratic spirit at the heart of our enterprise? And as true democrats, as true

5 For example, 'Ornament is Crime'.
See Safran and Wang, op. cit., p. 100.

Fat

believers in free speech, can we not bring ourselves to elicit even the slightest whimper in favour of elitism? Or would this, in a liberal climate which endorses all kinds of shallow worthiness, contaminate our purest and most heart-felt inclinations?

Much current thinking within what purports to be the Avant-Garde (an anachronistic idea today), is highly influenced by the acceptance, indeed encouragement, of another form of contamination, what is called the breaking down of boundaries between the arts and, in the case of architecture, that between fine art and architecture. Radical art theory from the 1960s, 1970s and 1980s is all the rage in schools of architecture, perhaps not surprisingly, given that the content of this language is liberal, emancipatory, romantic and anti-institutional. Is it not traditional that students display a touching weakness for such sentiments – against institutionalisation and yet institutionalised – how poignant!

However, in the language of current theory can be heard more than a whisper of elitism, of indeed, institutionalisation. The language, derived from highly specialised philosophical discourses, tends to display quite sufficient privilege while making a mighty and virtuous noise as soon as the problem of privilege is even remotely touched upon. Whilst preaching against oppression and repression, it remains highly elitist, with recourse to both its exclusivity and inaccessibility to those outside its discourse and, despite all talk of breaking down boundaries, in respect of its failure to break beyond the bounds of the academy and to convincingly cross the threshold of theory into practices outside of the academy. That the main targets of its attack are existing protocols and the established canons, which are represented as if they existed only to promote the ideologies of the white European male – would seem less ridiculous if only the jargon and self-righteousness could be toned down.

In relation to the user, this presents a paradox. For although the sentiments of much current debate may privilege the user (the predominance of the reader over the author in literary criticism)[6] the argument is often couched in such terms and uses such jargon as to do the opposite. On the other hand, one might be persuaded to posit the somewhat unfashionable idea (as Oscar Wilde nearly suggested, it is better to be unfashionable than boring), that the inclusion of the user or reader on their own terms leads to the reproduction of pre-existing prejudices and preconceptions and the undermining of complexity and depth. Such an assertion raises another ugly spectre – value.

6 R. Barthes, *Mythologies*, London, Paladin, 1973, p. 142.

> *Lavitorial graffiti is not to be distinguished in any qualitative way from the drawings of Rembrandt.*
>
> *No leisure activity is intrinsically superior to any other.*[7]

7 After R. Hoggart, *The Way We Live Now*, London, Pimlico, 1995, p. 55.

Fat

Current fashionable opinion states that there exist no boundaries between high and low culture, on the basis that there are no differences in value between them, that in the case of architecture, the apparent user preference for the Barratt house over the Le Corbusier villa should under no circumstances be subject to question. Under such circumstances, it is not difficult to understand Nietzsche's aversion to democratic instincts.

To take such a position is to want to have your cake and eat it. To proclaim any attempt to differentiate between the value of high culture against low culture is to invite accusations of elitism and of underpinning bourgeois hegemony. Simultaneously, we are subjected to the claim, that the penetrating critic can excavate information of high cultural value from forms of mass culture, can take on board uncritically the assumed desires of the user (or consumer) and allow these to dominate the product. Is there not the slightest temptation to ask of these penetrating critics, the sources of their methods – the means by which they engage in this archaeology?

Do not these sophisticates recognise a hint of irony (after all is not irony something they are meant to know of?) in the fact that the deconstruction of supposedly oppressive structures (although this notion is itself somewhat reductive and monolithic) requires a level of thought and intellectual abstraction which is located firmly in high culture, in an academic discourse which is not necessarily accessible to those outside of the academy?

And so we are presented with the ugly visage of the question of ideology, for the refusal to question value is little more than a privileging of ideology which simultaneously presents the paradoxical argument that cultural forms have no intrinsic ideological meaning. Hence, in the name of the democratic spirit, we can happily acknowledge the Wimpey house, the game show, the delights of Las Vegas, and accommodate the terms under which these cultural forms are produced whilst, at the level of ideology, condemn those who question these terms, for crimes of cultural hegemony and elitism. Hence, we are presented with a multi-faceted ideological contradiction which, on the one hand, on ideological grounds, conveniently ignores the ideology present in particular cultural forms and one the other, in the name of a questioning of all values, has no truck with the notion of value at all, nor with the idea that an artform of the 'higher' variety is not reducible to ideology.

> In attempting to define the nature of architecture's users, architects confront ideological delights that are usually swept under the carpet in polite discussions about space. The invention or reinvention of the 'user' has been a central issue in many contemporary areas. Right wing politics has attempted to turn citizens into consumers, dismantling the State's responsibility for the 'welfare' of those it governs – redefining NHS patients as customers of Hospital Trusts, tenants as homeowners. Meanwhile the new left proposes a society made up of individual stakeholders, sharing in the prosperity of the nation. Britain's lack of a written constitution with principles of citizenship provides fertile ground for the battle to redescribe the users of government and the rights of its citizens. The ideological status of the individual has a profound effect upon the way they inhabit their environment.

In situations where there aren't existing working definitions of the user – a scenario familiar to networked electronic environments – the user's identity has to be literally constructed prior to their presence. 'Habitat', an early MUD (an on-line text based interactive environment), developed an 'avatar', a composite character constructed by its users, choosing body parts, sex, name, age, etc. Users proceeded to interact with each other and the virtual environment via their avatar. The avatar is an example of an electronic identity, and as such, displays many of the common characteristics of this type of identification. A representation of an identity made up like a photofit, a combination of checked boxes, words or phrases, some kind of graphic, names, ages, etc. Once this identity has been formed, it then allows you to enter the realm of your choice and to act as this identity. This 'infofit' may be self-constructed, or thrust upon you, and already exists to varying degrees. From credit ratings and electronic tagging to e-mail and IRC nicknames – a collection of digital or electronic identities/representations of self which define limits of behaviour within certain (real or virtual) zones. The current slippery nature of the term 'user' (or identity) coincides with its increasing importance. As shifting or multiple and conflicting definitions pervade, and as electronic zones exert a greater presence in physical space, the architectural conception of 'user' will be forced to accommodate, negotiating real and virtual identities.

Does the suggestion that the accommodation of the user, reader and viewer on their own terms tends to reproduce, at the very least, the most conservative of values, mean that the users should be excluded from the production of high architecture, if not the production of space?

Such an assertion does not necessarily detract from the need to take on board the user in the process of design, nor to exclude the notion that the user through his actions contributes to the making of an architecture. For example, the presentation of architecture as a higher cultural form is conditioned by its use as a subject of contemplation, an act which itself produces a particular space with identifiable characteristics. Is it possible to facilitate an inclusion of the user which does not exclude a critical approach to notions of value and which stands apart from a prevalent and self-defeating cultural relativism which merely serves the interests of those it seeks to oppose? If so, what are the possible strategies for this inclusion of the user in the debate and process of architecture?

Perhaps we might begin to answer this question by setting out our terms as clearly and as unambiguously as possible, and to state that the subject at hand is architecture as the object of contemplation, 'high architecture', that which claims to be informed by a high level of intellectual engagement, intuition, and which consciously places itself within or against existing canons of high architecture and high architectural discourse, and which presents itself, in some respects at least, as a commentary on culture in general. This architecture is also characterised by its consciousness and reference to other cultural forms, be they fine art, film, literature or popular culture.

I like elements which are hybrid rather than 'pure' . . . ambiguous rather than 'articulated' . . . I prefer 'both–and' to 'either–or', black and white and sometimes grey to black and white.[8]

Robert Venturi

8 R. Venturi, *Complexity and Contradiction in Architecture,* New York, Museum of Modern Art Papers on Architecture,1966, pp. 22–3.

By employing the hybrid form to expose social and ideological contradictions, architects like Venturi partake of both the popular code of mass media and the 'high' code of art/architecture, of both the popular code of entertainment and a theoretically based political analysis of form, and of both the codes of information and the codes of the aesthetically formal.[9]

Dan Graham

9 D. Graham, 'Architecture in Relation to Art/ Art in Relation to Architecture', *Artforum*, 17, no. 6., 1979, p. 28.

This rhetoric, which would have us see A & P parking lots as the tapis verts of Versailles, or Caesars Palace in Las Vegas as the modern equivalent of Hadrian's villa, is ideology in its purest form.[10]

Kenneth Frampton on R. Venturi, D. Scott Brown, and S. Izenour,
Learning from Las Vegas, 1972

10 K. Frampton, *Modern Architecture. A Critical History*, London, Thames and Hudson, 1980, p. 291.

These statements identify an intrinsic element in the structure of any art – namely form – an element which unlike the other side of a much touted duality is somehow present as pure – uncontaminated – innocent. And yet, is not form the political element – the difficult bit – the thing that users or 'ordinary people' don't understand – the exclusive component, whereas content is supposedly inclusive – accessible?

McLuhan, prophet of the electric (sic) age, the epoch of inclusion, would not go along with this.[11] For McLuhan, form is defined as a type of technology and as such, form is the determining factor which allows inclusiveness or not. From this vantage point, the traditional roles of form and content are reversed. The content (the information, the aesthetic, the meaning) becomes form in the sense that it is material which has been manipulated. The form (how the information is manipulated) becomes the content. This is something understood by editors of tabloid newspapers, but not by Frampton in his dismissal of *Learning from Las Vegas*. The point of *Learning from Las Vegas*, is that Vegas becomes a subject – a site of representation – both as popular code and as art. Frampton's statement exposes him as an ideologue.

11 M. McLuhan, *Understanding Media, The Extensions of Man*, London, Routledge, 1994.

The approach outlined by Venturi and others is somewhat unfashionable today. However, although rarely acknowledged explicitly, it continues to inform architecture which *is* fashionable. It promotes the use of languages which are accessible in that they are drawn from popular codes, but whose meanings are questioned via altercation with sophisticated representational form. The language is therefore read on numerous levels, which are inclusive of intellectual analysis and popular understanding. This is not a new idea, it has been muted by amongst others, Dan Graham[12] and Charles Jencks.[13] The primary difference between this approach and the desire to facilitate inclusiveness today, is that it admits to difference in value between something that aspires towards art or a higher level of culture than the ordinary, and that which does not. As such, it is an idea that is out of sway with current tendencies towards wholesome political correctness which, in the name of an alleged democratic ideal, refuse to contaminate themselves with an ideology of difference lest it should expose

12 Graham, op. cit., p. 28.
13 C. Jencks, *The Language of Post-Modern Architecture*, London, Academy Editions, 1984, p. 6.

F at

The ability to exchange information across electronic networks has given people an ability known as 'telepresence'. Their degree of telepresence (or immersion) is dependent on the kind of information they are exchanging with their remote location (whether it be text, video, sound, touch, etc.). Teleworking allows you to conduct yourself as though you were at the office, facilitating access to any information you may need. It allows you to interact with your colleagues and clients, but to do so from a remote location – a hotel, airport lounge or from your home. Conversely, one is able to telesocialise . . . hang out with friends, conduct relationships, go shopping or indulge in various forms of cybersex. Currently, the machines that people use for word processing, spreadsheets, image manipulation, etc. (i.e. activities usually defined as 'work') are the same as the machines that they use for 'recreational' or 'social' time. Your screen could be showing, at any time, any kind of information – that is to say, files pertaining to a particular office commitment and a tickertape newsfeed of selected shareprices, news headlines, and a live video picture of your partner in the Northwest Territories, and a chat room full of other people killing time. . . . And your screen might be in the office, at home, at the beach . . . or wherever you have carried it. It will becoming increasingly difficult to define the nature of occupation of physical space; the association between the space you are in and what you might be doing in it is dissolving in a blurring of definitions, and a confusion of the different activities and roles we assume. This suggests that there may be a tendency for space
→

elitism, but which accepts an ideological content which would otherwise be considered reprehensible were it not the language of the hallowed lower orders.

The method employed by Venturi *et al.*, implicitly accepts and indeed affirms the limitations of architecture. However, one of the consequences of the notion that populist forms might become the subject of art forms which seek towards a higher form of culture, is that cultural form, as a subject of representation, becomes a metalanguage[14] – that which speaks of something other than itself. For architecture, this offers numerous possibilities, not least, that by speaking of things other than itself, the discipline becomes open to wider forms of communication and breaks out of its arcane, self referential language which is ultimately alienating to the users of architecture. In recent history, these references have been largely restricted to other forms of architecture, derived from historical sources. However, the idea of architecture as a form of communication implies a number of things. First, if architecture can communicate to other architects about other forms of architecture, it can presumably speak of a myriad of other things, be they mass media, politics, geography or place – a communication that can open architectural meaning to a wider section of readers, not just other architects.

Second, the notion of architecture as a form of communication is also intensified by the growing preponderance of other communication tools, such as mass media and electronic technology, which are becoming increasingly dominant in our culture and for that matter, are increasingly being incorporated into architecture itself, in ways that range from the use of technology on façades to its utilisation as means of organising buildings and, through the increasing promiscuousness of the drawing and the photograph as means of communication about architecture. Third, there exists the idea that this culture of communication, what McLuhan has called the electric (sic) age, is likely to break down specialisations such as art, architecture and literature which simply become competing communication systems.

For some, held in thrall to the prevailing ideologies of

academia, this collapse of specialisation, and of categorisation, is to be welcomed without reserve. After all, is not art an essentially bourgeois construct which serves the interests of the ruling class? The specialisation and separation of the arts into fine art, literature, architecture and the rest is seen as a structure intrinsic to this process. Hence the appearance of another strategy to include the user, a strategy which contrary to the approach of Venturi *et al.*, denies the limitations of architecture and seeks to redefine normative architectural practice beyond its present institutionalised categorisation.

to lose its defining tags, taking on a generic nature that is temporally informed as to its meaning by electronic data. These forces are redefining our personal, social, political and organisational principles. As Archigram proclaimed in 1971 'the electric aborigine is a social chameleon' or as Bill Gates put it in 1996 'Where do you want to go today™'.

Is the breaking down or blurring of categories really the road to freedom? Or do we detect a hint of linguistic conceit in this inclination? Certainly there is a lot to be said for cross fertilisation between disciplines, as a means of extending the methodologies within a discipline, but often these methods do not cross over as smoothly as one might like. The breaking down of boundaries between disciplines is perceived as being highly political and inclusive. However, joyous proclamations of the death of the artist or the architect seem as premature as the predictions of the death of the author appear to have been.[15]

14 Barthes, op. cit., pp. 124–5.

15 Any publisher will be only too glad to inform the enquirer that more authors are published and more books sold than at any other time.

The direct affect of attempted de-categorisation in architecture is the inclusion and partial legitimation of other activities which are in some way 'architectural' or 'environmental' within certain sections of the academic institution.[16] Work within this bracket tends to focus on a critique of the terms under which architecture is produced and defined, usually via means of engagement with other representational techniques, not usually considered architectural. Within these approaches lie explicit and implicit critiques of traditional techniques of architectural representation as both means of representation and as means of production. Hence, the argument goes, the architectural drawing is not innocent and is exclusive of issues of gender, social control, conflict and other politics of use or occupation.

A particular tactic, that has been vigorously pursued within the architectural academy, is the deliberate use of architectural drawing techniques to focus on the occupation of space rather than the discrete objects which, in the conventional and de-politicised definition of architectural space, form the elements which contain it. Implicit in this process is the idea that architecture might be defined as much by event as by the demarcation of physical elements. There are many instances where this is instructive in the excavating of political presences which can be shown to be not so much in space, but rather the very basis of the character of space. For example, drawing from Foucault's studies of the social relations of space made evident in the

16 Since the 1980s this has been a tendency in schools of architecture such as the Bartlett, the University of Westminster and the Architectural Association in London, and American schools such as the Cooper Union.

17 M. Foucault, *Discipline and Punish*, London, Penguin, 1975, pp. 195–230.

practice of Panopticism,[17] one might analyse the social structure of the lecture theatre and its relationship to the intensification of this structure in its physical make-up.

Within the lecture theatre, the perspectival conditions, which generated the Panoptican, are present, albeit, in a diluted form. Many of the conditions which have been identified as having to do with political power in space are also present: the perspectival concentration on the privileged individual who is the focus of vision, who has a clearly different social role, in that he has the power to command attention, from those who are privileged to view him. The speaker also enjoys a view of the audience that allows him or her to watch for and control dissenting activities. One might also imagine a reconstruction of this situation under a differing set of social relations whereby the lecturer is forced to sit on the floor and is surrounded by his audience who sit on high stools. Within a given space, a completely different set of psychological relations are set in place and a different space created, by instigation of the users who nevertheless produce a physical space. This is a condition which would be absent in an architectural drawing. But it is a definitive making of a space with particular characteristics which are experienced. This is an instance where the user might be said to make an architecture.

18 By practice, we refer specifically to the normative definition of 'practice', that is the design of buildings or events.

But this type of analysis, while highly illuminating theoretically, also has its limitations in the difficult context of practice.[18] For although attending to the issue of use and in doing so, attacking the terms under which architecture is produced, it allows for no viable alternative means of production unless one, once again, reduces the substance of architectural meaning to the role of fragmentary subject of contemplation. For the value of an event such as the reconstruction of the social field of the lecture theatre, lies in its very nature as a spontaneous and ephemeral occurrence which is not prone to institutionalisation. To design such events within the context of normative production is to institutionalise and hence, nullify them. And if one might dare to set limits on what might be defined as architecture, one is tempted to claim that architecture is determined by design, by the active intervention in the city. It is this, which at root, makes architecture, even in its most normative manifestations, potentially the most political and the most difficult of the arts. The observation of, speculation upon and subsequent representation of the occupation of space reduces the architect to the role of the anthropologist. In which case, why be architects at all?

Such a critique might also extend to the idea that architects might make manifest their production as film or as literature. But are not these disciplines, ironically, even more self-contained than architecture and hence, far less potentially dangerous than architecture? Is it not easier to manufacture difficult political moments in a film made in an academy, or within a piece of writing, not subject to censorship in the way architecture, as a presence in the city, is? Is not recourse to such tactics little more than a form of evasion? In this sense, the disintegration of all boundaries exists only on the level of a linguistic sleight of hand. Ultimately, film-making is film-making and writing is writing.

And of course, there is always the danger of hopping out of the frying pan of one category into the fire of another. Could this not be countered by an acceptance of the merits of boundaries? Might not one enter rather into de-differential practice – become architect and anthropologist and artist and writer – thus informing the extension of architectural practice by cross contamination rather than a blurring of boundaries to the extent that they disappear altogether leaving us only with an innocuous unity?

Dare we restate the idea that architecture might properly aspire to be a form of higher culture – complex, developed, challenging and difficult? And that architecture should remain the remit of certain specialists? And that in remaining a self contained discipline within defined limitations, become in itself, something quite different to the terms under which it is produced?

Or do we prefer, in the name of anti-elitism, to delude ourselves? To pretend that the language we speak from our ivory tower about inclusiveness is in fact, inclusive? To make believe that we will happily give up architecture's hallowed status as a kind of art?

If architecture implies use and contemplation, art denotes contemplation. Even that art which attempts to eschew contemplation is ultimately brought back into the gallery or at least, is reproduced in the catalogue. Thus, Duchamp's liberating tactic is cruelly inverted and constantly returns to haunt art. Does this not reinforce the impotence of art in the face of architecture which constantly overcodes and neutralises it? Even attempts to draw conceptually, the spaces generated by the user, are ultimately ensnared by the category 'art', if indeed, this status is not actively sought. Thus we are limited to pursuing our speculations on the safer territory of art.

In 1993, Fat instigated a project which sought to address the issues of contemplation and use. The project took place at the Edinburgh Festival and was repeated at a larger scale at the same venue the following year. In 1995, again at a larger scale, it took place at the Venice Biennale. Entitled 'Outpost', the project commissioned 100 works of art and 100 corresponding signatures (thus validating the art works by the authenticating mark of the artist) from a large number of artists. In 1993 there were 100 artists, in 1995 there were over 1,000 which meant that the project exhibited 100,000 works of art. All the works and the signatures were to be the size of a business card. Importantly, the art itself was to be anonymous. The card containing the

The definitions of the terms of engagement with certain zones or domains are successfully enforceable. The occupation of the golf course or the highway have been codified in such a way as to exclude deviant behaviours. These spaces are constructed or adapted for the specific pursuit of a singular activity – setting out (as far as possible) the possibilities of events occurring within their influence. By default, this conditions the users of these zones – their desires, actions, and their perception of space. In related ➝

architectural sites (the bathroom, the bedroom, the boardroom) architects retain a relationship with the idea of the space as something used, or at least that the projected occupation is more likely to be predictable – that the forms, colours, textures and materials used to construct the space engage with the activities and events occurring within them. This relationship becomes more tenuous the further one strays from spaces with specific and singular designated uses. At the other end of this spectrum is public space, a term which continually fails to provide any clues as to its identity as a zone of activity. Its illustration via the architectural drawing reveals occupation determined by the poses of Letraset figures. The current predilection for cappucino stalls, pavement cafes and jugglers is an uninspiring attempt to populate spaces between buildings with programme. As Robert Venturi remarked 'Americans don't need piazzas, they should be at home watching TV.' The idea that the user of public space is an individual (or a small family unit) who occupies these spaces at a quasi-domestic scale (the cup of coffee) limits the potential of programme. To identify 'the user' as a term referring to a number of people, rather than a singular individual might serve to open possibilities of use . . . kinds of occupation present in the football crowd, the battalion, or the gang.

signature was to be issued separately. The works were placed into a series of dispensers distributed throughout the city at a range of sites which included art galleries, post offices, blood banks and burger bars. The audience was invited to collect the anonymous artworks from the dispensers free of charge. On the back of each artwork was contained information which told the collector where to buy the validating signature of the artist and a catalogue of the exhibition which consisted of a book containing blank pages to be filled with the collector's selection of art works and corresponding signatures. The participating viewer would collect the anonymous art works from the dispensers located around the city and make a value judgement as to the quality of the work of art based purely on his or her reaction to the piece and free from the contaminating presence of either the artist's name (which might prejudice the viewer's judgement) or any form of curation (which would validate the artwork in the context of art history or a reading of current tendencies in the world of fine art). Thus, the viewer was free to judge the artwork on his or her own terms, rather than those of the art world. A work which did not entice the viewer would be discarded. However, the viewer was able to purchase the validating signature of the artist (at a price determined by the artist) of those works he wished to keep. He would also buy the catalogue and arrange the collected works and the purchased signatures as he saw fit.

Thus, the concept of use was introduced into the means by which art is seen and disseminated. The viewer was given an active role in which he became critic, curator and collector and became engaged in active participation rather than passive contemplation. The project's starting point was its use of a popular form – the collectible card, analogous to football stickers – which communicated to a wide audience and allowed the event to include a wide range of people ranging from families, whose members had no interest in art and who engaged in the project because it was fun and fostered a form of communication, to serious collectors. The project also fostered a network of interaction on an urban scale as participating viewers exchanged works of which they had more than one, for ones they did not possess. Thus, outside of the gallery, art was experienced with a freedom of percep-tion whilst simultaneously revealing the effect of architectural containers on the actions

Helen Chadwick

of the occupant. Dispensers were emptied at a far quicker rate from burger bars than from institutional environments such as art galleries where the dissuasive character of the space undermined the participating viewer's confidence to take something away free of charge. In these contexts, the issue of value was intrinsic to the project. The project allowed value judgements to be made and included work of high artistic merit as well as work with little or none. Outpost was an event operating at an urban scale, a macro event which promoted a multitude of micro events. Could this serve as a paradigm for architecture?

In a climate which fosters a blurring of boundaries between the disciplines, it is tempting, for a number of reasons, to define Outpost as a form of architecture: first on account of its promotion of a set of transactions which contrive to create a particular habitation of the city, and second because of its character as a form of intervention within particular sites (art gallery and burger bar) which changes the meaning of those sites whilst simultaneously revealing their existing codes and the way in which they control the character of occupation. On another level, Outpost, as a system geared towards a particular use of space, reconfigures a specific programme – the art gallery – as a dispersed entity integrated into the city, in a way quite different to normative gallery spaces. As an event, it also serves as an intervention which responds to, interrupts and and challenges the nature of given contexts. In this sense, as an organisation of space which is both oppositional and accommodating with respect to existing structures, it is open to an interpretation as architecture.

But this interpretation needs to be qualified, for it applies to the use of space as determined by a system which is fluid, a condition that is ultimately oppositional to architecture. For architecture is quite literally writ large in stone, and when the fluidity of an organisational system becomes cast in stone it tends towards determinism.

Figure 5.1 Helen Chadwick, Donor/Donee, 1994. Contribution to Outpost, commissioned by Fat. The donor card constituted the art work which could be collected free of charge from dispensers located around the city. The artwork was legitimised by the purchase of the corresponding signature card which, in this case, was the donee card. The price determined by the artist for this particular work was a pint of blood, to be donated at the local blood bank. Thus, the work set up a field of communication within the city mediated by the transfer of bodily fluids, becoming a metaphor for fluid space generated by the reconfiguration of the art gallery inherent within the project as a whole.

Could it be the case that the political possibilities of architecture lie not in architecture's tendency to intervene, to determine, but rather in its ability to remain fluid, to become the backdrop to events, to remain, on the surface at least, passive?

Intervention is a tendency that goes hand in hand with Modernist thought. Practised by governments and armies on a macro scale, and by architects on a scale only slightly smaller, intervention has also been the defining tactic in art since Dada. In

Figure 5.2 *Fat, Night Club, 1995. Interior showing the use of familiar iconographies derived from swimming pools, sports fields and airports.*

contrast to the excessively planned manoeuvres of architects which shared much in common with those of governments and armies, the interventions of the artist are meant to have, at least, an air of spontaneity and to have more in common with the operations of the urban guerrilla, who is the subject of the artist's unrequited love and the victim of his unwanted advances.

Both parties however, share a passion for the intervention which interrupts the normative programme and explodes the seamless myth of phantasmagorical reality to reveal the the political structures which underpin it. Of course, one of these parties is

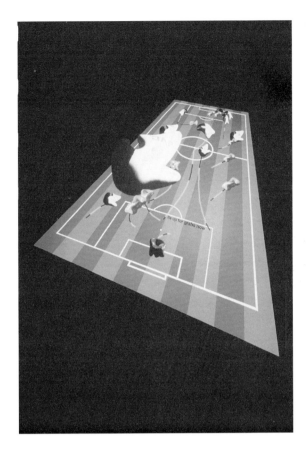

Figure 5.3 *Fat*, Spatial
Configuration, *1992. Model
describing the fluid spatial
characteristics of Michael
Thomas' last minute
championship winning goal for
Arsenal against Liverpool.*

prepared to go about fulfilling his passion with a greater degree of literalism than the other who pursues his desires on the safer ground of representation. If, in terms of the city, the guerrilla and the artist represent very different kinds of user, the architect who shares the passion for intervention represents the other. For the interventions of the architect, who can only determine programme in the most generic sense, are characterised almost entirely by their formal properties. What remains of the architect's interventionist inheritance is the overt and heroic aesthetic of difference, whose influence is felt in the idea of architecture as object, the object which inserts itself into the urban fabric and whose purity and separation is maintained by that most modernist of details – the shadow gap – a close relative of that unhygienic gap between kitchen objects. And so we come back to space and purity, for architecture's interventionist adventures rely on purity, on a purity that announces itself. Here, there is no room for discretion, for stealth, for these require a level of disappearance, a

Figure 5.4 *Fat*, Spatial
Configuration, *1994. Entry for
the Cardiff Opera House
Competition, using the
iconography of architectural
representation to describe space
as determined by modes of
occupation.*

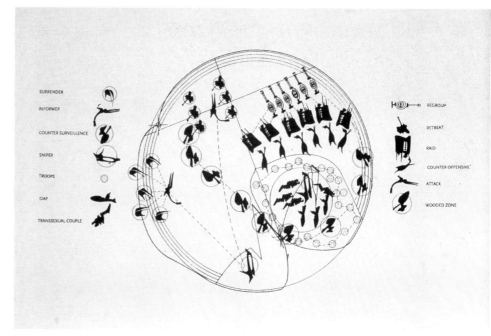

merging into the background, a desire to be contaminated by the surroundings. Implicit in this is the assertion that architecture can intervene alone and that there is no place for the contaminating presence of the user who should remain blurred into the surroundings from which architecture stands apart.

Writing about the particular needs of the scientific workplace, Robert Venturi describes a generic architecture of flexibility and accommodation which he contrasts to scientific buildings such as Louis Kahn's Richards Memorial Laboratory in Philadelphia, whose language of flexibility, made explicit in the heroic separation of servant and served spaces, is largely rhetorical. Venturi goes on to point out that, despite the expressionist bravado exhibited by such buildings, they are in fact highly inflexible and resistant to the accommodation of change. Instead Venturi calls for,

> the conventional laboratory building whose spatial and mechanical flexibility is particularly significant . . . for accommodating change inside, change that involves processes and technologies

and

Fat

Figure 5.5 *Fat*, House Interior, *1995. The familiar iconogra-phies of the exterior deployed in the interior.*

functions that are accommodated rather than expressed . . . for change that is more characteristically revolutionary than evolutionary and that is dynamically wide in its range – spatial, programmatic, perceptual, technical, iconographic – where in our time functional ambiguity rather than functional clarity can accommodate the potential for things not dreamt of in your philosophy.[19]

19 R. Venturi, *Iconography and Electronics upon a Generic Architecture*, London, MIT Press, 1996, pp. 220–1.

Is it possible that these comments express, in their implicit critique of ideology writ so large that its nullifies itself, a desire for occupations which are not announced and thus, contained by their own expression, occupations which slip in incidentally rather than explicitly? Is Venturi, in offering 'things not dreamt of in your philosophy', suggesting a flexibility that goes far beyond function, that embraces the incidental and the stealthy – dare we say the political?

The implication is that a generic openness which allows for normative functions, also leaves room for subversion, and that those buildings whose design results from the explicit expression of ideology, undermine the very subversion they seek to produce. Is it not the case, that however hard the radical architect tries to build-in subversion, he can never escape the fact that in one form or another, he is always the agent of power – a bureaucrat of a spatial reality determined by others more powerful than himself?

Deleuze and Guatarri have spoken of 'smooth space',[20] a concept that has been taken rather literally by those architects for whom these philosophers are a guiding light. For Deleuze and Guattari, smooth space is the space of the nomad, a space which stands in opposition to the striated space of the state and which is characterised by a form of free flowing occupation (the nomad creates territory by 'distributing himself in open space') which 'overcodes' the forces of institutionalisation. Smooth space, the desert and the steppe, a space free from codifications which determine behaviour, is a metaphorical allusion to types of occupation which resist the political restrictions the city places upon us. The desert and the steppe are presented as generic psycho-analytic terrains as well as physical and geographical environments

Could it be argued, that the smooth space described by Deleuze and Guattari has much in common with the generic iconographical space described by Venturi, for as Deleuze and Guattari make clear, smoothness is not something to be expressed and articulated, lest it should be subject to appropriation by the sedentary forces of striation. On the other hand, they suggest that smooth space never exists as a unified and singular entity but that it always exists in relation to, as well as in opposition to, striated space – the normative Western conception of measured static space.

> We must remind ourselves that the two spaces exist only in mixture: smooth space is constantly being translated, transversed into a striated space; striated space is constantly being reversed, returned to a smooth space. In the first case, one organises even in the desert; in the second, the desert gains and grows; and the two can happen simultaneously. But the de facto mixes do not preclude, or abstract, a distinction between the two parties.[21]
>
> Deleuze and Guattari

Hence, the space of opposition integrates and accommodates itself quite naturally into the normative generic space of the city. Its dynamic depends on this. The explicit expression of opposition is the very force that transforms the smooth space with its free flowing transformation of occupation into the coded striated space it seeks to overcome.

20 'It is the difference between a smooth (vectorial, projective, or topological) space and a striated (metric) space: in the first case "space is occupied without being counted", and in the second case "space is counted in order to be occupied".' G. Deleuze and F. Guattari, *A Thousand Plateaus*, London, Athlone Press, 1988, pp. 261–6.

21 Deleuze and Guattari, op. cit., pp. 474–5.

Fat

What is also clear is that smooth space is a condition of occupation which is fluid, not captured or writ large in stone. The nomad maintains jurisdiction over territory by fluid movement (distribution in open space), the architect builds walls. For architects to try to determine the nature of occupation, no matter how liberating the intention, amounts to little more than building walls. On the other hand to speculate on the nature of occupation is not to design and we must restate the fact that whatever its characteristics, to practise architecture, in whatever form, is to design.

Breaking beyond the limits of the conventional definition of architecture is a prevalent interest of the moment. As a strategy, it manifests itself in many ways ranging from the blurring of boundaries between architecture and other art forms, to an interest in how buildings and spaces are occupied and, in particular, the anthropological and sociological characteristics of this. Whilst work in these areas is often illuminating and instructive, the case for the abandonment of all boundaries, the creation of an idealised 'smooth space' is far from proven as either possible of desirable. Again, 'we must remind ourselves that the two spaces (smooth and striated) exist only in mixture'. Thus, it might be said that breaking beyond the conventional definition of architecture, paradoxically serves to illustrate and justify those very limits.

Architecture is unavoidably a form of intervention. Ironically, its strength might arise from its resistance to intervention, to its passive role as a backdrop (and through its resistance to intervention, its role as a facilitator) for events determined by people other than the architect, for its position as an object of contemplation which remains open to contamination.

space within

The concept of 'Space Within' tackles the issue of potential architectural space. It deals with the city as architecture. It is not a rejection or substitute for the orthodox approach to architecture, but attempts to reveal new territories for the active involvement of architectural concerns.

Venturing into these potential territories generates an inevitable critical edge which is of consequential rather than of primary interest. 'Space Within' aims to go beyond critique and requires direct involvement within real contexts. Reactions and criticisms are valid products of a process of investigation, but the true concern of 'Space Within' is architecture itself.

'Space Within' lies in the realm of the real: between the political and the everyday. It touches on life itself and is therefore accountable. This accountability is important, as it questions the validity of architectural actions and interventions.

The interest in, and the use of, actions and interventions stem back to the work of early twentieth-century avant-garde artists[1] and, in particular, the work of the 'Situationist International' founded in 1957.[2] Although the examples of work included below have a lot in common with the work of the Situationists they differ in that they attempt to define precise potential territories for diverse architectural interventions. The proposed architectural interventions consist of not only situations, but of precise combinations of situations and architectural and/or urban structures. The relationship between situation and structure is usually in constant flux and the appropriate balance is determined by the society and the time in which the intervention takes place. Occasionally this leads to apparent contradictions but, as history has proved, this is one of the inherent dangers of working within the Situationist tradition.[3]

The real contexts of these proposed architectural interventions remove these ventures or experiments from the mere reinterpretation of architecture and space. Invariably reinterpretation is part of the process, but it is not an end in itself. A fine line, at times difficult to discern, is drawn between academic enquiry and real architectural intervention. Dual accountability to the real and the academic allows for possible transgressions between these interconnected but at times hermetic realms. These transgressions themselves go through a process of reinterpretation and redefinition which reveals further potential territories for action. Action and proposed intervention evolve into the concept of architectural application. 'Space Within' consists of the application of situations and structures.

Any form of application within a real context automatically raises political issues, but the examples in this chapter attempt to engage with political realities without falling into the trap of politicising architecture.[4] They are politically resonant rather than political in nature. They function as architectural applications within the existing political context. Their purpose is not the ideal transformation of everyday life but rather to

1 Avant-garde artists and movements such as: International Surrealist Movement – André Breton and others (1920s), Movement for an Imaginist Bauhaus – Asger Jorn, Pinot Gallizio and others (1953), Cobra – Constant and others (1948) and the Lettrist International – led by Guy Debord (1945).

2 The Situationist International was founded in 1957, at Cosio d'Arroscia, in northern Italy. It was formed principally of the union of two prior avant-garde groups: The Movement for an Imaginist Bauhaus and the Lettrist International.

3 This refers to the many differences and disputes relating to ideology and the applications of ideas encountered by the different members of the Situationist International.

4 There is an intrinsic link between the Situationist tradition and Marxism. The examples in this chapter use the Situationist definitions of Constructed Situation, Psychogeography, Dérive, Unitary Urbanism and Détournement as tools that form part of the design process rather than as ideological statements within a political context.

Carlos Villanueva Brandt

intervene within it. This process does not lead to a subservience to context but, on the contrary, it develops a means of expanding beyond the existing social, political, economic and cultural constrictions.

The architectural application within these constrictions may take a variety of forms. It may affect them simultaneously or at different times. It may have a single, dual or multiple effect. It may take place at any moment from inception to completion and is not restricted to an eventual structure or consumable product. This is a subtle process and the balance between the application of situations and the application of structures is conditional on the contemporary social, political, economic and cultural forces. Although this balance changes accordingly, the resultant architectural application is always intricately connected to experience. 'Space Within' is dependent on experience.

The architectural application and its related applied experience blur the distinctions between design and product as well as the differentiations between creation and completion. The variables generated by the relationship between architectural application and applied experience are complex and are best described by means of the given examples.

'Space Within' may be a concept, a construct, a constructed situation, a building or a strategy, but when applied and experienced within a real context becomes architecture.

All the following examples are based on given projects for specific locations. They are independent projects which also form part of a common and evolving experiment with the city. Examples a, b, c, d and e are thesis projects applied to real contexts and example f is a constructed project applied within a real context.

'SPACE WITHIN': THE EXAMPLES

Example a: *A constructed event and radio broadcast instituted in order to influence the collective perception of a city.*

Location: Glasgow.

Author: Takashi Hasegawa.

Issue: The identification of an urban condition. An understanding of the urban decay in the docks of Glasgow not solely as the consequence of economic decline, but perhaps caused or at least perpetuated by a sense of nostalgia.

Carlos Villanueva Brandt

Figure 6.1 *Takashi Hasegawa,*
Example a: 'Nostalgia' Posters in
Glasgow.

Figure 6.2 *Takashi Hasegawa,*
Example a: Live Event in
Meadowside Quay.

Carlos Villanueva Brandt

Intention: To exorcise nostalgia.

Potential territory: 'Nostalgia'.

Application:

A proposed live event, addressing the issue of nostalgia, in the redundant Meadowside Quay site on the Clyde was advertised throughout Glasgow by means of posters and pirate radio transmissions. The event took place at the stated time. It consisted of a PA system set up on the site in order to disseminate views on nostalgia. It was also broadcast simultaneously from a radio transmitter located on the site. The author stated that unless the issue of nostalgia was addressed it would be inappropriate to propose more physical structures for the redundant dock sites. Residents of Glasgow were invited to participate in the debate. Unfortunately this dialogue did not take place because, even though four hundred posters were pasted throughout Glasgow and the event was advertised on local radio, no one turned up on the day. The live event did not work and nostalgia was not discussed. It was also impossible to ascertain the effects of the radio broadcast, so again nostalgia was not discussed.

    Nostalgia was not addressed as planned.

Example b: *An exchange between opposite but complementary sites. The sites are fragmented into points. The points are both cultural and physical and are transformed to form part of a proposed strategic network.*

Location: Glasgow.

Author: Knut Hovland.

Issue: The identification of physical points within the urban context by formally flipping or mirroring adjacent sites around the axis of the Clyde. The definition of these points as urban corners in order to establish an intermediary scale between architecture and the city. The identification and recognition of the cultural interrelationships between the transient and permanent populations of these sites. The identification of the cultural identities involved.

Carlos Villanueva Brandt

Figure 6.3 *Knut Hovland*, Example b:
Schoolboy and Painted Corner in
Govan.

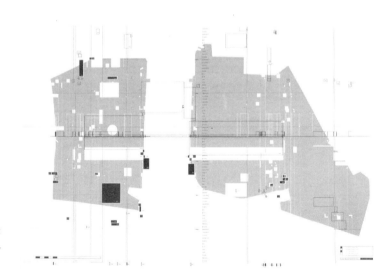

Figure 6.4 *Knut Hovland*, Example b:
Proposal for 146 Corners on Either
Side of the Clyde.

Carlos Villanueva Brandt

Intention: To bridge between the communities on the North and South of the Clyde by means of a proposed cultural and physical infrastructure.

Potential territory: Cultural differences.
The 'building programme'.

Application:

A schoolboy, Dominic, was identified waiting in a corner in Partick. This situation and its location were interpreted as constituting an urban point. Two actions were taken in relation to this point: the configuration of the physical location of the corner was recorded and then recreated, by means of painting its outline, on a mirrored flip-site on the South side of the Clyde and the schoolboy was asked to go to the new site in Govan.

The painting of the original corner on to its mirrored corner was not difficult to carry out and the local children were keen to help with the task. The schoolboy Dominic, on the other hand, was reluctant to cross the Clyde since, to him, this implied moving across a cultural divide. His uncertainty about a different community and a different religion led to fears, in his case real, of being beaten up. Eventually, he was persuaded by a fee of £5.

These actions established a first physical and social bridging process across the Clyde. This process was then questioned at a larger scale, over a greater time period and with a more complex structure.

Both the transient and permanent populations of this area of Glasgow were included in the process since it had been identified that they all had an active relationship with the points, corners and structures of the urban fabric. The transient population, although without permanent accommodation, share and have shared most of the institutions, services and urban spaces with the permanent residents. The concept of transience was a key element to the eventual application.

The idea of the corners was maintained and seventy-three corners were identified on the North bank. These were mirrored on the axis of the Clyde and a further resultant seventy-three corners were located on the South bank. All one hundred and forty-six corners became sites for potential interventions; all one hundred and forty-six interventions were proposed. The interventions ranged from actions to constructions. They varied in complexity from the simple renaming of existing conditions to the implementation of new structures. In one case, for example, the intervention consisted of muzzling a dog.

Whatever the nature of the interventions, they all formed part of a proposed cultural and physical network regulated by a seven-year 'building programme'. The

Carlos Villanueva Brandt

seventy-three interventions on one side were to be carried out simultaneously with their respective ones on the other. The seven-year period of building, its transient nature and its implications were integral to the proposed application. The proposed individual changes would affect the local scale, the proposed network of changes would address the territory of both communities and the proposed simultaneous 'building programme' would create a bridging structure across the cultural divide.

Example c:	*An appropriation of an existing museum institution in order to question the relationship between cultural objects and their spatial contexts. First an intervention within the existing institution, second an institutional intervention within the existing urban context.*
Location:	Glasgow.
Author:	Sara Cole.
Issue:	The establishment of the connection between objects and their respective cultural and economic structures. The use of the St Mungo Museum of Religious Life and Art to question the validation of cultural objects and events. The establishment of a definition of the city by means of the relationship between objects and their related urban context.
Intention:	To create three separate demonstrable sets of relationships between objects and the urban context. To create three 'Museums'.
Potential territory:	Selection, valuation and location: sampling. 'Museum 1': personal sampling. 'Museum 2': social sampling. 'Museum 3': spatial sampling.

Application:

A series of leftover objects were collected, at a particular time (12:30 am), on the Meadowside Quay site. The collected objects were considered as samples of particular social and economic relationships. They varied from on the one hand fragments such as 'Pigeon Feather' – smell of fox (sample 07) or 'Plastic Doll' – head, chest, arm and

Figure 6.5 *Sara Cole*, Example
c: Sample for 'Museum 2'.

16/05/94 - No. 3/10
Sample - Coffin on billboard
Elizabeth/ Scottish - / yrs.
Time - am Religion- none
Location - Gorbals Employed
farewell gesture from owner of only Italian / Irish pub in Glasgow.
"change in City pubs"

[1:1]

MUSEUM FOR 8mins

*[the time it took for a piece
of paper to shift in the wind]*

Samples - 24 points.
Date: - 08/06/94
Location - Site Specific- 99
Hutchinson St.
Glasgow G1.
A Living Museum
A Tour - Dialogue between Guide
& a Merchant dweller.

[-] merchant dweller.

Figure 6.6 *Sara Cole*,
Example c: Museum for 8
Minutes, 'Museum 3'.

Carlos Villanueva Brandt

one blue eye held together with string (sample 13) and on the other social remnants such as 'Surgical Syringe' – used to inject Amphetamines, Diamorphine (sample 01) or 'Diazepan 10 mg for rectal use' – batch No. 400858 (sample 12).

In total fourteen samples were used to investigate the structures of production as well as the structures of consumption. It was discovered, for instance, that certain corporate structures were responsible for not only the manufacture of the plastic used in the syringes but also for the establishment of drug rehabilitation programmes. The sampling established the complex interconnection between the objects and global economic structures. A comparison was also made between the samples and the exhibits in the St Mungo Museum, such as 'Religious Icons' or 'Ritual Circumcision', which established further relationships with complex social structures. This process of personal investigation formed the basis for 'Museum 1'.

In 'Museum 2', called 'The City – A Museum', the existing St Mungo Museum was appropriated as a ready-made institution. This time the sampling process was precisely explained by means of two formal documents of instruction: No. 1, the Sample Specification and No. 2, the Process Specification. Members of the public, visitors to the museum and Glasgow citizens were invited to provide the samples. The samples chosen by the citizens were recorded on a given form and located on a common map. They were subsequently photographed and catalogued in order to become exhibits, for a predetermined duration, of the museum within a museum; 'Museum 2' was created within the St Mungo Museum. It exhibited a structured interpretation, by its own citizens, of the city of Glasgow, it formed an integral part of the activities of the St Mungo Museum and it created a new museum within the existing one, thus avoiding the need for a new physical structure.

In the final phase, 'Museum 3', called 'The City – A Living Museum', the emphasis moved away from the sampling of objects and conditions to the sampling of spaces and experience.

A series of points, spatial samples, were marked by means of paint in their urban locations. These spatial samples were interrelated to the organisational core of 'Museum 3' which was part of an exhibition organised in a temporary gallery in Glasgow. In the exhibition space, the citizens and participants were introduced to the concept of the museum and were then invited on a guided tour of the marked spatial samples. This tour itself, shared between the participant and the guide (the author), became the basis for the living museum. The experience became an exhibit of 'Museum 3'. What was recorded in this case was not the spatial sample or the location, but the dialogue between the participant and the guide and the duration period of the experience. Again a museum about the city was constructed, it appropriated an existing structure, in this case: the city of Glasgow.

Carlos Villanueva Brandt

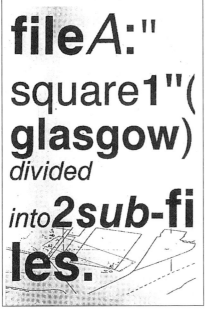

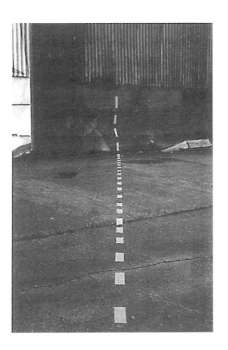

Figure 6.7 *Domenico Raimondo*, Example d: Drawing of 'The Square', Glasgow.

Figure 6.8 *Domenico Raimondo*, Example d: Taping out of 'The Square', Glasgow.

Example d: *An interactive construct between three different physical and cultural urban situations. In the construct, any changes in an individual evolving situation have a direct physical effect on the other parallel evolving situations.*

Location: Glasgow, Southall and Notting Hill Gate.

Author: Domenico Raimondo.

Issue: The identification of parallel and coexisting cultural structures. The identification and demonstration of an existing example. The establishment of an experimental structure (construct) to investigate the relationship between cultural fluctuations and physical changes.

Intention: To create an identical physical structure in all three locations.

Carlos Villanueva Brandt

To investigate the physical, social, political and economic factors affected by these structures; using these factors, to design an interactive construct between these structures. To speculate and design the physical consequences generated by social change within these structures.

Potential territory: Cultural territories.

The abstract construct.

Application:

5 'Discovering Glasgow Tourist Guide' is a conventional tourist guide of Glasgow.

6 'Spartacus the International Gay Guide' is a gay tourist guide that aims to identify gay lifestyle in varied international locations.

Two different guide books: 'Discovering Glasgow Tourist Guide'[5] and 'Spartacus the International Gay Guide'[6] were used to navigate the city of Glasgow. This process identified the varied interpretations of the same territory according to different cultural groups. It established that different cultural factors could directly affect the physical nature of the same territory. In order to further investigate these cultural inter-relationships and their effect on the physical environment an arbitrary formal intervention was devised. This intervention consisted of a simple rectangle of territory, unrelated to context, which was marked out with tape on the existing urban fabric. The dimensions of this rectangle were such that its extent crossed different lines of ownership, spanned between inside and outside, spanned between public and private and, at times, crossed different authorities and administrative systems.

The same rectangle was applied, taped, in three different locations: Glasgow, Southall and Notting Hill Gate. The physical activity of taping and its consequential social interactions were an integral part in the design of the proposed construct. On the formal side, these simple rectangles revealed the individual and complex physical, social, political and economic qualities of the different locations. Density, ownership, cultural value and economic value became easily comparable by means of the territorial rectangles and this process of comparison set up potential variables for the proposed interactive construct.

At the same time as the rectangles were constructed, an existing interactive and shared territory, the public toilet, was identified as a physical space governed by different social factors. It was recognised that the design of these spaces as part of the urban fabric was based on practicality, but their eventual use was influenced by strong and conflictive cultural forces: on the one hand they provided a civic service by means of a public convenience and on the other, when appropriated by a different cultural force, they provided an anonymous territory for social and physical interaction. These intrinsically interconnected influences, which were in a constant state of flux, directly influenced the design, material and physical qualities of the public toilet. The physical

Carlos Villanueva Brandt

changes, whether institutionalised or otherwise, reassessed the cultural significance of this shared territory. The nature of the physical changes and their counter-changes was small and precise: the changes of materials were countered by their removal, the creation of barriers was countered by drilling through them, the blocking of sight-lines was countered by creating new sight-lines, the restricting of access was countered by moving on to an alternative space and even the closing down of a convenience was countered by finding an alternative shared territory. The public toilet provided an example of the interrelationship between cultural forces and physical space.

The concept of this interrelationship was then addressed at the urban scale. The three taped rectangles became territories for action, potential spaces for change. A cultural interrelation between the territories was achieved by setting up an interactive construct that recorded social and cultural changes and determined the resultant physical changes. The interactive construct was put to work. Recorded and speculative changes were made in Glasgow that physically affected the territories in Southall and Notting Hill Gate, recorded and speculative changes were also made in Southall affecting the territories in Glasgow and Notting Hill Gate and the same process was carried out in Notting Hill Gate. The physical changes generated by the interactive construct were recorded and designed into their respective urban fabric.

The application of this abstract construct revealed the potential spatial possibilities generated by a culturally interactive urban development.

Example e:	*A fiction derived from within a physical reality followed by a fiction applied to a physical reality.*
Location:	Hackney, London.
Author:	Robert Bishop.
Issue:	The establishment of potential relationships between fictional space and real space. The involvement of the individual as a participant in fictional space. The involvement of the institution as a participant in fictional space.
Intention:	To create a fictional institution. To insert the fictional institution back within a real context.
Potential territory:	Fictional space.

Carlos Villanueva Brandt

Figure 6.9 *Robert Bishop*, Example e: Marking Out the Points of the 'Fictional Estate'.

Figure 6.10 *Robert Bishop*, Example e: The 'Fictional Estate' presented at the Kingshold Estate Tenants' Association Meeting.

Carlos Villanueva Brandt

Application:

A situation was set up consisting of a 24-hour intervention in a public space, Leicester Square. The author inhabited the square with a chair and table, creating his own space, and communicated exclusively by means of a typewriter. All social exchanges were carried out through writing, all institutional exchanges and confrontations were also carried out through writing. Observations, narratives and the author's dialogue were typed in lower case and all external dialogues or contributions were typed in the upper case. The beginning and end of the text was determined by the 24-hour cycle. The resulting document recorded the situation, dialogues, information, thoughts, comments, observations, facts, events, relationships and space. It constituted an interpretation of this urban situation and included the pertinent forces that make up the space of Leicester Square. It had its own internal fictional structure and was subsequently published as 'The Novel'.

This constructed situation identified the potential of a direct relationship between fictional and real space. This relationship was then addressed, at a larger scale, in the proposal for the Kingshold Estate in Hackney.

Through a series of daily interventions that lasted 100 days the concept for a fictional 'Estate' was established. By the use of varied systems a series of different fictional points were created and located throughout a specific area of the city. Two instigators, the author and the photo-journalist, worked together to record the points. One identified, fictionalised and marked the points whilst the other photographed them. The resultant sixty-four points, their locations, their photographs and their fictional interpretations were brought together into a book. This book became the 'Fictional Estate'.

The concept of fictional space was further investigated by a parallel but tangential intervention in Pentonville Prison. This institution was identified as an existing potential territory for a fictional interpretation of space. A parallel was also drawn between the difficulties of altering the design of prisons and the difficulties of altering a structure such as the Kingshold Estate.

Physical space and fictional space were considered separately.

A dialogue with the Home Office was initiated in order to suggest physical changes to the design of prisons. Communication was by means of faxes proposing possible changes to the details within a prison cell. All the proposed suggestions were rejected for clear objective and practical reasons. Changes to dimensions, heights, finishes and materials all created potential dangers and difficulties. It was concluded that it was extremely difficult to alter the physical configuration or the material quality of the prison cell.

After this process, the issue of the prison cell was readdressed by setting up an

Carlos Villanueva Brandt

interview with an inmate in Pentonville Prison. The prisoner explained his lack of concern with the physical design of the prison cell. He suggested that, in terms of space, the physical parameters of the prison cell were not problematic. All physical constrictions could be transcended by a more fictional interpretation of the space. Memory, desires and relationships could all exist within their own spatial structure. This intervention revealed an existing relationship between fictional and physical space.

It was then decided to introduce the 'Fictional Estate' to the real context of the Kingshold Estate. The 'Fictional Estate' was presented, at a formal meeting, to the Kingshold Estate Tenants' Association. The tenants acknowledged and accepted the notion of the 'Fictional Estate' and took part in the identification of further fictional points to add to the document. It was generally recognised that there was an essential relationship between the territory of experience, its fictional interpretation and the physical reality of the Kingshold Estate.

A real relationship was established between fictional space and physical space. An actual relationship was also set up between a fictional institution and a real institution. The 'Fictional Estate' became an integral part of the real Kingshold Estate.

Example f:
A physical manifestation of the relationship between space and landscape. A recognisable physical construct addressing the perception of space. A physical structure, a building, placed within a real political intervention.

Location:
Shogawa, Toyama Prefecture, Japan.

Author:
Carlos Villanueva Brandt.

Issue:
The proposal of a strategic project for the Toyama Prefecture as a whole, composed of individual architectural interventions in selected cities and towns.

Intention:
To create an architectural catalyst.
To create a strategic catalyst.
To set up an interactive cultural exchange.

Potential territory:
Civic space.
Intellectual space.
Political space.

Carlos Villanueva Brandt

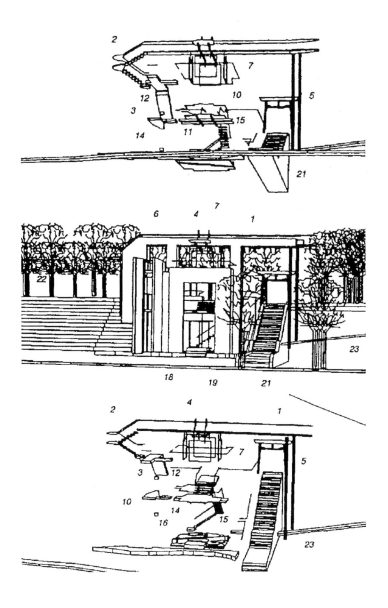

Figure 6.11 *Carlos Villanueva Brandt*, Example f: Sectional Sequence of Spaces in the Landscape.

Carlos Villanueva Brandt

115

Figure 6.12 *Carlos Villanueva Brandt,* Example f: The 'Shogawa Pavilion' Seen From the Park.

Application:

A strategic project, composed of independent architectural interventions, was proposed for Toyama in Japan by the Governor of the Prefecture. An advisory group, the Urban Factory, was set up to select, propose and administer the different independent projects. The concept of the overall project was both political and cultural and it was decided to invite international, rather than local, architects to design these projects. This on the one hand raised the universal awareness of the Toyama Prefecture and on the other introduced, to the Toyama Prefecture, the cultural inputs of the invited international architects.

The Urban Factory advised that the independent architectural projects should consist of appropriate public buildings required by the cities and towns. In all fourteen were chosen and the Urban Factory, along with the relevant local authorities, produced the respective architectural briefs.

The 'Shogawa Pavilion' was one of the chosen projects. The brief implied that the proposal had to work on four different fronts: the urban, the ceremonial, the architectural and, in terms of the overall project, the political. The proposed single structure addressed these implied fronts in different ways and also introduced a conceptual dimension. The interrelationship of these fronts within one structure was made easier by the openness of the brief.

The brief was interpreted, the project was conceived and the structure was built.

On the urban front, the structure links the town of Shogawa to the Funado Park which lies at the level of the Sho river and is otherwise invisible from the town. From the town the structure frames an existing ceremonial 'Torii' gate and forms a gateway to the park. From the park the structure transforms into a pavilion.

The park and the town are also brought together once a year by a traditional ceremony and festival. In the ceremony men of 25, 42 and 61 and women of 33 and 61, ages which are considered to be unlucky, administer 'sake' (a drink of religious significance) to carps, which are believed to take on a person's bad luck. The inebriated fish are then released into the river. This ceremony begins at the Shinto Temple and ends at the Sho river. The structure is designed to form part of the ceremonial route and provide an interlude along the procession to the river.

On the architectural front, the structure works mainly in section. Different sections create different routes through the landscape. These routes go through sequences of spaces that have different material qualities. All routes, sectional spaces and materials relate differently to the surrounding landscape. At its lowest point, the 'park and water level', the structure sits in a moat. Slightly higher and inside the structure, the 'gravel level' is split into two by an asymmetrical water channel, a 'river', creating a conceptual model of the town of Shogawa. Suspended above this, the 'timber level' and the central space of the structure, acts as a transitional space between the town and the park. On the roof of the main structure, the 'glass level', consisting simply of four glass walls without either ceiling or corners, unifies the key elements of the surrounding landscape: the town, the park, the mountain and the river. Their reflections intermingle with the views through the structure, creating a complex image of the whole. Finally at the highest point of the structure, the 'walkway and steel level', running parallel to the river, relates to the two dams that outline the boundaries of the town.

The 'Video Building' adjacent to this sectional sequence forms an integral part of the architectural space, but also establishes a more conceptual, constantly changing, relationship with the surrounding landscape. This is partly achieved by the architectural spaces which frame the landscape, but is reinforced by means of a video installation. Four video cameras, placed in inaccessible parts of the park, relay images at twenty-second intervals to monitors in the two video rooms within the 'Video Building'. These two rooms, with their changing images of inaccessible spaces, punctuate the experiential route set up within the main structure and create a further abstract involvement with the landscape.

The interrelationships between the urban, ceremonial, architectural and conceptual fronts of the 'Shogawa Pavilion' form part of the larger scale inherent in the political front. This front was and is addressed by the the strategy for Toyama as a whole: the 'Machi no Kao' (literally the 'Face of the Town') Project, which included all fourteen architectural interventions. Recognition for the architectural merit of this political front came from the Architectural Institute of Japan which honoured the Governor of the Toyama Prefecture, rather than the individual architects, with a special award for his contribution to architecture.[7]

These examples are an indication of potential architectural applications. They define new territories for the active involvement of architecture, create new definitions of architectural space and provide alternative experiential relationships within existing

7 In Spring 1995, the Governor of the Toyama Prefecture, Mr Nakaoki, received the Award of the Architectural Institute of Japan for his initiative in the Machi no Kao Project.

Carlos Villanueva Brandt

contexts. A constructed event (a), an infrastructural network of urban points (b), an appropriation of an existing institution followed by the appropriation of an urban territory (c), an interactive construct between different cultural situations (d), a fiction derived from a physical reality followed by a fiction applied to a physical reality (e) and a physical structure as part of a political intervention (f) show the latitude of potential architectural applications that form the evolving concept of 'Space Within'.

All the included applications are adapted to the society in which they take place, they come into being at different times and in different ways, they are more than an analysis of culture and society and they make cultural and political contributions by architectural means.

The future application of equivalent architectural situations and structures within real contexts will continue to question, reassess and expand the concept of 'Space Within'.

Carlos Villanueva Brandt

shared ground

'I was born in a house in Swan Street and I lived here for 41 years, then we got turned out and they built a block of offices and they weren't let. For three years they remained empty.'

'Look over the river. They built offices, offices, offices. They never left the space for green or something like that, for people enjoying themselves.'

'We would perhaps have preferred that site (the Tate) to be developed as an office complex and therefore we would have got more amenities, like another dry cleaning shop.'

'The office revolution of the seventies was going to finance the Globe. They produced plans which were a sort of Disney meets Shakespeare scenario.'

'It is as if layers of interest at different levels of influence have taken over and all the time an existing community has lived here and worked here and got on in spite of it all.'

'It is impossible for the private sector to achieve the kind of transformation we are talking about on its own. Even if it had enough capital to invest, it wouldn't on its own be able to achieve the kind of physiological change that is actually needed for the area to work. All of our projects will be funded through private sector money and public money and the views of all the people who live here and their participation in some of these projects is very very important.'

'If we could have even a small percentage of the business rate that is currently being sent out of London we could put that into public transport initiatives that would make a real difference.'

'Central government should devolve the power to raise and spend money much more, and that should apply to businesses. There should be a way of raising money from business through a local income tax.'

'We don't want our rents to go shooting up because the area is a better area now it has all these attractions because I'm sure our wages won't shoot up and we've still got to pay our rent.'

Muf Art and Architecture

'So we will start a dialogue to look at what are the needs of the Tate and what are the needs and aspirations of the local people.'

'I'd have a party, I'd open a big dance hall right over there.'

'We could develop some horticultural modern apprenticeships, park rangers who speak Japanese can also be tourist guides.'

'singing fa la la it's a lovely day, singing fa la la la la le oh.'

'The Tate themselves did a public consultation exercise which saw this as an important civic space, gave us, gave the community, plans of fountains and lovely statues from Italy and all of the rest of it, saying look what we can do, and yet proposing at the same time, and I don't actually think it is the Tate so much as the interest of the Globe more so, to bring coaches right into the area and destroy one of the most important spaces in the area which is of real value to residents.'

'This garden by the Tate is a vital lung in this part of London, in Bankside, which is lacking in green spaces.'

'You can say the river is a lung, you may say there is not much green space but one could theoretically see the river as the largest park we have in London.'

'There's no park round here with a swing in it.'

'Every time we play football round here all the parents complain. If we play in the square all the office workers complain.'

'You've got gardens proposed by the urban initiatives in the transport plan which are now car parks.'

Muf Art and Architecture

'What the area desperately needs is a commercial car park.'

'The residents clog the roads up as much as we do.'

'It's going to be great all that Modern Art. I'll be able to nick some of their ideas for down here in the community café.'

'My favourite thing is to play about.'

'If we play here they complain, if we play in Gatehouse Square they complain, if we play in the park there ain't no room.'

'As responsible adults we should allow them to concentrate on football.'

'I don't know what happened to the idea that when luxury housing was built certain units had to be put aside for social housing. That vanished years ago.'

'I'd like to see it go up-market and I think it will.'

'What the area needs is decent, low cost, good quality public housing.'

'I'm sick of the area, you want to come and live here and then you'll find out.'

'All these premises are empty because of the parking. People are so fed up with being hassled, he was in here eating his breakfast and they came along and he had to go, they wouldn't even give him 5 minutes.'

'It's not just here, it's in every high street. When the supermarkets have killed off all the other shops they'll start charging you for using their car park won't they. All this was shops, we had a grocer, we had a butcher, what's here now . . . nothing.'

'He was stripped of everything, his money, his home, his possessions, everything, and he died, he died in his fifties and he died in St Pancras Hotel which was the irony because that was built by his own father who he hardly knew.'

'I'm trying to bring people all along the little back streets, that's Disney that stuff along the river. People who visit here could understand how it was in the 1890s especially if you walk around to Octavia Hill's place. All those little cottages were owned by a Reverend somebody or other. He provided the money, but he wanted a 5 per cent return and she tried as best she could to guarantee his return. She didn't give things away.'

'Everyone of them died rescuing someone. There was a lady Alice Ayers, which is the name of Ayers Street through there. She died rescuing someone from a fire in that house and then he died. He dived into the water to rescue someone and was crushed by a boat and another chap he jumped on a railway line and of course was run over. Everybody died tragically.'

'And she took them all off the streets and she made a boys cadet force out of them and they were a rag tag bunch but she managed to twin them with Eton College and they fitted out these boys in the most marvellous uniforms and not only that they were issued with the latest rifles and these boys became London's first line of defence because they had these modern rifles and the others only had muskets or such like.'

'We used to have a mushroom farm there and now it's a night-club at night and car parking in the day. It's an odd area, it's mixed use, you've got residents who don't want change and businesses that are crying out for change.'

'They don't seem to like us, or maybe they don't like the club. We negotiate this minefield of problems and at the end of the day we're just exasperated and we think we'll just bin it. They should make up their minds. We are quite happy to know the rules and abide by them which ever *way they decide, but they have to decide definitely. If council policy is to support business, but they can't give an official OK until we make a planning application, then the risks are such it is worth doing, but on a well maybe – forget it. You've got to be prepared to upset someone because you are not going to please everyone all the way. Someone will be upset.'*

'The way I see it, it's either going to be a sort of dark urban office environment and very quiet the rest of the time, which might suit the resident, or you sow some seeds, you get some life. OK so there are a few more people at different times but at the same time it's possibly safer. There are people on the streets and more activity and then it snowballs, someone opens a café, and then someone opens a cocktail bar.'

His job is to find problems, it is always negative intervention, although I used to think he was quite a nice guy until he took me to court.'

'It was close to housing so we proposed a car wash. I mean it could have been panel beating or whatever because it had industrial use. So there we were, on balance being extremely considerate to the resident and one of my friends who's in Pimlico Opera asked if they could rehearse there on the weekend and I said yes. So the tenors were practising and in no time we had complaints from the residents about the noise.'

'We know we have a problem with traffic management. How can it work for all the parties, the residents, those who work here and the tourism industry?'

'The Romans settled Southwark before they settled London and one hopes Southwark will become a city just like London or Westminster.'

'It is an area that has been neglected and that has certain advantages – it hasn't suffered the boom and bust of the 60's and the 80's so in general the area is underdeveloped.'

'I think unfortunately that what happens with Londoners is they often need to see a development happen and then they look to see what is missing, but I think here there should be a certain

Muf Art and Architecture

projection to the future. There is an opportunity to create something on the street level, to spill onto the street. Life starts on the street.'

'Find the right anchor tenant to give the ripple effect, something to create a cosy quality of life on the main street that moves off into the side streets.'

'The people who live here fear they will be left on little islands while things go on around them. They fear they won't profit, that jobs will go elsewhere. A lot of people see the increase in tourism as hundreds of people go past their homes, leaving coke cans in the front garden, and the streets are used as a massive coach park. I don't think the interests of the tourist and business and residents are different. If you improve something for one, it should benefit the others.'

'There isn't a centre. There are lots of little places where people go.'

'The main problem is the male unemployed. Because it's a fairly traditional area the women have jobs as cleaners or receptionists. It's not great but they get by, but being traditional the older men are used to working in the printing and manufacturing industries which have gone now and younger men still feel they have to have a man's job and there just aren't any.'

'What I'm concerned about is that the sort of jobs they offer will be menial jobs and even for things like a receptionist they think you need an ex art student. My fear is that they will offer security jobs, loo cleaning jobs and washing up jobs and anything more they think you have to have an artist. The big offices who moved here bring their work force with them. I'm sick of this business of "we provide hundreds of jobs". They don't.

'If you don't have a job you're not going to be able to eat out in the little restaurant that has popped up. If you have no money at all then you're simply not part of it.'

'There's older people like myself, 40 or 50 with no hope of another job.'

Transcript from '100 Desires for Southwark Street'.
A video produced by Muf Art and Architecture.

Muf Art and Architecture

SOUTHWARK STREET – SHARED GROUND

In February 1996 Muf were commissioned by Southwark Council in London to propose improvements to the urban environment of Southwark Street. This project was one of seven commissioned for different sites in the north of the Borough. In June all seven

initial schemes were publicly exhibited in the old car wash on Southwark Street. This public exhibition *Future Southwark* was also a forum for discussion and formal consultation.

We drew the street not as four lanes and two footways but as a moving sight line – *as far as the eye can see* – where the eye does not respect the lines of property ownership nor the parallel geometry of the street. Our designated site – Southwark Street – expanded to include empty ground floors and long views off the street towards housing or the river.

On Sundays Southwark Street is deserted, a place where one person might be seen in the distance criss-crossing the street on the way to far away shops or the river. Southwark Street is a place where anything can happen but often nothing ever does.

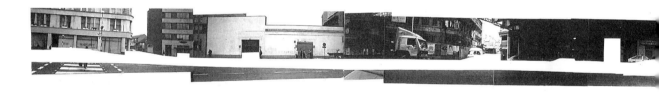

Public consultation was a stated requirement of the brief, even so there seemed to be a tacit limit to how far one should go. There was a fear of either raising people's expectations or of giving the impression that demands could or would be met. The project balanced on the edge of the abject territory that the public realm had become. We moved amongst a history of discontent, opportunism, resentment and *laissez-faire*, between discrete packages of funding and the desire for finite deliverables before the next financial year.

Muf Art and Architecture

We began talking to people in the street, in their houses, in shops, offices and cafés. Each time calling on the next person someone mentioned. We spoke to over 100 people. We learnt not to foreclose a response with the multiple choice question. Instead we asked: 'What is you wildest dream scenario?' 'Where would you like to be in five years time?' These conversations were documented in a video '100 Desires for Southwark Street.'

People who lived and worked in the area spoke not only to us, the commissioned professionals, but also through the video to one another and to the larger political bodies that were responsible for the implementation of the proposals. The video was the first site for a shared ground.

The principle of shared ground expanded into a strategy for the public space and private property of Southwark Street. The designer as outsider has to act as mediator/negotiator or as interloper, moving on and off the street, to develop new relationships of give and take, across the boundary of public and private.

The principal proposal is to widen the south facing pavement as if the foreshore of the river Thames had been turned inland, to occupy the sunny side of the street. The new pavement will undulate and lift to create level access to the elevated ground floors of former warehouses. It will also form furniture, public benches that can overlap the licensed territory of the café forecourt. This proposal gives form to new planning policy which allows offices to change to retail.

Improvement relative to what? And for whom?

The pavement proposal is held in a web of proposals for lighting, landscape and information which stretch from the river to Union Street and make connections across the borough from the south and the east.

Muf Art and Architecture

A PILOT PROJECT FOR SOUTHWARK STREET – LINES OF NEGOTIATION

A year after the initial commission Muf were asked to implement the strategy as a pilot project. The aims of our *Future Southwark* proposal were telescoped into 200 metres of Street frontage. The client intimated that the pilot could have 'far reaching consequences' for the whole site in the future. Our investigations had taken us beyond the street and into the social networks which informed our strategy. Would 200 metres be too densely packed to hold all of the proposals presented at *Future Southwark*?

The proposals became evident as rules, as a brief, as the impetus to pursue partnerships and as liberation from the search for a building to be built. Strangely obedient to these original precepts, almost all of the original injunctions can be found however minutely in the pilot project.

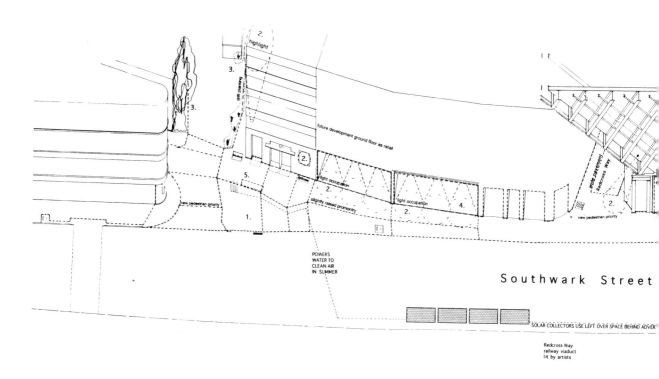

The first drawing shows the street as existing. The dotted line sets out the territory for negotiation across the boundaries of ownership and responsibility between ourselves, the official and unofficial client, the building owners, the designers of adjacent projects, the highways department and the Director of Traffic for London.

Muf Art and Architecture

Although the line is broken to allow you in, it also marks out exclusions. The building owner and design professional understand this line as the threshold of vested interests, but the child's sense of territorial demarcations is absent from this drawing.

The drawing aims to make space for other knowledge to influence the design process, for example the expertise that comes with living somewhere for twenty years or being aged five.

Children are themselves 'Future Southwark', but they are usually spoken for and have no stake in the formation of the places they will grow up to own and inhabit. To expand our understanding of how children perceive the places they live in, and how it might be possible to include their knowledge in the design, we set up a parallel project. We invited children from a nearby school to shadow us in the detailed development of the design.

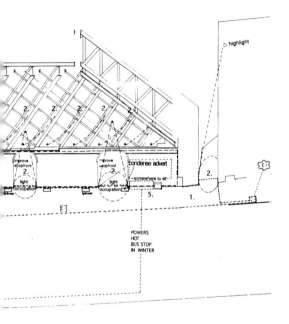

The work the children produced both overlapped and separated from our own. For them, time moved at a different pace, they soon forgot what we thought they would remember. They described the city as they saw it on the way to school, but Southwark Street was a vague territory which held little interest until it was re-imagined as an international funfair, as a stage for the Spice Girls or visited by a stranger/tourist. Then the attractions became more obvious.

What will you not give up?

The children clearly reiterated to us the territory where no distinction is made between things that are real and things that are not real, the pens and colours used to make a picture are as real as the thing drawn.

Some of the designs the children made will be embedded in the project like logos or tags on the new street furniture. The project will also be theirs because they were the first ones to know about it. They too had passed with us behind the scenes to make proposals for what the street might become.

Muf Art and Architecture

A PILOT PROJECT FOR SOUTHWARK STREET – DESIGN PROPOSAL

1   The south facing pavement is widened by between 2 and 9 metres, taking up one lane of the highway and is levelled where side streets cross. The pedestrian has a new priority over the car.

2   The geometry of the pavement wavers and opens up, lateral joints between cast in-situ concrete panels are drawn along the street.

3   Trees appear from the side street, Thrale Street, as if flowing into Southwark Street

4   The landscaped view out of Southwark Street is formed by vertical planting against a flank wall and planting along Maiden Lane drifting into the hinterland.

5   A black precast concrete bench/sofa outside Wilcox House, 4500 × 500 × 500 mm high with a smaller white seat inset 1350 × 250 × 350 mm high.

5A   Logos, based on the children's designs, are embedded in the surface of the concrete:

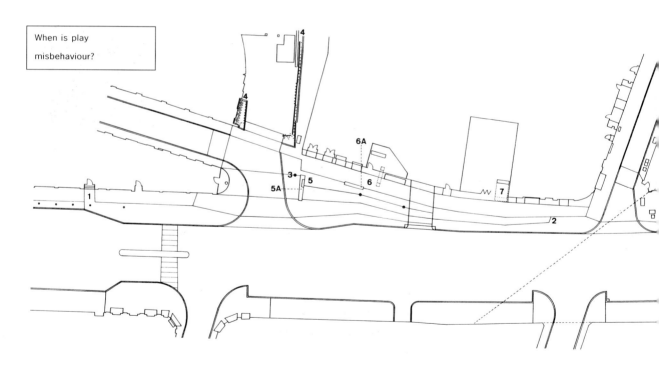

When is play
misbehaviour?

Muf Art and Architecture

Pottery From Wilcox House: 'My design is for pottery from Wilcox House to put on Southwark Street. It is a broken pot which tells people about the pottery in Wilcox House.' Jake.

A Stage For Geri: 'The stage is red and it has Geri written on it. It has little stones on it and shining glitter all over it. The height is 900 mm and the length 1500 mm.' Sanna.

Paving Stone For Emma: 'The paving stone is pink. I had Baby Spice written on it and it is 900 by 600 mm. The paving stone will stay there all the time, but Baby Spice will only stay there for a week. I also have decorations.' Leanne.

6   A bench is shared with a new café terrace licensed to spill out onto the street. It is 2900 × 500 × 400 mm high.

Figure 7.4 *Jake, Pottery From Wilcox House.*

6A   A logo is embedded in the surface:

Posh Spice: 'For my Posh Spice stage, I want a gate around it, some barbed wire and a padlock on it and I want some stone for the stage and to paint it purple with two lights over it and it is going to be 900 × 1000 × 100 mm.' Kane.

Figure 7.6 *Kane, Posh Spice.*

7   A new mini-market is licensed to use the street beyond the existing 900mm line of privately owned pavement.

8   The Ace café slips further out of the railway arch to catch the morning sun and is lit by an 'ACE' neon sign at night.

9   Hop Cars, a 24-hr mini-cab office, shares a new 'hot seat' with the tourist visitor at the coach drop off.

10   New lighting is introduced to the railway bridge. Lights set between the beams highlight the existing structure, lighting the highway and shop fronts.

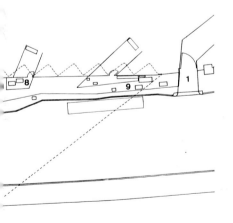

Muf Art and Architecture

A PILOT PROJECT FOR SOUTHWARK STREET – DURING CONSTRUCTION

The pilot project for the street begins construction in September 1997 and will be finished the following Spring. The pavement will widen to make a south facing pavement as if the foreshore of the river had been turned inland. Muf will culminate this part of the project with an intervention to make the fantasy of the foreshore temporarily 'real'.

At the Spring tide a 24-hour video projection will bring the ebb and flow of the incoming tide onto the facade of one of the buildings which border the site to make a temporary and imaginary beach.

We will take the children on a trip on a boat down the river to the sea to film the tide. The journey will connect the place they live to the faraway sea and show how places are linked by geography – the river runs from Southwark down to the sea – as well as through the imagination.

Figure 7.7 *Bosun*, River Thames.

DESIGN TEAM

Muf Art and Architecture: Caterina Almada, Marie Alix Beaugier, Juliet Bidgood, Katherine Clarke, Liza Fior, Cathy Hawley.

Ove Arup and Partners: Carol Christie, David George, Florence Lam, Strachan Mitchell.

Landscape: Carolyn Roy.

Typography: Tamasin Cole and Richard Hollis.

Southwark Council: Craig Bradley, Project Officer.

Muf wish to thank the RSA for funding '100 Desires for Southwark Street' and The Arts Council and the University of North London for funding work with The Cathedral School of St Saviours and St Mary Overie.

an other architect

Figure 8.1 *Swimming pool,
Los Angeles.*

Los Angeles is a city of ghettos, wealthy or impoverished islands defined by their occupants and patrolled by the police, who ensure that the diverse economic and ethnic groups are isolated from each other. The freeways are the essential tool for the policing of Los Angeles. They provide routes through the metropolis so that the inhabitants of each ghetto never enter hostile territory. The freeway in Los Angeles is analogous to the road which linked West Berlin to West Germany before the unification of the state. It is an umbilical cord between related bodies. The purpose of the freeway is to prevent unwanted connections and permit desirable ones, to deny and conceal difference, to reinforce the apparent autonomy of each ghetto.

The actor Dennis Hopper's house in Los Angeles is located in Venice. During the day the beach front unconsciously parodies the image of Los Angeles propagated in films. Absurdly sculpted sun-lit bodies lumber along the sea front. If this is the land of opportunity, why does everyone look like a cartoon? At night, the boardwalk is a violent no-go area. Hopper's house is a high-security container for art with a window-less façade and surveillance cameras patrolling the exterior. Movie stars do not live in Venice. Hopper is in alien, hostile territory. He is in the wrong ghetto.

The city of Los Angeles is an analogue for the discipline of architecture because it is divided into a series of discrete ghettos that prevent an overview of the whole. The fragmentation of the city of Los Angeles and the discipline of architecture into seemingly autonomous, mutually exclusive and carefully controlled areas of activity is of course compatible with the regulation of society required by capitalist ideology. Ideas, icons and bodies are reduced to the level of capitalist detritus. Radicality is a product for sale. In Los Angeles, the police contain the boundaries of the ghettos. In architecture, the profession is the police force. The freeway is the essential tool for the policing of Los Angeles and the practices and procedures of the architect are the essential tools for the policing of architecture.

Jonathan Hill

The term 'architect' is enshrined in law and every architect has a number. Now who is this designed to protect? Seemingly the architect as much as the user. The architectural profession claims a monopoly over a specific area of architectural production for the purpose of economic and social self-protection. The aim of the profession is to provide the products and practices of its members with an iconic status and a cultural value, to suggest that only the work of architects deserves the title architecture. Although unregulated by the law, the architectural historian claims a similar monopoly within the field of history. Architects and architectural historians monitor and patrol their domains in order to exclude critics from within and intruders from without, especially each other. They protect their territories by deriding incursions from outside as ignorant or mistaken, implying that there is a truthful and correct interpretation of a fixed body of knowledge. Of course, a politically correct Post-Modernist is just as likely to use this tactic as a didactic Modernist.

Professionalism is a state of mind as much as of law. The control of architecture by its police force(s) is partial and mythical and a myth sometimes does most harm to the social group it seems to protect. Professionalism acts as a restraint on architects because it encourages them to be parochial and obsessed with their financial and social status. Ideas and actions that challenge the authority of the architectural profession are marginalised and, consequently, the language of architectural practice acts as a restriction as much as a liberation. So many of the important qualities of architecture appear only fleetingly in the architectural drawing and text. Therefore, they are not designed by the architect. We must ask two simple but important questions. How do we produce architecture? What is left out of this process?

Architectural discourse usually focuses on the individual project and ignores the terms that frame discussion. The most essential subject is often the least discussed but its absence can be painfully visible. The major currency in contemporary architecture is the image, the photograph not the building. Two-thirds of the city of Los Angeles is covered in roads. The photograph occupies an equivalent position of importance within architecture. The architectural photograph has two contradictory roles. First, to present architecture as a higher form of cultural production to defend and promote the class it represents and, second, to further architecture's absorption into consumer culture. The combination of these two demands reduces the architectural magazine to the level of a travel brochure. Photographs in architectural magazines all have similar characteristics. The profusion of blue skies and balmy weather turn the shiny pages of the magazine into a sanatorium in which the architect is the patient and the photograph the medicine. The photograph presents the myth of its own reality to convince the architect that outside lies a diminished reality or even unreality. Of course withdrawal symptoms may be suffered after we leave the magazine's reassuring embrace but under its bright skies we can simulate the clean fresh air and brisk healthy exercise that are important components of life in the sanatorium.

The pre-eminence of the photograph in contemporary architecture is exemplified by the Barcelona Pavilion. The Pavilion was built for an exhibition in 1929. It was, therefore, constructed and demolished in the same year. About ten years ago, it was rebuilt from photographs. On the cover of the issue of *Blueprint* published to celebrate this event, the proud instigator of the Pavilion's reconstruction stands in front of the building.[1] Unseen behind him, an errant piece of late twentieth-century technology, a rubberised expansion joint, droops from the gap between the sheets of travertine. To add further irony, the existence of a post-war concrete building, standing directly in front of the Pavilion and obscuring the latter's relations with its original context, is rarely mentioned in architectural articles. Can you imagine the frantic contortions of the photographer to exclude it from photographs? Since the reconstruction of the Pavilion, the concrete building has been demolished. Maybe its destruction was performed for the photograph not the site?

Figure 8.2 *Mies van der Rohe, Barcelona Pavilion, 1929. Reconstructed 1986. The post-war concrete building, since demolished, is to the right of the photograph.*

In confusing the photograph of the Barcelona Pavilion with the building of the Barcelona Pavilion, the emptiness of the former is often assumed to be the agenda of the latter.[2] However, sometimes, the most silent space is also the loudest. The Pavilion is so open to different forms of use because it is physically specific but functionally non-specific. Consequently, rather than permanently empty, the seductive spatiality and materiality of the Pavilion is waiting to be filled.

> *We make a vessel from a lump of clay; it is the empty space within the vessel that makes it useful. We make doors and windows for a room; thus while the tangible has advantages, it is the intangible that makes it useful.*[3]

The Barcelona Pavilion is not the same as its photograph. It is an icon of twentieth-century architecture for the wrong reasons, not because it is a building with a subtle and suggestive programme but precisely because it existed as a photograph and could *not* be occupied. Between 1929 and 1986, while the Pavilion did not exist, it was probably the most copied building of the twentieth century. The photograph was being copied not the building. To imagine the extent of the appropriation, we just need to visualise the Pavilion with a few petrol pumps on its forecourt, a cashpoint machine in the wall or a barbecue by the pool.

At the beginning of the 1990s, the baby was the ultimate advertising accessory for a 'caring decade'. However, in architecture, the baby did not, even for cynical reasons, appear in the photograph. The most obvious and important action of the architectural photograph is to empty architecture of its inhabitants. The absence of people from the architectural photograph is the physical manifestation of a deep fear of the user within the architectural profession. For the architect, the occupant is an intruder, analogous to dirt, in the sense defined by Mary Douglas as matter out of place.[4]

Architects often dream of a captive audience and rarely credit the inhabitants of architecture with any initiative. A building functions on a psychological and a physical level. It demonstrates control as a physical structure claiming dominance by scale and as an ideological tool of the political and social system it represents. Movement within, and around, the structure is constricted by a combination of psychological and physical controls which permit, or deny, access to all, or part, of the building. Individuals and groups are excluded from the dominant power structures by the process of mythification manifested in architecture, which makes a situation or system appear impenetrable and defines the identity of the outsider. Fortunately it is easier to control the people in a photograph than in a building. Even the most static and stereotypical architecture only indicates, it does not determine, behaviour. It is still

Jonathan Hill

Figure 8.3 *Stephen Harty*, Individual Acts of Terrorism Are Entirely Pointless But They Feel Fantastic at the Time, *1992. Photograph, Hugo Glendenning. One leg of the chair ends in a light bulb. Sitting down destroys the light and the chair topples over.*

possible to slouch in a straight-backed chair because social codes are manufactured by the complex interplay of ideological mechanisms. Of course, this does not mean that breaking the rules is easy. Sex on the kitchen-table might not be a transgression but exactly what we are supposed to do.

The purpose of the architectural photograph is to convince architects that they control architecture, but it is essential that they recognise the opposite. Paradoxically, such an admission would increase rather than diminish the· role of the architect because it would facilitate the subtle investigation of issues which are at present simply ignored, especially the role of the user.

In architecture, there are two occupations. First, the activities of the architect and, second, the actions of the user. The architect and user both produce architecture, the former by design, the latter by inhabitation. As architecture is designed and experienced, the user has as creative a role as the architect. This understanding of architecture is indebted to Roland Barthes' text 'The Death of the Author'.[5] Barthes states that a text often contradicts the intentions of its author and each reader constructs a new text through the act of reading. His denunciation of the symbolic purity of language recalls, first, Benjamin's support for allegory as a more plastic form

Jonathan Hill

of communication than the symbol[6] and, second, Surrealist practices that shift the emphasis from the single author to hybrid author-readers who both make and consume a work.[7] Barthes recognises that a profusion of ambiguities and interpretations inhabit the gap between writing and reading but does not imply that the writer should be without ideas. Instead, he proposes that the writer should be aware of, and indeed use, the limitations of his medium.

Barthes, therefore, argues for the death of the traditional author and the creation of a new type of writer, aware of the importance of the reader. Barthes' reformulation of the author also suggests a new model for the architect, one who recognises the creative and active inhabitation of architecture. 'The Death of the Author' has a considerable, and comparatively unexplored, relevance to architecture. However, a building is not directly comparable to a text. Rather than linking one term within literature to another in architecture, I suggest that author–text–reader relations, as a whole, are analogous to architect–building–user relations. Architecture is the gap between building and using, just as literature is the gap between writing and reading. Of course, whatever the agenda of the architect, the most powerful occupations of architecture will often be accidental. In London, the concrete undercrofts to the cultural institutions alongside the Thames are cold, dark, uneven and seemingly useless. It is hard to imagine the purpose for which they were conceived. However, they are constantly occupied by skateboarders because the ramped forms and ready audience are so appropriate to the sport. Paradoxically, the space is so potent and available for occupation because it is undefined by the architect. A more clearly political appropriation of space occurred in Paris. The ordered linearity of Haussmann's boulevards facilitates the speedy movement of troops around the city. In 1968, students acted against the institutions of the state. The protesters dug up the cobbles from the streets and hurled them at the police, for a few minutes turning a weapon of the state against the institutions it represented. The government responded equally pragmatically by tarmacking over the cobbles.

In searching for an architect who recognises the disjunction of use and form, it is obvious to focus on Bernard Tschumi. In the 'Advertisements for Architecture' he states: 'to really appreciate architecture you may even need to commit a murder. Architecture is defined by the actions it witnesses as much as by the enclosure of its walls.'[8] In *The Manhattan Transcripts*,[9] he cites the montage of forms and events as a rejection of the rigid separation and delineation of activity that occurs in authoritarian architecture. However, Parc de la Villette is simply too uniform to invite the diverse relations between form and event described in Tschumi's writings. In contrast to *The Manhattan Transcripts*, Parc de la Villette is a work of the derrière-garde not the avant-garde. Parc de la Villette resists a negative present but does not propose a positive

Jonathan Hill

future. However, in no way does the disappointment of La Villette invalidate the principles of *The Manhattan Transcripts*. The differences between the two are revealing. 'The Death of the Author' is 40 years old, Walter Benjamin's text 'The Author as Producer'[10] and the strategies of Surrealism and Dada are much older, but their influence on architectural production is slight, largely because of the status of the architect as a professional. First, because many architects are comparatively ignorant of developments in art and literature and, second, because ideas that threaten the limits of the architects' power are consciously marginalised.

Knowledge without action is not a threat. The former does not necessarily lead to the latter. Clearly, it is not enough to question the architectural profession as a whole because the familiar procedures of architectural practice resist the user in specific ways. Therefore, a reassessment of architect–building–user relations must dismantle and re-cast the detail of architectural discourse and production. In the following pages, I discuss two fragments of this process, respectively function and the architectural drawing.

In this century, discussions on the inhabitation of architecture have centred on function.[11] The latter's dominant position in early twentieth-century architecture is superseded by its present guise as the shadowy and unwanted ghost of practice. In planning applications and building regulations, architecture is still defined in terms of function because the quantification of all the spheres of production is a central tenet of the Capitalist system. However, the reputation of Functionalism is now so tarnished that it deters serious investigation into the ways in which architecture is occupied and inhabited. Function is merely one attempt to understand how we occupy architecture. However, its history is so recent and threatening that it is often assumed to be the only theory available. In architectural discourse, use is often fatally coupled with function and, consequently, they are both ignored. Therefore, function must be dissected and then detached from use before a reassessment of the latter can be made.

With a few exceptions, early twentieth-century Modernism discarded visual references to the human form.[12] Instead, it concentrated on the actions and processes of the body. Functionalism supposes that only the quantifiable is real. It disregards non-productive, 'irrational' actions and focuses only on actions deemed to be 'useful'. In 1927, Grete Schütte-Lihotzky designed the mass produced, standardised Frankfurt Kitchen for the city's social housing programme. In applying the scientific management of labour to the production of architecture, Schütte-Lihotzky analysed the actions performed within the kitchen, so as to eradicate unnecessary labour and allow each function to be performed with the minimum effort and in the minimum space. Efficiency rather than pleasure was the agenda. The Frankfurt Kitchen is an appropriate emblem for the rational, waste-free society propagated by Functionalists, in which the paradigmatic form of the body is the technician at labour in the factory and the home. Le Corbusier's phrase, 'a machine for living in',[13] is only an accurate description of Functionalist sensibilities if the human is a component of the machine, not the machine a servant of the human. The 'machine for living in' is a totalising and all-pervading model for society not just architecture. The desire for a society of scientific progression and functional purity is similar to the obsessive hand-washing in individuals. They are both a product of social anxiety but on different scales. In Alvar Aalto's Paimio Sanitorium, an iconic Functionalist project, the surfaces of the wash hand-basins are carefully angled to silence the running water as its falls into the basin below, both to deny the presence of dirt and to hide the process of cleansing. The silent flow of dirty water disappearing into the drains is the sound of guilty minds at work, 'improving' society through architecture.

Determinism[14] is the central theory of Functionalism. It is also the most contra-dictory and alarming aspect of the Modernist agenda because, from the architect, it demands a faith in science that cannot be validated scientifically and, from the user, it expects merely obedience. In witchcraft, the cut on the doll results in a pain in the body. In determinism, the decision of the architect results in the action of the user. One perverse response to the perceived failure of Modernism has been to dismiss all large-scale architectural propositions as inherently regressive and morally suspect, a scenario that ironically accepts the link between architecture and deter-minism. The result is an oppressive status quo in which large-scale architectural action is frowned upon. However, as Rem Koolhaas says 'Architecture is a paradoxical mixture of power and powerlessness.'[15] That architecture influences many things but determines very few should be a source for optimism not pessimism. Extricated from the burdens of determinism and Functionalism, architects can acquire a far subtler understanding of the two occupations of architecture, the activities of the architect and the actions of the user.

Determinism assumes that the user is passive and predictable while this text suggests that the user is active and unpredictable. The fact is that both are true. The oscillation between passivity and activity is more apparent in the experience of architecture than in any other cultural phenomena. Value, authority, and the 'correct' reading of a film, book or exhibition is disseminated to its public through hype, reviews and the codes of the space in which it is displayed. The more pervasive mass media have both the largest audience and the most sophisticated means to publicise a 'correct' interpretation. As a text or artwork usually has a much smaller audience than a film, the mechanisms for the dissemination of the former are less pervasive than those of the latter but they are as intense because the cultural value ascribed to art and literature is higher than that of film and, consequently, greater authority is accorded to

Jonathan Hill

the statements of the artist and writer than the film-maker. In contrast, very few buildings reach mass consciousness. They are experienced without any knowledge of the architect's pre-publicity, of which only other architects are usually aware. A building is perceived for the first time in a different way to most artworks, films or books because it is experienced cold without any prior knowledge, except in relation to other buildings known to the user. A film, artwork or book is experienced at most a few times but they have a second and equally powerful existence in memory. A building, however, is usually experienced over a long period of time and even the occupant of a large city frequents a narrow range of places and routes. Therefore, while the other media are experienced in a state of focused, but often submissive, concentration, architecture is experienced in a state of distraction. The attention of the user is seemingly focused on everything but the architecture.

Ironically, an architect's experience of architecture is more akin to the contemplation of the art object than the occupation of a building. Unfortunately, architects often choose to ignore this simple distinction. For architects, the classification of architecture as an art is an issue of social and financial necessity. A plethora of social and cultural codes reinforce the superiority of art over the everyday, of contemplation over distraction.

Habit is the ballast that chains the dog to his vomit.[16]

Architecture is, it appears, demeaned by its association with habit. However, in the example of a car driver, Stan Allen suggests that distraction is not necessarily simple or passive: 'You can concentrate and perform actions necessary to keep the car on the road and, at the same time, think and actually do all kinds of different things.'[17] Distraction is not a state of unawareness but a particular type of awareness that enables a person to perform, at the same time, a series of complex activities that move in and out of focus from a conscious to an unconscious state. Habit, memory and experience are coupled with the sensual disembodiment of twentieth-century forms of communication to form a complex compound of spatial and temporal layers. Someone talks to you, caresses your back, while you listen to the phone, read the fax and peer out of the window.

There appears to be an enormous gap between the complexity of architecture and the simplicity of a sheet of paper and yet architects make drawings not buildings. The drawing is the principal language of mediation between the architect and the builder. Therefore, architects can only build what they can represent in words or images. For architects, the gap between the drawing and the building is an uncomfortable truth to be forcefully denied because it threatens their authority over architecture. Consequently, in an act of self-protection and self-promotion, the architect presents the drawing and the model as truthful representations of the building. However, the languages of architectural discourse and production are ideological not neutral. All forms of representation omit as much as they include. The traditional means of architectural representation emphasise the dimensional and compositional but architecture is defined by the actions and events which occur within it as much as the walls that mark its dimensions.[18] How can we consider the inhabitation of architecture in drawings that have no means to describe that occupation? This dilemma suggests a three-fold investigation of the architectural drawing. First, to consider how the drawing and building are similar and different, second, to develop new ways to visualise the qualities of architecture excluded from the drawing, and, third, if these cannot be drawn, to find other ways to describe and discuss them.

The term 'white paper' is an appropriate one for the reassessment of the architectural drawing because of its double meanings. It is a programme and a site. As the former, a white paper alludes to the formulation of a law in the British parliamentary system as it passes through a series of discussions, debates and transformations. It is an instrument of politics. The more obviously architectural interpretation of white paper defines that luscious moment when the paper is seemingly empty.[19] The most important word in the previous sentence is 'seemingly' because the sheet of paper is really a site with edges, surface and depth. In the shop at the Rietveld Museum in Amsterdam, there is a jigsaw puzzle of a painting from Malevich's *White on White* series (1917–1918). Try to imagine yourself piecing it together. If we can construct a white on white jigsaw puzzle, maybe the architect's drawing paper consists of not one but many whites. You just have to look hard enough to find the differences. To manipulate the white paper, the architect must use it spatially, as a site, as a space with depth, smell, sounds, material and even use. Disposing the elements of a drawing around the edges of the paper is a quite different proposition to a centralised image. Each composition implies a distinct proposition for the draw-ing and, through analogy, for the building site. All architectural drawings are scaled. Occasionally they have more than one scale but the scaled elements are isolated from each other. If instead they are juxtaposed to each other, the drawing immediately acquires a third dimension with distance and depth. The elements of the drawing recede back and jump forward from the plane of the drawing. Most important of all, the paper can be treated literally cut, erased and marked. In architecture, a line on a drawing is an action in its own right and a description of another action outside the drawing. Build a drawing and draw a building.

Jonathan Hill

Figure 8.4 *Jonathan Hill,*
Building a Drawing, *1992.*
Photograph, Hugo Glendenning.

However, if this text were to only focus on the transformations to the architect's means of production it would discuss just one part of architecture. The term 'architect' is enshrined in law. Fortunately, the word 'architecture' has no legal protection. Architecture is not a strong, coherent discipline with internal self-validating codes that safely protect its members and exclude 'ignorant' outsiders. As Mark Cousins suggests in this book, architecture is a weak discipline, not weak in a pejorative sense, but weak in contrast to a self-validating discipline. The interior of a strong discipline is precise and stable, its boundaries equally certain; decisions are made only in reference to what is already inside the discipline. In architecture, the boundary between inside and outside is confused and there is no shared idea of what constitutes its interior. The 'weakness' of the discipline of architecture is deeply threatening to the architectural profession. Consequently, architects attempt to prevent two intrusions, one into the body of *their* profession, the other into the body of *their* architecture. The former occurs when the work of an 'illegal' architect is recognised as architecture. The latter occurs when the user occupies architecture. To repel these intrusions, architects assume that architecture is a physical phenomena with specific materials and dimensions, a building but not any building, *their* building unoccupied. However, a more appropriate definition, and one that threatens the profession, is that architecture is not just a building. It is, primarily, a particular relation between a subject and an object, in which the former occupies the latter, which is not necessarilly a building, but can be a space, text, artwork or any other phenomenon that displays or refers to the subject–object relations particular to architecture.

Architecture is a far larger category than the work of professional architects and some of the most thoughtful and speculative contemporary architecture is made by illegal architects. Two distinct cultural disciplines, for example art and architecture, cannot be fused into a cohesive whole because distinct forces frame each activity but an artist may produce architecture and an architect can make art. A film, artwork or text is not necessarily architecture but it can, at the very least, be architectural in specific ways, whether spatial, material or temporal, especially if it is considered as a series of strategies, elements and techniques rather than an indivisible whole. This suggests that anyone wanting to produce architecture should, first, discard the preconceived boundaries of the discipline and, second, be prepared to learn from architecture wherever it is found, whoever it is produced by.

An architecture that responds to the creative unpredictability of the user is more likely to be produced by an illegal architect rather than a professional one. However, as I use the term, the illegal architect is not simply a person who produces archi- tecture without a professional qualification. The illegal architect questions and subverts the conventions, codes and 'laws' of architecture, and, therefore, could even be a registered architect critical of the profession. Ultimately, 'what is architecture?' is a challenge not a limitation.

About a year ago, I bought a copy of the catalogue to the Rebecca Horn exhibition at the Guggenheim in New York. When I turned to Figure 94, I was surprised to recognise the particularly grotty hotel room in Barcelona that I stayed in in November 1992.[20] My room in the Hotel Peninsular being one of seven rooms in which Horn had installed her work for three months earlier in the same year. Of course, the insalubrious nature of the location adds immensely to the character of the project. The room is easily recognisable because the transformation is so subtle. Curiously, by the time I arrived, the room had lost its number and the concierge could find neither the numeral nor the room. As Duchamp claimed a urinal as his own and Manzoni canned his shit in the name of art, maybe Horn's appropriation of my hotel room transformed it from architecture into art.[21] Its disappearance from the hotel register signifying the room's passage from the realm of utility. When I spent five nights in Barcelona, was I inhabiting the art or architecture of Rebecca Horn?

Pair of men's shoes, flashing light, motor and bed, dimensions variable. The diverse materials in Horn's installation at the Hotel Peninsular challenge the reductive

Jonathan Hill

abstractions of architectural construction, while her emphasis on the minute indicates that power does not always correspond to scale. Artists exploit the soft underbelly of idiosyncratic and everyday experiences but architects usually limit themselves to conventional materials and identifiable programmes. The realisation that art can be made of anything has had little effect on how architects produce architecture but it has had an effect on how artists make architecture. As art can be made of anything, it can also be made of architecture. The sites for architectural practice are now so expansive that architects without architecture is one side of this coin and artists with architecture is the other. Although analogous to a fragment rather than a whole project, Richard Wilson's *20:50* (1987) is surely architectural, even if the material is unexpected, the author an artist and the site unfamiliar. A steel container filled with sump oil forms the floor. The viewer enters along a gently sloping and narrowing walkway cut into a mirrored floor, reflecting the ceiling above. The powerful smell of the oil contradicts the visual experience of the artwork and reveals the true nature of the floor.

Figure 8.5 *Richard Wilson, 20:50, 1987. Courtesy Matt's Gallery and The Saatchi Collection. Photograph, Edward Woodman.*

In 1991, with the assistance of the architects Baratloo-Balch, Dan Graham completed the *Rooftop Urban Park Project* at the DIA Center for the Arts in New York. The park referred to in the title is not just the rooftop of the DIA building but the roof plane of the city. Consisting of a cylinder within a cube, both walled in two-way mirror glass, the pavilion is an entrance lobby to gaze on the city of corporate modernism through its own (distorted) architecture, the reflective glass overlaying the image of the viewer on to the view.

The work of the artist James Turrell is an even more original architecture. In a famous phrase, Le Corbusier described architecture as the play of forms in light,[22] suggesting that the latter is an essential component of architecture. Turrell uses light with greater skill than any twentieth-century architect. In Le Corbusier's phrase, form and light are two separate entities, while the presence of space is implied but not mentioned by name. In Turrell's light-work *Rayzor* (1991) colour saturates and flattens architectural space until all sense of depth and distance is confused while his 'building' at the Israel Museum in Jerusalem (1992) 'frames' the sky and 'collects' the shadows. Turrell combines light, space and form into a single entity. Is he or Le Corbusier the better architect?

The diffuse light and intense colour of Yves Klein's *Blue Monochrome* (1960) radiates a slippery spatial zone similar to Turrell's lightworks. Space here is a heavy, tactile, sensual substance in which the body is immersed, like a fish swimming in water.[23] The contradictory sensations of density and weightlessness create a space that is utterly flat and infinitely deep. So often, space is assumed to be the void between objects. But Turrell and Klein's understanding of space, as a material presence, inverts the conventional perception of architectural space as the void between material, tangible architectural elements – the walls, floors and ceilings. Turrell and Klein suggest an architecture of space rather than an architecture of lines, where the former is solid and the latter inconsequential. As ephemerality and speed of change are the most distinctive qualities of the contemporary city, space may be more tangible than lines and more physical than mass. 'All that is solid melts into air.'[24]

Space is the subject and substance of the work of both artists but Klein offers a more interesting model for architectural production because his work suggests a spatiality of process as well as product.[25] Space is usually classified in two ways, as a perceptual phenomena and an intellectual process.[26] To design space has a fairly clear meaning. To think spatially, the ability to make unexpected non-linear connections between diverse phenomena, is a more complex and ultimately more important proposition. Most systems of thought, including conventional notions of architectural history and design, adopt the hierarchical model of a tree in which a leaf is traced to the roots via the branch and trunk. However, with the exception of Salvador Dali's

Jonathan Hill

Paranoid Critical Method[27] and the mathematical logic of the engineer, the linearity of thought is a burden on architectural design.[28] A few years ago, I overheard a conversation between two scientists. The physicist said to the biologist: 'You've got to have a model.' The latter replied 'But I am a biologist. We evolve things. It might end up as a golden eagle or a wart hog.' Obviously, I am on the side of the biologist. Applied to architecture, the spatiality of cultural production suggests a series of parallel but dependent procedures, so that the form, materials and site of a project are chosen because they are desired not merely expected. The architect can be a musician, the project an experiment and the site an operating theatre. Architectural research is an accumulative process but the best does not necessarily come last.

The biologist's story is so appropriate to an understanding of space because it describes a process in a state of non-linear flux. Architects are primarily interested in form, a condition reinforced by the architectural photograph. However, space is occupied, form is not. Space is particularly seductive because it is so hard to grasp and define. Pleasure and love are still not respectable subjects for architecture. Most theories of architecture allude to rationality, which by implication denies and demeans pleasure. Of course, if we try to understand love, we may miss the point. The majority of architecture is prosaic because it is so obviously architecture. Maybe the unpredictability of actions is related to the desirability and seductiveness of the spaces. Architecture may, paradoxically, be most suggestive when we do not know how to occupy it. Only fragments of Yves Klein's elemental architecture of air roofs, fire walls and water columns were built but they suggest a use that is certainly tantalising, if dangerous. Burn this house down. The incompletion of architecture is implicit in my argument. However, I am not referring to physical flexibility. Instead, I propose an architecture in which actions rub against spaces. Feeling the taste and texture of the building on the tongue. Licking the loose pigment until none remains.[29]

Many of the qualities I describe occur in a border. Although it is normally assumed to be a line, a border has a thickness and edges. Within it there is a zone with height, width and depth, between distinct territories. A border is not empty, rather it is a liminal space, a site with its own rules and codes of behaviour, even if these are obscure. Sometimes the edges of a border are monitored but not its centre. The stereotypical conclusion of a prisoner of war movie, when the heroes and villains fight for supremacy, occurs in the bend of a mountain road between two national borders. The characters are literally out of sight and out of mind. The border guards of the first country have already forgotten the protagonists, while the guards of the second do not even expect their arrival. Consequently, the fight between the characters is unrecognised and ignored. So often we assume a place is empty, when it is actually full of what we do not see.

Jonathan Hill

Figure 8.6 *Yves Klein*, Fire Wall and Fountain, *1961. Copyright ADAGP, Paris and DACS, London 1998.*

The film *Brief Encounter*[30] details a tentative romantic meeting between two people. The site of their meeting is appropriate, the platform of a railway station. Here there are two borders crossing. The entrance to the station and the door to the approaching train are the edges of one border. The space between the man and the woman is the other. The paradox is that to cross one border, between themselves, they have to deny the purpose of the other border, the station platform. The edges of the platform are more temporal than spatial. The tension in the film derives from the characters' desire for the train not to arrive. For their relationship to progress, they must ignore their original purpose, to catch the train. *Brief Encounter* is understandably recognised as a classic example of English formality and reticence. The protagonists find it so hard to recognise and respond to their desires. It truly describes a liminal zone, a place between alternative states. Those immersed within it must transform themselves if they wish to benefit from the space. *Brief Encounter* shows that a border is a space, not a line. A border is a site of spatial flux because it is not recognised and defined to the same extent as the territories to each side of it. The manner in which a person crosses or occupies the space within the border influences its effect upon them.

The encounter in the film is brief because we tend not to linger on a railway station platform. A space cannot determine the events within it but neither is the former completely isolated from the latter, rather they affect each other loosely. If the liminal

Jonathan Hill

qualities of the platform can increase the chances of an encounter occurring, could it influence the chances of love succeeding? If architecture includes actions, as well as forms, the delay of the train would help. How would more obviously architectural qualities intrude on this encounter? Would a champagne bucket in a broom cupboard, a sumptuous sofa instead of a hard bench, or a warm fire on a cold night, prolong the romance? Can the surface of a wall increase the chance of love?

One of the aims of this text is to identify and exploit the spatiality of border conditions, both physical and conceptual. However, the other side of this strategy is to question and dissolve boundaries, first, the division of theory from practice and, second, the isolation of one architectural protagonist from another. Therefore, as an architect, historian and user, it is appropriate that I conclude this chapter with an architectural project that addresses all these issues.

The social contract between the state and the profession, by which the title architect is a protected term, offers a (potential) monopoly to the profession in return for the safe management of an area of (unsafe) knowledge.[31] The 'guardian' of a strong discipline, such as the lawyer, is able to fulfill his side of the bargain, the architect is not. It is possible to argue that a weak discipline, even more than a strong one, requires the protection of the professional. However, a profession is compatible with a strong discipline but not a weak one because the professional denies the value of subjectivity, which is essential in the latter. The status of the architect is confused because it is dependent upon the contradictory demands of the 'objectivity' of professionalism and the 'subjectivity' of art.

My agenda is the dislocation of architecture from the narrow confines of professionalism and its development within an expanded cultural field. In place of a term protected in law, I propose an architect who does not need a number after his or her name to identify a skill. This suggests, first, the transformation of the legal, professional architect, and, second, the development of the illegal, politicised architect.

Figure 8.7 *Jonathan Hill*, Exterior, The Institute of Illegal Architects, 1996. Model, Bradley Starkey. Photograph, Edward Woodman.

To give my criticism of the architectural profession a tangible target, I have focused on the Royal Institute of British Architects.[32] My proposal is for an 'other' institute of architecture, one that is neither Royal or British, sited in the street directly in front of the RIBA building in London.[33] The Institute of Illegal Architects is a research facility for the production of architecture by non-professional architects and active users, who may of course be the same person. Its five spaces are each conceived for a specific form of sensual or perceptual production – smell, sound, sight, touch and time – but a tight fit between space and occupation is undesirable. Mis-use is expected, a healthy contradiction itself. In addition to the spatial zones, the project contains a collection of transient elements, the number and character of which is in a constant state of flux.[34] The juxtaposition of the spatial zones and the transient elements is based on the rules of the Surrealist game, 'Exquisite Corpse',[35] suggesting that the seductive power of architecture relies as much on the gaps as the elements.

Figure 8.8 *Jonathan Hill*, The Transient Elements, The Institute of Illegal Architects, *1996*.

Jonathan Hill

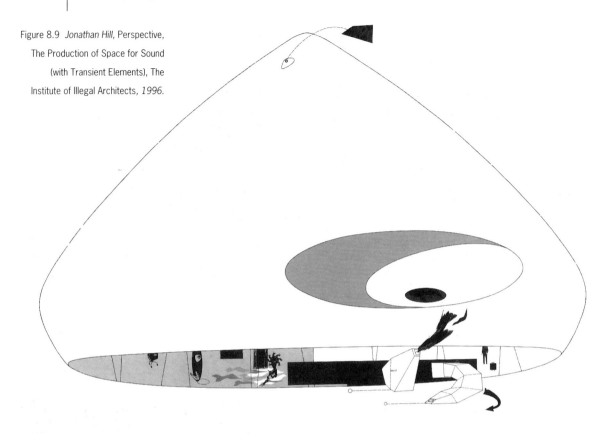

Figure 8.9 *Jonathan Hill*, Perspective, The Production of Space for Sound (with Transient Elements), The Institute of Illegal Architects, *1996.*

The relationship between the RIBA and the Institute of Illegal Architects is similar to that between the body and the fairground mirror that fattens, thins and distorts the original, inviting both laughter and nightmares. While the RIBA rises vertically from the pavement, the new institute is horizontal, submerged into, and rising from, the street. The Institute of Illegal Architects inhabits the public domain of the street rather than the private realm of the familiar building site. It is an urban park as much as a building. In designing the project, I was reminded of a famous phrase from the 1960s, beneath the pavement is the beach, suggesting that desire not utility is the motor of everyday life and our relations with architecture. So it seems appropriate that I finish this text with a quote from an interview with Yves Klein, an artist who deserves the title architect:

> *'Mr Klein' I asked, 'if the sky over Nice had been grey, on that day in 1946 when you and Arman and Pascal decided to divide the world between you, would you still have chosen the sky and signed it on its underside as your first monochrome work?' 'No' said Klein 'If the sky had been grey, we would not have been on the beach.*[36]

Jonathan Hill

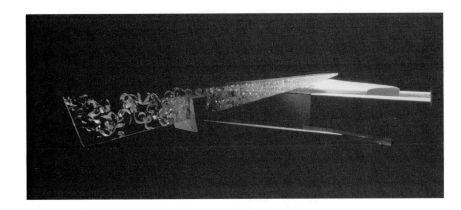

Figure 8.10 *Jonathan Hill, Exterior, The Institute of Illegal Architects, 1996. Model, Bradley Starkey. Photograph, Edward Woodman.*

Figure 8.11 *Jonathan Hill, Exterior, The Institute of Illegal Architects, 1996. Model, Bradley Starkey. Photograph, Edward Woodman.*

Figure 8.12 *Jonathan Hill, Exterior Detail, The Institute of Illegal Architects, 1996. Model, Bradley Starkey. Photograph, Edward Woodman.*

Figure 8.13 *Jonathan Hill, Interior, The Institute of Illegal Architects, 1996. Model Bradley Starkey. Photograph, Edward Woodman.*

NOTES

1 Designed by Mies van der Rohe as the German Pavilion for the Barcelona International Exposition of 1929. The pavilion was reconstructed by Ignasi de Solà Morales, Christian Cirici and Fernando Ramos in 1986.

2 The emptiness of the pavilion is a common theme within architectural criticism. While it is not possible to prove that certain critics equate the photograph with the building, I believe it is a plausible assumption. For example, J. Quetglas, 'Fear of Glass: The Barcelona Pavilion', in B. Colomina (ed.), *Architectureproduction*, New York, Princeton Architectural Press, 1988, pp. 123–51 or M. Tafuri, 'The Stage as Virtual City', in *The Sphere and the Labyrinth*, trans. P. d'Acierno and R. Connolly, Cambridge, Mass., MIT Press, 1987, pp. 111 12.

3 Lao Tsu, quoted in C. van de Ven, *Space in Architecture*, Amsterdam, Van Gorcum Assen, 1978, p. 3. The quote derives from Lao Tsu, *Tao Te Ching*, *c.* 550 BC, ch.1, book 1. Translations of this text differ. I have used the one in *Space and Architecture* as it is particularly architectural.

4 M. Douglas, *Purity and Danger*, London, Routledge, 1966, p. 2.

5 R. Barthes, 'The Death of the Author', in *Image-Music-Text*, trans. S. Heath, London, Flamingo, 1977, pp.142–8.

6 W. Benjamin, *The Origin of German Tragic Drama*, trans. J. Osborne, London, New Left Books, 1977.

7 D. Ades, 'Dada and Surrealism', in N. Stangos (ed.), *Concepts of Modern Art*, London, Thames and Hudson, 1981, pp. 110–37.

8 B. Tschumi, 'Illustrated Themes from The Manhattan Transcripts', *AA Files* No. 4, 1983, p. 66.

9 B. Tschumi, *The Manhattan Transcripts*, London, Academy, 1981, p. 7.

10 W. Benjamin, 'The Author as Producer', in A. Arato and E. Gebhardt (eds), *The Essential Frankfurt School Reader*, New York, Urizen Books, 1978.

11 Buildings were rarely designed to the rigorous functional criteria proposed by the early Modernists, to whom, even if they claimed otherwise, aesthetic decisions were often as important as functional ones. In its purest form, Functionalism proposes an architecture that is a-cultural, purely organisational and therefore impossible to build. Consequently, the most convincing example of Functionalism occurred in words rather than concrete when in 1930, as Director of the Bauhaus, Hannes Meyer erased the word architecture from the institution, renaming the School of Architecture the School of Building. As a Scientific Marxist, it is easy to understand Meyer's advocacy of Functionalism, a strategy that affirms the dominance of production over culture. However, the Functionalist agenda is also similar to that of Taylorism and Fordism, two essential strategies of early twentieth-century Capitalism. Although it is too simplistic to say that Functionalism is a Capitalist strategy, it did extend the values and techniques of industrialised production into areas which had previously claimed 'autonomy' from the demands of Capitalist society.

12 Le Corbusier's 'Modulor' being one.

13 Le Corbusier, *Towards a New Architecture*, London, Rodker, 1927, p. 10.

14 Determinism assumes that human actions are predictable and that every event has a cause.

15 R. Koolhaas, *El Croquis*, No. 53, February–March 1992, p. 6.

16 S. Beckett, quoted in B. Massumi, *A User's Guide to Capitalism and Schizophrenia*, Cambridge, Mass., MIT Press, 1992, p. 47.

17 S. Allen, 'Dazed and Confused', *Assemblage*, 27, 1995, p. 48.

Jonathan Hill

18 B. Tschumi, *Architecture and Disjunction*, Cambridge, Mass., MIT Press, 1994.

19 The glow of the empty computer screen is equally seductive. The computer has superseded the drawing board in many architectural offices. However rather than slipping into technological determinism a judicious combination of the two would use each for its specific qualities. For example, the luminosity of the screen and the physicality of the drawing.

20 Rebecca Horn, *River of the Moon: Room of the Earth*, 1992, published in *Rebecca Horn: The Inferno Paradiso Switch*, New York, Guggenheim Museum, 1993, Figure 94.

21 In 1917 Duchamp signed a urinal 'R. Mutt' and renamed it *Fountain*. Over forty years later Manzoni labelled, numbered and signed ninety cans of *Merda d'Artista*, each filled with 30 grams of his excrement.

22 Le Corbusier, op. cit., p. 202.

23 Speaking about the education at the Illinois Institute of Technology in the 1950s: 'At that time, we were made to feel the tangibility of space, we could swim in it; like a fish swims in water. Space was a metaphysical solid. You didn't have to confine yourself to the surface of a wall to imbue a building with symbolism; space itself had iconic and symbolic value.' James Ingo Freed, quoted in B. Diamonstein, *American Architecture Now*, New York, Rizzoli, 1985, p. 93.

24 K. Marx and F. Engels, 'The Communist Manifesto', in R. Tucker (ed.), *The Marx-Engels Reader*, New York, Norton, 1978, p. 476.

25 Klein's work must be considered selectively. The highly sexist anthropometry performances, in which the male artist used a naked woman as a painting tool is certainly not a useful model for architectural practice.

26 A subtler understanding of space, as perceived, conceived and lived is posited in H. Lefebvre, *The Production of Space*, trans. D. Nicholson-Smith, Oxford, Blackwell, 1991, p. 89.

27 A strategy devised by Dali in which an initial, irrational decision is pursued to the limits of its logic, exemplified in his statement: 'The only difference between the madman and me, is that I am not mad.' Salvador Dali, quoted by D. Ades in 'Dada and Surrealism', N. Stangos (ed.), *Concepts of Modern Art*, London, Thames and Hudson, 1981, p.132. For a discussion of the Paranoid Critical Method in architecture, see R. Koolhaas, 'Europeans: Biuer! Dali and Le Corbusier conquer New York', *Delirious New York*, Rotterdam, 010 Publishers, 1994, pp. 235–282.

28 With regard to history, the myth of historical linearity and progression must be exposed for all its clumsy pretension. It is normal for a historical text to be structured chronologically. But what if history is not simply linear and progressive but spatial as well? An event in 1998 may be closer to one in 1923, than another in 1992. Instead, of a model of historical progression, I suggest one of oscillating flux, in which change does not happen simply in a linear sequence. Ridley Scott's film *Blade Runner*, Warner, 1982, presents a convincing allegory for the spatiality of history, in which umbrellas exist along futuristic machines and the narrator is both a Chandleresque detective and an android assassin.

29 In 1992, Ganit Mayslits, at that time my teaching partner at The Bartlett, and I asked our students to occupy a building in Barcelona, in a manner that was unexpected but exposed qualities latent within the architecture. Carolyn Butterworth chose to lick every surface in the Barcelona Pavilion, recording the experience in a set of photographs and analytical drawings. Her actions are discussed further in Ben Godber's chapter.

30 D. Lean (dir.), *Brief Encounter*, Pinewood Films, 1945.

31 R. Dingwall and P. Lewis (eds), *The Sociology of the Professions: Lawyers, Doctors and Others*, London, Macmillan, 1983, p. 5.

32 The Architectural profession in Britain is dominated by the RIBA and ARB. I have concentrated on the former as it has the more 'public' role.

33 The avant-gardist denial of the institution of architecture collapsed on the myth of its own anti-institutionalism and resulted in either the withering away of radical practice or the incorporation of its de-politicised husk within an expanded institution. In excepting the original principles of avant-gardism, so many of the radical projects produced in recent years have concentrated on the minor. However, marginality is insufficient, and the role of the outsider is self-fulfilling. Institutions should be formed or re-formed not destroyed. They are essential to the advocacy of change.

34 The users, physically and conceptually, affect the spaces and the transient elements. For example, 250 m long and 40 m wide, the Production Space for Time occupies Portland Place between Devonshire Street and Cavendish Street, blocking the Royal processional route between Regent's Park and Regent Street. The space is initially very thin and, later, very deep. Its upper surface is flush with the pavement of Portland Place. The ground plane is divided into two equal halves. The northern half is made of a hard black stone covered with a 50 mm layer of soft white chalk, the southern half is made of a hard white stone covered with a 50 mm layer of soft black chalk. Movement across the surface gradually erases the chalk surfaces, so that the northern half changes from black to white, the southern half from white to black. The chalk is carried through the city on the soles of shoes. Once all the chalk has been removed, the surface erodes more slowly. Transient Element No. 43 (Table-Bench) has four sequential sections, each the same colour, orange, and formally homogeneous, but made from a different material – plastic, steel, wood and soap. The location, form and surface of the element all influence its use.

35 'Exquisite Corpse' is a form of montage that shifts the emphasis from the single author to hybrid author-readers who both make and consume a work. It is a game played by several people, who compose a sentence without anyone seeing the preceding collaborations, each player in turn writing a word or phrase before folding the paper to conceal their contribution and passing it onto the next player. André Breton stated that 'With "Exquisite Corpse" we had at our disposal – at last – an infallible means of temporarily dismissing the critical mind and of fully freezing metaphorical activity.' Quoted in J. Marcel (ed.), *Autobiography of Surrealism*, New York, Viking, 1980, p. 222. The first sentence produced by the game created its name 'The exquisite corpse will drink new wine.' Ibid., p. 220.

36 Y. Klein, quoted by J. Reichardt in *Yves Klein Now*, London, Hayward Gallery, 1995.

Jonathan Hill

the landscape of luxury

It is not necessity but its contrary, 'luxury', that presents living matter and mankind with their fundamental problems.

Georges Bataille

LUXURY AND CATASTROPHE

North of downtown Las Vegas, set within 320 acres of silent flat desert, an immaculate little yellow flag hovers 30 ft below, across a lake. The lake is a mirror of still water, the green, a saucer (3,000 sq ft) of billiard smooth grass, gently pitching and rolling into three grades of trimmed border against a mountain waterfall cloaked in aspen pines. There are swans on the lake and a pheasant pecking in the long grasses under a willow tree. To the right there is a bunker, a pure dish of fine sand, above, treetops give way to the purple hues of the distant Spring Mountains, a pastel backdrop to the deep shadows of the trees glancing long over the fairway.

This is the view from the seventeenth tee of Shadow Creek, the private golf course of Steve Wynn, CEO of Mirage Resorts Inc. Left to nature it would be a scalding rattlesnake pit, enough to suck the breath from any casual visitor; now the tee markers at your feet are floral arrangements of violets, every blade of grass lush (springing from imported sod), with clumps of pampas grass lining the fairways and trees individually selected to replicate the natural wooded sand hills of temperate North Carolina.

It is a unique aesthetic experience, as Wynn explains:

The seventeenth is an obvious crowd pleaser because it's so theatrical. I'm not sure people will believe that Mother Nature created something this nice. Had we delivered this kind of treatment too often, it might have been excessive. But, it was irresistible to do it once.[1]

For most of us our only chance to savour this unique experience will be through the pages of a lush Mirage Resorts publication.[2] If you do drive out to the site, there is nothing spectacular about the miles of barren chain-link fencing behind which low pine trees appear to struggle for ground. Shadow Creek is miraculous, invisible from the dusty track that leads to its unassuming gate house but vivid in the imagination.

Despite Wynn's deference to Mother Nature, Shadow Creek is considered an affront to nature and to those values associated with the natural. The profligacy of buying and slowly draining the artesian well to sprinkle each green, contrive each soothing view and support over twenty thousand trees in a pit of desert scrub is one thing, the unusual selection of wildlife another, and the politics a third.

An expert on Los Angeles gangland warfare, and author of *City of Quartz*, is perched on a desert rock in blue jeans and sneakers to deliver the unequivocal doomsday scenario: years of relentless and extravagant expansion by greedy

1 S. Wynn and T. Fazio, *Shadow Creek from Barren Desert to Desert Oasis*, Las Vegas, Mirage Resorts Inc., 1995, p. 124.

2 J. L. Smith, *Running Scared: The Life and Treacherous Times of Las Vegas Casino King Steve Wynn*, New York, Barricade Books, 1995, p. 244. Playing Shadow Creek by invitation may demand a healthy expenditure of over $100,000 at the tables of Mirage Resort Casinos. Otherwise play is restricted to friends. The souvenir publication is $40.

corporate developers, moneymen oblivious to the beauties of the desert and blind to the value of its most basic resource, dictate Las Vegas will simply dry up. An art critic from *Harper's Bazaar* sips cappuccino on the terrace of Spago, enjoying artificial sunrise and sunset every half hour in the convivial atmosphere of Forum Shopping at Caesars. He savours a Biblical apocalypse; a shrinking water table under the desert flood plain finally cracking to swallow the entire city.[3] A journalist for the *Las Vegas Review Journal* wonders, at a cost of $48 million and with a membership of just one (Steve Wynn himself), what the real purpose behind Shadow Creek might be.[4]

Las Vegas, Spanish for 'the meadows', once marshy plains amidst the Nevada desert fed by artesian wells, must now strike deals with neighbouring states to pump water to the greens of upwards of thirty golf courses, into the luxurious plumbing of 100,000 hotel rooms, associated spas and pools, into artificial buccaneer bays, volcanoes, tropical rain forest and even the south west's largest privately owned lake; to cascade surrealistically down the side of a stucco submarine surfacing from the desert floor,[5] and then to fizz from the rows of tiny nozzles that aquify the air over the heads of the crowds on Las Vegas Boulevard. Steve Wynn can boast of the 150,000 gallons a minute pumped through the lagoon at his Mirage casino resort for the benefit of his customers; for Mike Davis sitting on a rock, the town has only ten years left before it sucks the Colorado River dry.

Las Vegas' phenomenal growth within the most affluent Western economy, almost entirely funded through the leisure industry, is accompanied by a chorus of critical disapproval marshalled with respect to the balance of nature but extrapolated to render Las Vegas an economic, social and aesthetic catastrophe. There is little mention of Mirage Resort's comprehensive high-tech water recovery systems that ensure upwards of 97 per cent of water is recycled, or even to the water level of Lake Mead behind the Hoover Dam which is threatening to rise by five feet during 1997. Whatever the political and technical realities behind the city's water usage Las Vegas is considered profligate against the 'nature' of its physical geography.[6]

Meanwhile, within the global economy, the city flourishes with over 30 million visitors per year and an unprecedented building boom. For every pair of hotel rooms built it is estimated that 1.5 jobs are created, and while almost as many people move out as well as move in to the city of last chances, they do so with the certain knowledge (or experience) that it is a city devoted to a principle, common in the minds of its millions of visitors as well as their hosts, that it is in their mutual interest to accelerate the exchange of wealth.

Risk has become an everyday encounter in modern economies. The balancing of risk was the preserve of a few investors as recently as the last century, but today active

3 *Virtually Las Vegas*, BBC Television, 1994.

4 John L. Smith, author of Wynn's controversial biography is a columnist for the *Las Vegas Review Journal*.

5 'Dive' restaurant, a joint venture between Steven Spielberg and Steve Wynn, rises from Las Vegas Boulevard.

6 Nevada water rights from the Colorado were first negotiated in the Colorado River Compact of 1922, prior to the planning and construction of the Hoover Dam. The Colorado, fed from snow fields to the north flowing 1,400 miles to the Gulf of California, once tamed by the dam, would feed the explosive growth of California and Los Angeles as well as Nevada and Las Vegas. Presently those original agreements regarding water allocation to each state are disputed by the water hungry Las Vegans, who believe that any water shortage is political rather than natural. For history see J. Stevens, *Hoover Dam, an American Adventure*, Norman, University of Oklahoma Press, 1988. For immediate threat of flooding in 1997, see *Las Vegas Review Journal*, 12 February 1997.

Paul Davies

participation in investment markets, and the awareness of the consequences, is commonplace. This has made the percentages represented by the gaming tables more respectable, and the casinos have changed their emphasis, paradoxically, toward value for money; presenting a high-quality supportive environment where gaming means quality time.

Coinciding with the Reagan administration, the liberalisation of the gaming industry in the USA began in earnest in the early 1980s; the early years of this administration were marked by a recession where Las Vegas suffered under competition with a resurgent Atlantic City, with an image tarnished by the fatal MGM fire in November 1980, and a second fire at The Hilton in 1981. This recession set the context for the boom that broke in Las Vegas in the mid-1980s. The talisman of that boom was the $650 million Mirage, created by Steve Wynn.

The mid-1980s also saw speculation in financial markets symptomatic of the *laissez-fare* policies of 'Reaganomics' and epitomised by a vigorous re-capitalisation based on the issue of so-called 'junk bonds'. The innovator in this field was Michael Milken, then working with the New York firm of Drexel Burnham Lambert from Beverly Hills CA, where Milken preached his economic theories to ranks of aspiring corporate raiders via his 'Predators Ball' seminars, and where he met Steve Wynn.

The events on Wall Street and in particular the crash of Black Monday in October 1987 restored debate surrounding the boundary between 'real' and 'illusory' economics; a 'conventional wisdom' represented by J.K. Galbraith and the 'unconventional wisdom', 'voodoo' or even 'casino economics' of Michael Milken.[7] In particular the freewheeling economic policies of the time found representation, literally, in the luxury of The Mirage, as junk bonds raised the fresh capital, newcomer Steve Wynn needed to build America's finest casino resort.

The context for these policies was by no means parochial, recognising the technological change evident in manufacturing production as well as in the information systems of the world's trading floors. Given the events of November 1989 and the collapse of the Berlin Wall, they coincided with the final collapse of the Iron Curtain economies, and victory in the ideological conflict of the Cold War.

In 1989 The Mirage opened to record monthly profits of $40 million at the tables alone. Even traditional loss leaders such as food, beverage and rooms were turning profits. While the old 'carpet joints' are nostalgically celebrated in the media as hotbeds of authentic vice, The Mirage celebrated comfort, luxury and service to make the corny con-trick obsolete. The value of pleasure was suddenly redefined in a complex equation no longer satisfied by the casino economics of banal exploitation relying on the catch-alls of free rooms and cheap food.

How has the architectural profession responded to this new competitive order?

7 For background see J.K. Galbraith, *A Short History of Financial Euphoria*, London, Penguin, 1990. P. Bronson, *Bombardiers*, London, Secker and Warburg, 1995. B. Burrough and J. Helyar, *Barbarians at the Gate*, London, Jonathan Cape, 1990. C. Bruck, *The Predators Ball*, New York, Penguin, 1989.

Paul Davies

Modern architecture is littered with calls for less; 'existence minimum', 'ornament and crime', even 'less is more'. Even when these aphorisms have been called into question, the tendency has been to elaborate upon fresh territories whilst applying the same sensibility. In particular there has been the struggle to define appropriate responses to geography, either advocating a quasi-mystical identification with issues of 'place', or at least formalising issues of 'context', and latterly closely associating both of these with 'sustainability'. In short modern architects have found their moral obligations, taste for the abstract, even work processes conspiring toward the appearance of bare necessity, and they have constructed that necessity as natural.

Las Vegas architecture, in its engagement with the luxury of waste on the one hand, and fakery on the other, challenges the basis of this practice, for if Las Vegas has a characteristic view of place, it is that other places should somehow reconstitute themselves across its naturally inauspicious landscape for the delight of consumers.

Importing glamour to the desert was the original idea for Las Vegas; Bugsy Siegel brought Miami modern to the strip with The Flamingo in 1946. But transit to the monoculture of Las Vegas brings with it some spectacular shifts. All casino resorts are not the same, although they cater for almost identical, luxurious, activities. This differentiation is not dependent on architectural authorship, for where individual architects elsewhere distinguish themselves in a consistency of approach across different projects, the design hierarchy and the complexity of consultancy demanded by today's Las Vegas casino resort programmes work against architects' personal expression. In general, the work of the individual architect is invisible to the eye of the tourist on The Strip.

If there is a critical resistance to the consideration of luxury within architectural discourse it is because it is conservatively aligned with catastrophe; it is also because it threatens the social role and livelihoods of architects. The combination of environmental market appeal and innovation in Las Vegas is analogous to the effect of Michael Milken's junk bonds on those staid yet respectable banking institutions. Even *The Economist* still refers to The Strip as 'Armageddon in neon'.[8] Modern architecture established protocols which ranked luxury with waste, vulgarity and poor taste. Conventional economic wisdom holds Wall Street's periodic booms as illusory; yet as the cycle becomes regular, as economic trends assimilate intangibles such as confidence, faith and even bluff (those attributes well known to the seasoned poker player), Wall Street's precocious cousin Las Vegas matures, emerging from an image sharply defined by a black and white morality into one of Technicolor ambiguity. Where once the gaudy neon appeared an anachronistic irritation to the conservative tastes of a socially responsible architecture, now it is the quality of The Mirage that outshines conventional competition.

8 *The Economist Pocket USA*, London, Penguin, 1994, p. 137.

Paul Davies

165

If as Georges Bataille states:

The living organism, in a situation determined by the play of energy on the surface of the globe, ordinarily receives more energy than is necessary for maintaining life; the excess energy (wealth) can be used for growth of the system (e.g., an organism); if the system can no longer grow, or if the excess cannot be completely absorbed in its growth, it must be necessarily lost without profit; it must be spent, willingly or not, gloriously or catastrophically.[9]

9 G. Bataille, *The Accursed Share*, New York, Zone Books, 1967, p. 21.

Gaming offers a more luxurious space for waste than the literal burning of dollars, and what appear to architectural eyes as wasteful, excessive, vulgar casinos may indeed be considered as 'natural' as an adobe home in the desert. Meanwhile the scale of the development illustrates mass participation in the gaming phenomenon; a mass once represented by modernist architects as a passive, objectified whole, now crowds the Las Vegas Strip, fragmented in taste, yet united in their active search for just the right excuse to dispose of hard-earned leisure dollars.

THE MIRAGE

The first thing Steve Wynn removed from the casino vocabulary with The Mirage was neon. He erased the dominant signifier of Las Vegas as a 'place'. Further refuting expectations he imported the modernist clean lines of Joel Bergman's architecture for its form, but dressed it in a golden corporate surface of suncool glass to dazzle Las Vegas Boulevard. As the sun goes down, instead of the fluorescent glow of a sign, a volcano erupts periodically to growling thunder and flickering torchlight, set within $30 million worth of lush lagoon landscape.

Customers move past the lagoon along travelators to the religious tones of Steve Wynn himself, encouraging their choice of menu across twelve intercontinental restaurants to theme their day. Wynn has transformed what Ian Fleming once termed 'the gilded mousetrap' school of architecture[10] into the very gentle massage of arcadie.

10 I. Fleming, *Diamonds are Forever*, London, Coronet, 1988, p. 115.

In the foyer two golden mermaids rise heavenward; behind, a rainforest fills the atrium, gushing waterfalls with spotlit original sculptures and historic artefacts set within its leafy glades. Sunlight shimmers through a trellis-work of tropical blooms to dapple the marble path cut through to the casino; where soulful bands play sensuous bass lines through the mist from the Lagoon Saloon. The detail is exquisite, the balustrade a finely wrought translation of jungle twine into marble, its finial an elaborate transformation of a pineapple into a jewel.

Figures 9.1–9.5
Progression From Desert to
Pool. *The Mirage, Las
Vegas. Photographs, Paul
Davies.*

Across the vast interior the palette of The Mirage is muted, a raft of rich mahogany compliments each swathe of soft cream across an interior that demands a new architectural vocabulary. The conventional structure is dressed in hearth stone, Polynesia magically subverted by an internal sea of Wrightian domesticity. In the elaborate canopies that hover over each gaming area east meets west in a new strangely contradictory style where ancient and modern combine to evoke a long-lost innocence; the super-primitive in the service of 'die neue gemütlichkeit'.[11]

11 'The new comfort'.

This super-primitive is Tarzan at Tiffany's, or perfectly finished rustic log structures whose exposed endgrain sparkle with brass caps embossed as rope fastenings. It is an undercroft detailed as woven lattice, while the upper edge tumbles over as swirling thatch moulding. Along the beams supporting the open lattice of logs run thin mirror strips carrying sparkling miniature trains of lights – one of five kinds of accent lighting that illuminate each gambler's next hand.

Paul Davies

Eight years on, The Mirage is still a sell-out every night, and Wynn has been voted Favourite Male Las Vegan for twelve consecutive years. In 1996, his casinos won Best Downtown (Golden Nugget) and Strip Hotel (Mirage), Best Hotel Attraction and Best Hotel Theme, Best Production Show and Hotel Lobby. He also took Best Looking Las Vegan, Best Dressed Las Vegan, Las Vegan You'd Like to Know More About and Las Vegan You're Tired of Hearing About.[12]

Transforming the environment was no less an achievement than Steve Wynn's transformation of the casino owner's reputation. Despite the legacy of a long line of colourful Las Vegas entrepreneurs, Steve Wynn has achieved the status of clean white knight. Wynn could be interviewed and frankly remark that he had never run into any mob activity within his casino business. In 1997 Mirage Resorts Inc. was voted America's second most admired company by *Fortune* magazine.[13] His employees adore him, partly for working conditions far from the norm in the tourist industry, where facilities backstage are seen as comparable to those front of house, and where employees are welcome to bring family members in to eat with them during their breaks.

Milken's innovation had been to recognise that statistically debt was good, that high debt investment capital encouraged lean and mean companies which moved quickly in competitive markets. Within the highly competitive environment of the Las Vegas Strip, Wynn's company pushes harder, continually restructuring its debt with new projects each overshadowing the last, performing equally for both consumers and stockholders.[14] The Mirage is a machine, a vast, relentless, self perpetuating luxury machine. On a Friday afternoon, as the weekenders pour into town and The Strip clogs with California registration plates and offroaders from the desert, it starts to purr.

This success relies on a complex interplay of themes where ambiguity triumphs over literal representation; where international dreams are played against domestic myths, the ancient with the modern, the far east with the wild west; the vast with the intimate; the natural with the synthetic, in a symphonic totality simultaneously threatening and comfortable. Even when it comes to the personalities; Wynn is clean in a dirty business, Milken a financial guru who lived modestly despite vast wealth.

Just as you leave The Mirage, having witnessed the 'industrialisation of pick pocketing' (Davis 1994) that includes the birth of dolphins, you may notice adults hugging the cuddly toys of Siegfried and Roy mechandising. Siegfried and Roy, tiger conservationists by day, who earn millions per year by magic, make tigers disappear each evening in the Mirage Theatre, only for them to reappear as comfort toys and pyjama cases for the children left back home.

In fact, within the temple of luxury there lies much that is strangely instructive. The Dolphinarium not only provides the largest area of water per dolphin in the world (while

12 '1996 Best of Las Vegas Readers Poll', *Las Vegas Review Journal*, 24 March 1996.

13 'Annual Peer Review Poll', *Fortune Magazine*, March 1997.

14 Wynn's next casino venture in Las Vegas was 'Treasure Island' which opened in 1993, his next the 'Bellagio' on the old Dunes site. Bellagio is a $1.4 billion resort due to open in 1998; it will include a special collection of European Modern Art within a facsimile of the Renaissance town of Bellagio on Lake Como.

Paul Davies

the shark maintains a state of arrested development in the huge aquarium behind the reception desk) but is free to parties of local school children. Whilst critical cynicism is predictable, the crowds are treated to explanations not just of the birthing of the dolphins and the need for conservation, but of the regime of 'freedom' that ensures their continual happiness and, despite being the Atlantic species, their adoption of Nevada as their natural (sic) home. On from the dolphins, Siegfried and Roy's Secret Garden is a form of miniature game reserve for their collection of big cats and Indian Elephant. Also instructional, their garden allows an intimate encounter with the rare Siberian Tiger under the hot desert sun, with tips as to each predatorial personality, doubled with exhortations to man's duty to save the planet, received via personal headset.

Hence, whilst some new resorts by their sheer size take on the complexities of cities in themselves, with interior boulevards and street scenes simulating the anonymous drift of city life, The Mirage remains steadfast in presenting cosmic concerns within an intimate and personal context, encouraging the personal revelation at the altar of economic power. It refutes any opposition between the natural and the artificial with an environment loaded with immaculately controlled signifiers. A world where fear of the otherworldly has replaced the threat of communism, and where the workings of the economy are, in the popular imagination, best represented by magic shows.

GOLF DESTINATION CITY

Mid-October, above the Baccarat bar, the television screens are tuned to the Golf Channel and the Nike Tour Championship. The Nike Tour features professionals who have lost their coveted PGA Tour cards but are getting back up to do it all again. A lone figure stalks the course, in his mid-thirties to mid-forties, subtitled with soothing exclamations about the value of the game:

> *I am inspiration*
> *I am perseverance*
> *I am the Nike Tour*
> *I am not afraid to do what I want for a living*
> *I am down to my last $100*
> *I have no regrets*

15 *Las Vegas Golf Magazine,*
July–August 1996.

Golf is the fastest growing sport in the modern world, and Las Vegas has become 'The Newest World-Class Golf Destination City'.**15** In fact, urban growth in Las Vegas can

Paul Davies

be measured by golf course demand, for each golf club comes with a condominium development, and with each condo a golf course. Presently *Las Vegas Golf Magazine* estimates a demand for seventeen new golf courses.

In the unpromising heart of the Mojave desert, Las Vegas boasts a reputation as a venue within three professional tours (including the PGA tour); its own golf guide; even a university golf team, The Rebels, ranked number one in the USA. Tourists now want to do more than just gamble in Las Vegas.[16] Many want to play golf, meaning it is in the interests of the major resort companies to restrict the availability of tees to locals. The traditional battleground between tourists and local users is no longer the public space of the city, but the availability of a green. In Southern Nevada, one of the biggest user interest groups is devoted to the state provision of golf courses for the aspirational middle class.

The Nike promotion weighs in on the side of such a player, temporarily down on his luck. Meanwhile *Tin Cup*[17] is in heavy rotation at the box office. Sensation Tiger Woods won The Masters in April 1997 to be hailed as America's most influential personality by *Time* magazine,[18] but his path to conservative Augusta and the green jacket ran via victory at the Disney Classic (with a hug from a life-size Disney 'Tigger') and Las Vegas International (played within the famous Spanish Trails gated community considered the model for Las Vegas development).

The stratospheric rise of golf, like Las Vegas, has become a theoretical *bête noir*, while simultaneously a cipher for the new spirit of competition in the post Cold War environment. It has become an adjunct to social and physiological well-being with the health of golfers and their families an obsession. From nagging finger injuries to cancer, from diet to lack of confidence or lousy luck; the relaxing walk has become its opposite, a cipher for faith in the individual. Golf, and some wily tax breaks, made Las Vegas Preferred Middle-Size City for Business in the US for *Entrepreneur Magazine*.[19]

For golf is fundamentally attractive to business minds, not just for the country clubs central to the workings of middle-class social life. This recreational landscape has come to be entwined with the work ethic and business practices. It is played one-on-one with people of any age without any prescriptive advantage for the younger competitor, the element of chance is so volatile that even the best players can be struck by mysterious bad patches, and your game constantly requires attention, 'hard work', even tuition, in the hope that it will finally come right. *Tin Cup* shows us golf can even be poetic, unmask deceit and land the partner of your dreams. It is also individual competition based on having to pay to play, the rewards of golf being determined purely by performance. While played with partners, golf is competition against yourself and the course; unlike any other sport, there is no opponent except the landscape which has been created for play.

16 Statistics of the Caesar's Palace Public Relations Department show that for every $200 lost gaming, $300 is spent on related items and entertainment.

17 The romantic golf movie starring Kevin Costner.

18 *Time Magazine*, 21 April 1997.

19 *Entrepreneur Magazine*, June 1996.

Paul Davies

DESIGNING A SHORT WALK

Golf takes longer to play than most other sports. Yet in a round of as much as four hours the golfer is in play only between two and three and a half minutes . . . with each stroke taking less than a couple of seconds the golfer spends very little time – not even two per cent of the game – in physical play. And that leaves one hell of a lot of time to be thinking about all the wrong things.[20]

20 R. Masters and J. Burns, *Mind Swings*, Aurum Press, 1995.

In a city where golf is a highly tangible quotient in urban development, Shadow Creek is mythological territory. In 1991, Mirage Resort's vice president for publicity, Alan Feldman remarked:

What we were seeking to do is find an extraordinary incentive to bring the highest level players to Las Vegas and the casino . . . in our business you look for things that are special – we are always trying to do things that no one else can . . . Shadow Creek gives us a marketing edge over the competition.[21]

21 *Las Vegas Golf Guide*, 1996, p. 74.

While Steve Wynn commented:

This golf course is an entertainment first, last and always. This is a recreational sport and the course is a recreational entertainment. It has no other reason for existing.[22]

22 ibid.

Functionally Shadow Creek is thoroughly ambiguous. Bugsy Siegel and Wilbur Clarke first provided golf courses as adjuncts to their Strip casinos, but the far eastern obsession with golf that became a phenomenon throughout the eighties, alongside the financial and technological boom, provided a new challenge to the aspiring casino mogul.[23] Golf tournaments, sponsorship and celebrities pepper the pages of eighties power dramas. Generally, talk of business is excised from actual play, yet the bonding and positioning fostered between players in their shared recreation has nevertheless become a crucial, compensatory, component in business. Without speaking their name those take-overs and buy-outs were leveraged as much over golf as they were secured by junk bonds.[24]

23 Pacific Rim high rollers contributed 17 per cent of revenue at The Mirage high stakes baccarat tables. Ken Mizuno, a keen golfer, dropped $75 million into the Mirage coffers in two years. See Smith, op. cit., p. 237.

24 See negotiations over RJR Nabisco – the biggest buy-out of the 1980s, in Burrough and Helyar, op. cit.

To build the perfect course Wynn enlisted the talents of top designer Tom Fazio. He says the pair:

constantly talked about what the golfers would see, what they would say, and what the course would say to them. We wanted it to stimulate conversation and camaraderie. The social aspects of the game were always in my mind, and, I think, were as much a controlling element in the design as anything else.[25]

25 Wynn and Fazio, op. cit., p. 21.

At first Fazio entered into the project with some trepidation; rising to the challenge would mean trying something entirely new, constructing a piece of Carolina in the middle of the desert. His reputation was at stake and at the mercy of a charming, yet ruthless client. First Wynn does not like traditional links courses, he finds them ugly;[26] and second, he wanted the heart of the golfing establishment transposed to one of the most hostile 'natural' environments on earth.

Steve Wynn has a very narrow field of vision: a victim of the degenerative eye disease retinitis pigmentosa. To communicate clearly, they had a scale model of the proposal prepared that was itself 40 by 50 ft. With the help of individual model trees and a video camera with a micro lens they shot footage of the views from each tee, along the fairways and around the greens, each taken as if from the vantage point of a six-foot golfer. Photographs of the existing mountain backdrop were then patched into the video. The result, according to Fazio, 'looked like something you'd see on the television during the US Open'.

Steve 'kept pushing us to make the holes narrower, to create distinct settings for the creeks, and to bring the shadows closer to the teeing areas which enhanced the framing'. The framing of views is traditional in landscape design, but the artifice of Shadow Creek, combined with the meticulous layered composition made possible only by the latest technology, was conjured for a man whose physical sight was failing.

When they were finally happy with the video work they began creating a test hole on site. Like a scaled-up model, the contours were excavated, three hundred trees positioned and even the fairways sprayed two shades of green and the creek dyed blue. Wynn visited the site, and called for an extra two hundred trees. Step by step the course was manicured into shape, with the careful placing of objects in the service of each total composition. It is a staggering achievement, a masterly play of shadow, form and contrived perspectives continually playing with the golfer's eye, with dramatic surprises such as the abyss number 5 hole, where the ball is struck over a sixty-foot canyon, and the Shangri-La hole 8, where the green is entirely enclosed and inward looking, an exotic garden fresh from the pages of *Lost Horizon*.[27]

The result, the audacious translocation of 'place', tested the conservative golf establishment. 'Gaudy' and 'classic' quickly became interchangeable adjectives in reviews. Nouveau riche publication *Cigar Aficionado* termed it 'the greatest golf course you'll (probably) never play' and it was voted best new course in 1990 and eighth best in the country by *Golf Digest* in 1994. Such an audacious re-creation was deemed tasteless by the establishment for whom the golf club is a definitive statement in social standing. Many saw Wynn as buying himself into his own very exclusive club.[28] Even Donald Trump was reduced to sniping 'he's got a great act. He's a smooth talker, he's

26 *Las Vegas Golf Guide*, op. cit., p. 74.

27 Wynn states James Hilton's *Lost Horizon* as the inspiration for the hole – 'where travellers find everlasting youth and wisdom'. See Wynn and Fazio, op. cit., p. 71.

28 Smith, op. cit., pp. 243–9.

Paul Davies

29 D. Trump, *The Art of the Deal*, New York, Random House, 1988, p. 157.

perfectly manicured, and he's invariably dressed to kill in $2,000 suits and $200 silk shirts. The problem with Wynn is that he tries too hard to look perfect.'[29]

UNCONVENTIONAL WISDOM

Luxury is more ruthless than war.

Juvenal

Trump implies that the successful entrepreneur should not have to try too hard, that success comes 'naturally'. Yet we can see that the relaxed atmospheres of The Mirage and Shadow Creek are contrivances of staggering complexity, marshalled under twin pressures of customer power and investment debt. Trump implies that contrary to this, powerful individuals do not, by their nature, have to try so hard to please.

To extrapolate a conversation about the power relations between architects and users, it is clear that the natural place of things relates to a wider order than that represented by mere geographical co-ordinates, and that Steve Wynn's assault on convention reflects both his own sense of ambition and that of the consumers who flock to The Mirage.

Modern architecture prescribed the appearance of less no matter what the circumstances, within a conventional appreciation of both 'natural' forms and social roles. Robert Venturi's critique was the first to publicise 'less' as 'a bore'. Escaping Yale to find inspiration in Las Vegas in 1968, Venturi, Scott Brown and Izenour arrived on the strip when Jay Sarno's Caesar's Palace was its latest addition. They cautiously incorporated its vulgarised image of Rome (a 'lush oasis with gleaming statuary, gorgeous gardens and fabulous fountains' and where 'toga clad attendants eagerly await your every summons')[30] into a respectable critique on the presumptions of American modernism.

30 Caesar's Palace Tourist Brochure included in R. Venturi, D. Scott Brown and S. Izenour, *Learning From Las Vegas*, Cambridge Mass., MIT Press, 1977, p. 55.

But Venturi's team believed the time was not yet right for a broader appreciation of the morality of Las Vegas. The social roles of 'toga-clad attendants' in an industrial society would defer to a critique of the academy's love of ancient Rome with Venturi's subversive rendition of Las Vegas presented in the manner of the Renaissance Noli plan of Rome. Their paradigm was the study of gothic cathedrals, which they believed 'need not include a debate on the morality of medieval religion'.[31] What Venturi's team self-consciously excised from their formal analysis of Las Vegas was the social, presumably because a black and white rendition of social responsibility had been struck as formidably within the architectural academy as it had been corrupted and

31 Venturi, Scott Brown and Izenour, op. cit., p. 6.

exploited in Las Vegas backrooms. However, the resultant practice of Venturi Rauch Scott Brown architects (Robert Venturi and Denise Scott Brown dated in Las Vegas), whilst maintaining an academic respectability, did shift toward a latent political engagement with the mythmaking of the capitalist marketplace and the comfort of consumers within it.

Thirty years on, it seems that the issue burns brighter, for we recognise the limits of Venturi's formal strategy all the more clearly as Las Vegas represents not so much a challenge to the form of contemporary buildings, but to professional conceits.

Today's new economic 'medici' have followed the pre-modern model when commissioning architecture. The guild structure of fifteenth-century Florence ranked stonemasons and fabricators below the cloth merchants and traders, and architects and artists of the Renaissance deferred to the wisdom of their patron Cosimo Medici whose enlightened scholarship was considered their guide. Mirage Resorts operates under the directorship of Steve Wynn through all matters of detail. He worked directly with Fazio to create Shadow Creek and reputedly had his own drawing board next to Joel Bergman during design for The Mirage.[32] Wynn's 'vision' supplants the 'eye' of the professional architect, and the co-operation of the building team is assured by conditions of almost guild-like co-operation across a mass of carefully selected consultants. Meanwhile the tools with which to realise the vision diversify in response to the latest technology, and fading eyesight.

Notwithstanding any crisis in visual culture as anticipated by Marshall McLuhan,[33] this destabilises the question of authorship in architectural production and has serious repercussions for architectural criticism. The process is exemplified within Mirage Resorts Inc., but is no less evident when Disney CEO Michael Eisner discusses his new-found interests in commissioning the best-known architects for Disney Company:

> Buildings, architecture, are something that stay with you in a way nothing else does, it's subliminal. You don't even know what you know about architecture. Yet you get angry or you feel good and you don't understand why you feel good.[34]

The sensibility emphasises issues of empathy, mystery and 'feeling good'. These are prioritised over traditional, abstract, professional concerns. If big name 'signature architects' are employed within these corporations, they are employed precisely for their 'signature' within the broader scheme of multi-disciplinary teams fine-tuning their work specifically in response to active markets of expectant consumers. Mirage Resorts is successful because its architecture responds to the desires, conscious and sub-conscious, of its guests within the mono-culture of the Strip where environmental

32 Smith, op. cit., p. 196.

33 Marshall McLuhan recognised that the age of perspective, of the visual, was passing. A shift in either the media of production (computer visualisation) or construction (environmental technology) will change the terms for the appreciation of the architectural product away from the confines of perspective.

34 Michael Eisner quoted in B. Dunlop, *Building a Dream – The Art of Disney Architecture*, New York, Abrams, 1996, p. 63.

Paul Davies

qualities attract business from competitive facilities offering the same basic range of services.

Both Mirage Resorts and Walt Disney Company spend more on design than their competitors. Michael Milken's economic regime demanded high performance, including repayment clauses on bond issues which favoured profitability 150 per cent higher than market expectations. Wynn's products have to succeed in the marketplace. His second Strip property, Treasure Island, completed 1993 and oriented toward a less exclusive market than The Mirage next door, holds the world hotel occupancy record of 112 days totally sold out.

To achieve success Wynn employs a rich ambiguity in a landscape so often dismissed as literally false and banal by architectural critics, critics whose viewpoint is predicated on an interpretation of natural behaviour held in question here with reference to George Bataille in the field of anthropology and Michael Milken in the field of economics. That booming Las Vegas is constructed as imminently and perpetually catastrophic is symptomatic of an impasse haunting conventional criticism. Meanwhile we can be certain that no matter the particularities of boom and bust that may face Las Vegas in the future, the mechanisms at work in the construction of this extraordinary test-bed for architecture, are those now endemic to Western culture.

Once, the Casino Resort was a carpet joint whose gilded mousetrap interior became the home solely of victims and the asset of crooks. Today The Mirage presents an entirely different phenomenon, whose architectural precedents lie even closer to the great cathedrals. Taking Venturi's argument a step further, far from creating an irreconcilable atmosphere of gloom and doom, touching on the religious and moral aspects of The Mirage may reveal a rich territory.

If The Mirage is the cathedral, then Shadow Creek is the hunting lodge of the New Medici. Originally, golf was an amusement played across the tricky meanderings of the coastal estuaries of western Scotland. The holes were conveniently tended by rabbits and other wildlife and the ball a hopeful inculcation of feathers stuffed inside a roughly stitched leather skin. James II of Scotland had to ban the game, for it interfered with his soldiers' compulsory archery practice.

The hunt celebrated a necessity (food) as a ritualised luxury (festival). Today, golfers meet to celebrate a specific moment of leisure amidst the twenty-four-hour competitive global economy. They compete against a contrived natural landscape as a representation of power over external circumstances. At Shadow Creek these circumstances range from the forces of the global market and political power to those of personal tragedy.

Architecturally modernists have had difficulty in considering leisure as anything other than a regime unto itself. Modern conceptions of health and fitness have tended to be regimented, waste or excess were not permitted, and the spaces of leisure were neutral and self-contained. They were also set within a regime of architectural protocols which have been careful to delineate precisely what may be considered architecture and what may not. Both these territories proved highly exclusive.

Venturi was not able to encompass in his study architectural events such as Frank Sinatra singing 'Fly me to the Moon' to packed audiences at The Sands in the early 1960s, or Dean Martin relaxing nonchalantly (as usual) on the golf course. Yet I cannot imagine a critique today that would not include Siegfried and Roy in a discussion of the architecture of The Mirage, since this entertainment has become integrated, synergised, into a world far beyond that which Venturi was inclined to abstract as figure against ground.

Thirty years on from *Learning from Las Vegas*, I wonder whether architects can come to terms with these spectacular inversions to their assumed wisdom, a world where, as Siegfried and Roy believe:

> Fantasy is stronger than Wisdom;
> Myths are more convincing than History;
> Dreams are more persuasive than Facts;
> Hope will triumph over Knowledge;
> Laughter is the medicine for all Sorrow;
> And that Love is stronger than Death.[35]

35 Robert Fulghum, quoted by Siegfried and Roy in the souvenir edition of *The Magic Begins at Home*, Las Vegas, The Mirage, 1996, p. 91.

Paul Davies

the knowing and

subverting reader

Was John Major an architect? Were his works, the means, modes, codes and rituals of their production, representation and dissemination, inherently architectural? It is not uncommon to hear or to read the title of 'architect' being bestowed upon heads of state, diplomats and elder statesmen, usually in recognition of their roles in establishing historic pieces of legislation. And although upon closer inspection this phenomenon may prove to be little more than a mass-media cliché based on popular, though outdated, preconceptions, I suspect that such an enquiry may reveal much of what are, by convention, perceived to be the essential characteristics of that which is 'architectural'.

I have, therefore, chosen as one of my objects of study the Downing Street Joint Declaration published by the British and Irish Governments that forms the basis of the 'Northern Ireland Peace Initiative'. My concern is specifically for representations of the text itself, of its production, 'and of its immediate consequences as a product of contemporary culture. I have chosen to couple this first object of study with a conventional work of high modernist architecture, and in so doing I hope to reveal something of an 'architectural' territory common to both. The building I have chosen is the German Pavilion built for the Barcelona International Exposition of 1929 and designed by the German architect Ludwig Mies van der Rohe. The relevance of this building stems not simply from its iconic status within modernist architecture but also from its brief role as stage set for, witness to, and object of an act of international diplomacy and statesmanship.

The Barcelona Pavilion and the Downing Street Declaration are two very distinct projects, one: the highest icon of high modernist architecture, the other: a text forming the basis of a political quest for peace in Northern Ireland. One: a three-dimensional construction in travertine, onyx and marble; glass, concrete and steel. The other: a two-dimensional text printed on a series of ordered pages. The obvious physical and material actualities of the two projects have little in common. I intend, therefore, effectively to remove myself from that physical and material actuality and through their photographic representation to arrive at those points of connection and regions of overlap.

The furniture inside Mies' pavilion was designed specifically for the ceremonial inauguration of the pavilion by the then King and Queen of Spain in the presence of Dr Schintzler, the German General Commissioner for the Barcelona Exposition. This ceremony was itself symbolic of a renewed acceptance of Germany within Europe after the First World War. The Barcelona Pavilion has attracted much conjecture, as to its role within what was a highly sensitive political climate, and not least about Mies' own political sympathies. Critical opinion seems divided between the likes of Giedion who describes Mies as 'standing quiet but firm in his enlightened modernity, as night

Ben Godber

descended around him',[1] and José Quetglas who describes the pavilion's 'useless, silent, marmoreal vacant qualities' as being 'premonitory symbols of Prussian militarism'.[2] It seems all too obvious to observe that the truth must lie somewhere in between. Robin Evans asks 'some of the mud sticks but does it stick to his [Mies'] buildings?'[3]

Both projects are political animals and it is quite deliberate that I have chosen to compare a work so heavily laden with political and historical associations with another work of an unashamedly political nature and of historical portent. A quest for publicity would seem to be coincident with any political aspiration, and since there can be no publicity without first seeking representation, to choose two such political projects seems apt given the need to approach them first through their representation in photography.

Both projects have attracted the attention of commentators, polemicists and theorists alike, although for distinctly different reasons. The Downing Street Declaration is a measured document stating the positions of the British and Irish governments with respect to a quest for peace in Northern Ireland. A quest which aims to dissipate a heritage of many generations of religious distinction, entrenched factional hatred and violence in the province of Northern Ireland. It has a neutered tone stemming from a resolute understatedness which is quite deliberate on the part of its authors, who recognise its emotive potential as an intervention into an already volatile climate. It is precisely because of this climate that the Downing Street Declaration and its immediate consequences have attracted so much written commentary. By contrast, the Barcelona Pavilion continues to attract commentary of a very different nature. Whilst its gestures are similarly measured, it is by virtue of its understatedness, and the very 'uselessness' and 'silence' alluded to by José Quetglas, that the Barcelona Pavilion has found itself to be such an accommodating vehicle for the assorted causes célèbres of so many theorists and academics.

Yet it is not the writer who is courted by the architect or statesman in seeking representation of their works, it is the image maker, the photographer. Seeing is, after all, believing and in the same way that we would look to a person's face to betray the true sentiments behind what they say, we seem far more alive to the agendas and subtexts; to political intent contained within a piece of writing than we ever are to the same agendas and subtexts within an image. The building and the head of state's signature have ceased to be the dominant currencies within the economies of both architecture and of international diplomacy. They have been displaced by the publishable image.

Yet to refer to the pre-eminence of the image in contemporary culture as if it were a recent phenomenon is I feel something of a fallacy. The primary sense organs of the

1 S. Giedion, *Space, Time and Architecture*, Cambridge, Mass., Harvard University Press, 1954, p. 548.

2 J. Quetglas, 'Fear of Glass: The Barcelona Pavilion', in B. Colomina (ed.), *Architectureproduction*, New York, Princeton Architectural Press, 1988, p. 150.

3 R. Evans, 'Mies van der Rohe's Paradoxical Symmetries', *AA Files*, No. 19, 1990, p. 57.

Ben Godber

human being are its eyes and the pre-eminence of visual media is, therefore, no coincidence. Rather it is its proliferation and mobility, come to rival that of text based media, which is the contemporary phenomenon.

One cannot help but be aware that the photographic image has an increasingly seductive materiality of its own. If the building and the statesman's signature have been displaced by images as dominant currencies within their respective disciplines, must we conclude that, as material actualities and as objects of study for this enquiry, the Barcelona Pavilion and Downing Street Joint Declaration have also been displaced by their representative images?

The practices of architecture and of international diplomacy are dominated by their respective, politically motivated institutions. Institutions whose prime objectives are not necessarily architectural and are more likely to be concerned with the perpetuation of the mythical status of their own members. The corollary to this is that the images of currency within the economies of architecture and international diplomacy are rarely seductive enough in themselves to assume primacy over their subjects since this would serve the photographer rather than the architect, statesman or diplomat. It is, therefore, the political intent of the institution, which ensures that the subject of the image retains primacy over the image itself.

The image may have the capacity to inform and reinform our understanding or indeed the creative processes which gave rise to the subject of that image. And whilst much of what we know, or think we know, comes to us through our experience of it in the two-dimensional photographic image, that image is none the less wholly contingent upon the materiality not only of its own media but also that of which it depicts. These are not the rhetorical or narrative images which are an experience in themselves; the images of currency within the disciplines of architecture and international political affairs are simply intended to promote an awareness of the existence of the works themselves. As such it remains the case that the objects of study for this enquiry are the Barcelona Pavilion and the Downing Street Joint Declaration as material actualities.

A discussion of this kind seems particularly relevant given my choice of the Barcelona Pavilion as an object of study, since as a work of high modernism it existed for more than forty years not as a building but as a dispersed collection of sketches and working drawings, as text in the writings of contemporary architectural theorists and, importantly in this context, as photographs. In short, the only material manifestations of the Barcelona Pavilion for many years were two dimensional. This fact renders Mies' Pavilion a perfect object of study for an enquiry which declares an interest in photographic representation.

The unusual, disjointed chronology of events surrounding the pavilion may appear to contradict my earlier renunciation of the idea that, in architectural photography, the image might transcend the materiality of its subject. The existence of the re-constructed pavilion may raise the question as to which is the true pavilion or even as to whether the images of the pavilion of 1929 are in fact of greater value than the pavilion now standing in Barcelona? I shall leave such questions to others since I suspect this territory is already well trodden and of little relevance to my enquiry. I shall simply point to the fact that the pavilion was reconstructed, which would seem to suggest that the images alone could not sustain the Barcelona Pavilion.

During any enquiry into photography one must inevitably encounter the photographer, although any such encounter would appear to be prefaced or hindered by the terms 'amateur' and 'professional' . Similarly any rigorous enquiry of architecture forces one to grapple with the terms 'architect' and 'user' and by extension, if the statesman or diplomat may be referred to as an 'architect' it must follow that we as their electorate must assume 'usership'.

For the purpose of this enquiry, however, our concern is for representation of the objects of study and what such representations might betray of their subjects and their means of production. Having established representation as a prime concern I feel that the terms 'author' and 'reader' are rather more meaningful than either 'amateur' and 'professional' or 'architect' and 'user'. In establishing my definition of the author's representation with respect to photography I am in many ways linking the title of 'author' to the status of 'professional'. By professional I mean one whose work is procured through his or her affiliation to an institution which through rituals, codes and modes of practice seeks to establish the exclusivity of its members. I have taken the title of 'author' to mean one who whilst not necessarily the sole progenitor of a piece of work, or even one accredited with its production, is able to represent that work in such a way that it would be recognised and acknowledged by the institution, i.e. of architecture or of international political diplomacy. This means that the author has to be well versed in the modes, codes, rituals and conventions of that institution. Conversely, the title of 'reader' is bestowed upon one who, by representation of a piece of work, demonstrates one or more interpretations of that work which would not be recognised by the institution. In short, the reader's representations of works are those excluded from the institutions of architecture and of international diplomacy.

I would suggest that we are so conditioned to recognise and acknowledge the author's representation, that we have long since ceased to recognise the codes and conventions which define that representation. In this climate of ignorance it is at times almost impossible to distinguish the author's from the reader's representation since the reader may often unwittingly attempt to mimic these codes and conventions of authorship. The distinction may often be defined by little more than technique.

Ben Godber

The title of 'reader' does not necessarily confer upon the individual an ignorance of the conventions of authorship and it is at this juncture that we arrive at the definition of the 'knowing reader'. A title which is bestowed upon one who is well versed in the conventions of authorship but who knowingly acquiesces in, distorts or subverts them. In this way the status of reader is reaffirmed with reference to but in direct contradiction of that of the author. Within the construct of the author/reader relationship the influence of the knowing and subverting reader exerts little change; it remains the case that the identity of the author is autonomous whilst that of the reader is still wholly dependent upon that of the author.

Sinn Fein returns to the fold

Britain quibbles, but Dublin hails a historic handshake as a new beginning, writes David McKittrick

THE HANDSHAKE between an Irish taoiseach and a Sinn Fein leader which took place in Dublin yesterday was hailed as a historic milestone in the Irish peace process.

The meeting between Albert Reynolds and Gerry Adams of Sinn Fein, the first time since the Irish Civil War period in the 1920s that such an event has taken place, was viewed in Irish political circles as a momentous entry for the IRA and Sinn Fein into legitimate politics.

Together with the SDLP leader, John Hume, the two men issued a joint statement which said: "We are at the beginning of a new era in which we are all totally and absolutely committed to democratic and peaceful methods of resolving our political problems."

But even as the world watched, the British and Irish governments remained at odds on the question of whether the IRA's campaign was really over, and on how republicans should now be treated.

Downing Street remained impassive and was still examining the statement last night to judge whether it conveyed the "permanent" cessation of violence commitment it has demanded.

While striving to convey a continuing positive tone towards the ceasefire, No 10 resisted calls for an immediate response. A spokesman said: "We want to look at the statement very closely."

Earlier a Downing Street meeting of senior ministers had reiterated the Government's position that the IRA had to show by "words and deeds" that its ceasefire was permanent.

But at another meeting at No 10, John Major took decisive action to stamp on what he views as highly damaging interventions in

THEY HANDLED it pretty well, this little moment in history, this moment with its possibility of new beginnings, of new directions in Irish history.

They were suitably grave as they came down the ornate steps of the Taoiseach's office, with its elaborate entrance and its grand columns.

Albert Reynolds, the Taoiseach, shook the hand of Gerry Adams, leader of Sinn Fein, then they both shook the hand of John Hume, leader of the SDLP, who had helped to bring them together. Mr Reynolds, in his familiar persona of a brisk, no-nonsense businessman, might have been closing a deal with a commercial partner. Mr Adams, whose party has not been officially welcomed by the Dublin government for 25 years, exuded the personal dignity which so infuriates his opponents.

Not so long ago Mr Reynolds viewed Mr Adams as a subversive, while the Sinn Fein leader thought of the Irish government as quislings and the puppets of Britain.

It was a moment in history, but there are so many precedents of welcoming violent prodigals into politics that the Irish reckon they know instinctively how to deal with such happenings. The drill is not to stand on ceremony or dwell on formalities but to get the miscreants in before they change their minds.

Mr Reynolds's Fianna Fail party went through just such a transformation in the Twenties and Thirties. At least two of his predecessors as Fianna leader and Taoiseach were intimately acquainted with Mausers and Lee-Enfield rifles before rising to

'The beginning of a new era in which we are all totally and absolutely committed to democratic and peaceful methods of resolving our political problems' — from yesterday's joint statement issued in Dublin by (from left) Gerry Adams, Albert Reynolds and John Hume *Photograph: David Rose*

Figure 10.1 Adams, Reynolds and Hume Shake Hands in Dublin, The Independent, *7 September 1994, p. 1. Photograph, David Rose.*

The image I have chosen as representative of the Downing Street Declaration and exemplifying a typical author's representation within the institution of international diplomacy, appeared in *The Independent* newspaper on 7 September 1994 a week after the declaration of an IRA cease-fire. Taken by David Rose it depicts three of the most prominent statesmen of the 'Northern Ireland Peace Initiative': Gerry Adams, Albert Reynolds and John Hume shaking hands on the steps of the Taoiseach's office in Dublin.

Ben Godber

Whilst their mode of dress is almost identical: uniformly sober, dignified and 'respectable' as would befit a statesman's public persona, the three men's identically smiling faces are easily recognisable since all three look out of the image towards the world's press. Nothing in the composition distracts from these three men. Albert Reynolds, the most senior of the three both in years and in terms of his political status, is in the centre of the composition, the implication being that he has brought these men together. The importance of Albert Reynolds within the composition is further accentuated by the device of a rigid vertical axis of bilateral symmetry. It is by virtue of this device that this grouping of men is perceived as one of significance and of contrived formality. Nothing in the image subtracts from the basic explicit narrative, which is that these men have come to an agreement. Both their smiles and the physical contact between them suggest their concurrence. Everything is done to obscure their respective personalities, these men are not represented as individuals but rather as icons, as figureheads for their respective organisations, the populations and communities which they represent.

There is a stasis to the image, they appear almost as motionless as the building used for a backdrop behind them. The implication, typical of such formulaic representations, would seem to be that their agreement symbolised in the tripartite handshake has all the gravitas and durability of the very edifice upon which they stand. In this instant these three men have become not so much the 'architects' of a great act of diplomacy and statesmanship but rather the architecture of a great act of diplomacy and statesmanship. In the front-page article which accompanied this photograph, David McKittrick seemed anxious to convey the symbolic significance of this instance of physical contact between the three men. A reference to 'this little moment in history with its possibility of new beginnings, of new directions in Irish history' is followed almost immediately by a reference to 'the ornate steps of the Taoiseach's Office, with its elaborate entrance and its grand columns'. David McKittrick not only couples the language of international diplomacy with that of architectural commentary, but in so doing implies the enduring quality of a 'moment in history' through its close proximity to a significant, conventional architectural phenomenon.

The image I have chosen as representative of the Barcelona Pavilion and exemplifying a typical author's representation within the institution of architecture, depicts the reconstructed pavilion as seen from one of the same vantage points used to represent the original pavilion. It was this representation perhaps more than any other which helped to sustain the myth surrounding the original pavilion after its demolition. The intention in re-representation of this kind may have been to imply a seamless lineage between the two buildings.

The image shows the main mass of the pavilion in the middle ground, reflected in

Ben Godber

Figure 10.2 *Mies van der Rohe,*
The Barcelona Pavilion, 1929.
Reconstructed 1986.
Photograph, Eloi Bonjoch.

the large pool which occupies the foreground. All of which is set against a backdrop of foliage provided by the trees behind. The composition of the image is spatially dramatic and the perspectival foreshortening severe, which may have less to do with the image than with the building itself. The infinite planes suggested by Mies' walls, floors, pools and roofs of marble, travertine, water, concrete, onyx, marble and glass, easily generate such dramatic effects. The pavilion, having no axis of symmetry concurrent with its built surroundings, sets itself apart through the device of a rigid, horizontal axis of bilateral symmetry.

In much the same way that the three statesmen fill out the entire frame of their image, the pavilion fully occupies the entire composition. No attempt is made to portray it in its true context. The only part of another building to feature is the spire of a nearby church which could quite easily be mistaken as part of the backdrop of

Ben Godber

foliage. Seen in isolation, this image gives the impression of a pavilion set in lush, perhaps even pastoral, seclusion. The reality is that the pavilion is bounded by busy roads on two sides to the south and west, a dusty car park to the north and the blind wall of the Palau de Victòria Eugenia to the east. The pavilion as a whole is marginalised on the edge of a vast triumphalist, baroque composition. Almost all such images of the pavilion are taken from a vantage point within the curtilage of the pavilion itself, a territory carefully demarcated by Mies' white plinth of travertine upon which the pavilion stands. All such representations serve to demonstrate the selectivity of the photographer's lens, under its influence the pavilion is decontextualised and objectified.

The only dynamic elements within the composition are perhaps the clouds and, as is typical of nearly all conventional architectural photography, the building appears almost completely unpopulated. That is, except for two security guards, officious and motionless, on the steps which form the main means of access to the pavilion. Identically posed, side by side, clad in dark uniforms replete with handcuffs, their own hands characteristically clasped behind their backs which are turned to the viewer. These guards, in dissuading anyone from attempting to populate the image, serve to preserve the authoritative integrity of the author's representation.

Whilst both authors' representations are of widely differing subjects, they share certain characteristics. Through the device of the photographer's lens the author, in representation, is afforded the privilege of exclusivity, he or she may remove all evidence of context for the subject of his or her image. Perhaps it is not so important what comes to be represented by the image but rather what is not represented by the image.

Through the device of the shutter a stasis is imposed upon the composition, crystallising what otherwise might be construed as an imperfect entity. Under the influence of the camera any dynamic element is rendered a static one. Whereas for the authors' representation of great acts of statesmanship the concern is to preserve the momentous significance of an ephemeral gesture, for the building the author's concern is rather to exclude any dynamic or ephemeral gesture or consequence of an otherwise static architecture. For both objects of study, however, the desirable condition remains one of stasis.

It is arguable the extent to which the symmetry observed in both images, typical to all such authors' representations, can be considered to be 'an artefact of photography'[4] or whether it is rather a function of the subjects themselves. In his essay 'Mies van der Rohe's Paradoxical Symmetries' Robin Evans argues that this symmetry is more a function of the building than of its representative images, although he concedes that this phenomenon is rendered 'easier to discern' through the agency of

4 ibid., p. 63.

Ben Godber

the photograph. In both instances, however, the intention of this device seems clear: to establish both projects as authoritative entities, distinct from their surroundings. In the case of the act of diplomacy and statesmanship the concern is to formalise the composition. The author is anxious that the fact of their meeting and the concurrence of these three men, should be perceived and interpreted as momentous and worthy of history.

In the instance of the pavilion, the author's representation helps one to observe a horizontal axis of symmetry. A device employed by Mies to ensure that his pavilion be perceived and interpreted as distinct from its built surroundings, not simply by contrasting his minimal high modernist aesthetic with the exuberant baroque of the Palau de Victòria Eugenia, but also by contrast with its ubiquitous vertical, bilateral symmetry. In both these examples of typical authors' representations, the net effect of the devices deployed in representation, appears to have been to limit the number of possible interpretations to one.

Figure 10.3 Bill Clinton Meets Gerry Adams, The Times, 1 December 1995, p. 3. Photograph, A. Lewis/Sygma.

THE TIMES FRIDAY DECEMBER 1 1995   4M **CLINTON VISIT** 3

President stops off at the baker's for a bag of buns and walks out with Gerry Adams

Fruitful visit is hailed on streets of peace

By Alan Hamilton
IN BELFAST

BILL CLINTON popped into McErlean's bakery in the Falls Road yesterday for a bag of Irish potato cakes and who should be having a coffee in the back shop but Gerry Adams.

It is, to say the least, unlikely that as the motorcade snaked its way through the Roman Catholic heartland of West Belfast, the President of the United States turned to the First Lady and said: "Hey Hillary, I'm kinda peckish; you wait there and I'll go get us an ethnic snack." Spontaneity is not the overriding feature of presidential progress.

Yet, despite the presence of a huge media circus including the fearsome White House press corps, only a couple of amateur photographers were on hand to record the moment when the Sinn Fein leader put down his coffee and emerged on to the pavement to shake the hand of his visitor and welcome him to West Belfast.

Presidential security men talked frantically to their sleeves as the substantial crowd on the pavement broke ranks and pressed around the two men as they walked together into the shop. Mr Clinton smiling broadly and, clearly at ease, shook hands with all the shop assistants. Pauline Leonard, the manager, who swore she had had only 20 minutes' warning, hastily put a selection of potato

The photograph taken by a bystander of the President and Mr Adams shaking hands in a street encounter outside McErleans' bakery in Belfast yesterday

Operation Venice ensures watertight security

By Martin Fletcher
AND Nicholas Watt

MORE than 3,000 police officers and 100 American secret service agents, many of them armed, stood guard in Belfast and Londonderry as part of Operation Venice to protect Mr Clinton.

The operation dwarfed the extensive security which used to surround John Major on his visits to Northern Ireland. This time, however, British soldiers were nowhere to be seen; they have been absent from the streets of Belfast and Londonderry for almost a year. While the police were in overall control of security the secret agents had the task of close protection should there have been an attack.

Mr Clinton travelled through Belfast and Londonderry in a bulletproof limousine that formed part of a lengthy convoy. The limousine has gun ports, air filter system and supplies of blood.

It was followed by armourplated Jeeps and a second limousine which sometimes changes places with the President's vehicle to confuse would-be attackers. It is said that the military aide, who carries the secret codes to launch US nuclear weapons, travels in the second limousine. The convoy also had a military ambulance for emergency operations. A doctor and nurse always travel with the President.

Roads along the route were closed two hours before the convoy passed. Police marks-

Picture that was almost missed

By Martin Fletcher
IN BELFAST

PRESIDENT CLINTON finally shook the hand of Gerry Adams in public yesterday, but the world's media very nearly missed the remarkable picture of America's leader embracing a former terrorist. It was left to an amateur photographer to capture the historic moment.

Mr Clinton has met Mr Adams twice before in Washington, but on both occasions behind closed doors. This time the White House, wanting to encourage the Sinn Fein leader in his pursuit of peace, decided to abandon its earlier coyness and laid plans for a "semi-spontaneous" street encounter between the two men.

The idea was for Mr Clinton to drive down the Falls Road after visiting a factory on Belfast's "peace line", and to stop his motorcade outside McErlean's bakery, near Sinn Fein's headquarters, where he knew Mr Adams would be waiting.

The motorcade stopped. Mr Clinton got out. But as he and his bodyguards walked towards Mr Adams the two men were instantly engulfed by a huge crowd of excited people, who utterly obscured the long-awaited handshake from the squads of photographers and television crews who follow the President's every move.

A few people waiting had cameras and snapped wildly in the direction of Mr Clinton. One passer-by managed to capture the moment and within no time the picture was being flashed around the world.

Mr Adams said he greeted the President with a Gaelic phrase meaning "a thousand welcomes". The President then stepped into the bakery to say hello. Earlier he and his wife, Hillary, had gone into Violet's grocery shop in the Protestant Shankill Road in another display of well orchestrated "spontaneity".

Ben Godber

188

The image that I have chosen as an example of a reader's representation of the Downing Street Joint Declaration depicts Gerry Adams and Bill Clinton during the American President's visit to Belfast in late November of 1995. Appearing in *The Times*, the photograph was taken by an amateur photographer.[5] Under a superficial analysis, this image might appear almost indistinguishable from an author's representation; in capturing the two men it mimics the codes and conventions alluded to earlier. It is a familiar image: that of two prominent political icons shaking hands. Yet that handshake is of no import to anyone other than the individuals engaged in it. They seem unaware of the camera, their attentions are directed solely towards one another. Whilst both Clinton and Adams, the two most prominent and readily recognisable figures, are placed firmly in the centre of the composition, there seems to have been no effort on the part of the photographer to decontextualise them. To the left of Clinton both in front and behind him, we can clearly make out his body guards and in the background a crowd of people who seem largely unaware of his presence. The composition does not share the same rigid symmetry so common to typical authors' representations, there is none of the contrived formality that we would associate with such images.

Other newspapers published precisely the same photograph, but attempted to establish it as closer to the typical author's representation by cropping the original photograph so as to show only Clinton and Adams. The uncropped version was carried by *The Times* because their concern was specifically for the provenance of the image and the unconventional circumstances in which it was obtained, rather than for the content of the image itself. In this image Gerry Adams does not play the role of figurehead for the republican movement in Ireland, similarly Clinton does not play the role of President of the USA. They are simply two men, previously acquainted, seen to be greeting one another in the street. The fact that their sober and statesman-like apparel is concealed beneath their respective overcoats of different colours, in addition to the fact that neither of them has addressed himself to the camera, would seem to further establish this image as one made without the institution of authorship. They do not stand before a symbolic edifice, their concurrence is private not public. There is an implicit movement, a dynamic to the image, we are witness to a fleeting moment not an uncomfortably prolonged pose.

The fourth and final image depicting the reconstructed Barcelona Pavilion is an example of what I would classify a representation by a *knowing and subverting reader*. The photograph depicts Carolyn Butterworth in close-up, licking one of the travertine panels which form the walls of the Barcelona Pavilion. The tight framing of the image could be said to work to its detriment since, without prior knowledge, it is unlikely one would guess that this image depicted the Barcelona Pavilion. Indeed it could be argued

5 The photograph was taken by a high-ranking member of Sinn Fein who was able to take the photograph due to his association with Gerry Adams. Photo-journalists were unable to get a photo opportunity due to the President's limousine being unexpectedly re-routed.

Ben Godber

Figure 10.4 *Carolyn Butterworth, Licking the Barcelona Pavilion, 1992. Photograph, Emma Cheatle.*

that the subject of this image is Carolyn Butterworth rather than a work of high modernist architecture. Yet the fact of our interest in the image and indeed the fact of Butterworth's licking this particular surface, are both entirely contingent upon the fact that this is a representation of Mies' pavilion.

The image immediately establishes itself as being outside the canon of conventional architectural representation by depicting interaction with the pavilion. It has, by virtue of this interaction, an inherent dynamic, it portrays movement and makes use of the mechanisms of the shutter and the high speed photo-chemical processes within the camera, not to restrain, but rather to represent that dynamic. The image seems quite deliberately irreverent and provocative, even in the absence of any prior knowledge of the pavilion. Having acknowledged this image as a representation of a work of high modernist architecture, however, it assumes an almost iconoclastic quality. Is the implication one of edible and, therefore, consumable architecture? This is not an empty irreverence, however, no marker pen moustache on the face of the Mona Lisa, since, in representation, Carolyn Butterworth has equally articulated the rich textural nature of the materials and the unexpectedly sensual quality of Mies' pavilion.

A close-up of this kind would in any author's representation be reserved for the purposes of detail fetishism, never interaction. In this instance, however, the notion of a traditional author's representation of a detail has been pushed far beyond that recognised or acknowledged by the institution of architecture. In depicting direct experience of the material and textural quality of the pavilion not by the primary sensory mechanism of sight but rather by promoting an alternative sensory experience of architecture: by taste, Carolyn Butterworth has subverted many of the codes and modes of representation recognised by the institution of architecture.

Both of the examples of images displaying the codes, modes and conventions of authorship within the disciplines of architecture and international diplomacy seek to portray perfected and completed, finite entities. Nothing in the images betray process, the tools or means of production. The image of Gerry Adams, Albert Reynolds and John Hume presents us with nothing more than the fact of their agreement, nothing suggests the way in which that agreement was reached.

The image of the reconstructed pavilion similarly betrays nothing of its means of production, we are presented with nothing more than the fact of its existence. Through the decontextualised stasis of both representations, the tools, means, modes, codes, conventions and rituals of production remain the privileged preserve of the author operating within the institution.

Those images sanctioned by the institutions of architecture and of international diplomacy not only appear to conceal the means of their production but also to limit as far as possible the ways in which such an image may be interpreted. The compositional device of bilateral symmetry revealed by the camera in the photographic image serves to further reinforce the authority of the author's representation, in establishing the subject of the image as distinct from its surroundings.

My chosen examples of readers' representations similarly betray little of their means of production. The reader does not, however, seek to conceal these means of production in the same way that the author does. The reader's intention is not to reproduce the experience of that entity but rather to posit an alternative interpretation of it. This interpretation in turn becomes an entity in its own right but one which betrays the source and means of its own production through its contingency upon, not only the materiality of its subject, but also upon the author's original representation. This can be seen in the image depicting Bill Clinton and Gerry Adams. Whilst this image betrays nothing of their codes of practice as heads of state, it portrays them as having a relationship which is not subject to those same codes of practice, rather as two men, previously acquainted, greeting one another in the street. It is significant by virtue of its non-conformity to the conventions of authorship. And yet the fact of their meeting and the fact of our interest in these two men remains wholly contingent upon their roles as statesmen and as icons for the organisations, populations and communities which they represent.

The basis for this enquiry was to test the validity of referring to those engaged in international diplomacy as 'architects' by comparison between a conventional work of

Ben Godber

high modernist architecture and an article of statesmanship. The intention being to reveal an architectural territory common to both. Both the architect and statesman function as productive or creative operatives for their respective disciplines. Yet it would seem that it is not only by recognition of the creative processes involved in the production of a building or the establishing of international accord, which confers upon an individual the status of architect. It is equally by recognition of his or her affiliation to an institution that the status of architect is given credence. Since the role of the institution is first and foremost to perpetuate the cult of expertise for its members it is not necessarily the case that the prime objective of the institution will be an architectural one. Yet it is only by recognition of his or her expertise that the 'architect' retains that very status, and that recognition can only come about through representation of his or her works.

I have sought to demonstrate, with reference to photographic representations of the objects of study, that the 'architect' is established by the representation of his or her works as an author within the institution. All other such works, coming from outside the institution are by extension established as being those of a reader. An author's representation may be defined by the intent to objectify that which it depicts through both temporal and geographical decontextualisation and by the imposition of stasis upon its subject; by its refusal to betray process or the means of production; and in so doing to limit the number of interpretations for the viewer, to one. The reader's representation is, in contrast, defined simply by reference to how it differs from the typical author's representation. The corollary to this is that a reader's representation may by virtue of this difference permit a multitude of interpretations.

The binary construct of the author/reader relationship, hinging as it does upon membership or otherwise of the institution, would appear to hinder the creative processes which might rightly be considered to be architectural. This becomes especially apparent when one observes that the reader may often attempt unwittingly to mimic the stylistic conventions of a typical author's representation. Given the pre-eminence of the publishable image within the economies of both architecture and international diplomacy, the author's representation becomes increasingly pervasive within a climate of architectural stagnation, as the reader's mimicry becomes increasingly adept in aping the codes, modes, means and conventions of authorship. Unwittingly the reader's representation, possessing scope for multifarious inter-pretations, has become almost indistinguishable from that of the author's which permits us only one.

The knowing and subverting reader, however, emerges from between this binary opposition of author and reader, being at once within and without the institution, and is by virtue of his or her knowledge of the conventions, rituals, codes, modes and means

Ben Godber

of authorship able to posit a number of challenging and provocative interpretations for the viewer. Interpretations which call into question those same codes, modes, rituals and conventions which define the author/architect/professional and his or her works and their representations. Interpretations which rail against the intransigence and exclusivity of the institution, suggesting perhaps more responsive and inclusive, richer, more diverse and potentially divergent methods of production and representation for both international diplomacy and conventional architecture.

In reinforming the processes of production and representation, the knowing and subverting reader breaks down the distinction between the author/architect/professional and the reader/user/amateur. Under the influence of the knowing and subverting reader, the emphasis shifts away from the institution and towards the act of production itself. It is perhaps the *knowing and subverting reader* operating from within a new non-institution of architecture who deserves the status of architect.

Ben Godber

body architecture

SKATEBOARDING AND THE CREATION

OF SUPER-ARCHITECTURAL SPACE

1 A. Benjamin, 'Time, Question Fold', AA Files, Autumn 1993, no. 26, p. 7.

The relationship between philosophy and architecture not only works to position one in relation to the other, it also opens up the possibility that one may already be figuring in and thus would already be present within the other.[1]

Andrew Benjamin

2 H. Lefebvre, The Production of Space, Oxford, Blackwell, 1991, p. 94.

Surely it is the supreme illusion to defer to architects, urbanists or planners as being experts or ultimate authorities in matters relating to space.[2]

Henri Lefebvre

Andrew Benjamin's statement is, in its first part, one with which many would agree; the relation between architecture and philosophy has a long history. But what if we not only explore the more tentative, second part of his assertion – that somehow philosophy and architecture are present within each other – and simultaneously rethink philosophy away from the academic or metaphysical practice divorced from daily life, and toward

3 H. Lefebvre, Everyday Life in the Modern World, New Brunswick, Transaction, 1984.

one that, as Henri Lefebvre has consistently argued, is or should be embedded in the everyday?[3] What happens to the architect and to architecture when critical thinking is rethought as a quotidian procedure, and when appropriations of space, the space of the body, and representations as lived experiences are brought to bear on consciously designed construction as manifestations of philosophy-as-everyday-practice? The exploration here treats the activity of skateboarding for precisely these considerations, using, in particular, Lefebvre's considerations of space and the everyday as levers to open out meanings and possibilities.

The architecture of skateboarding falls into two interdependent categories, one closer to the conventional realm of architecture as the conceptualisation, design and production of built spaces, the other closer to the realm of the user and the experience and creation of space through bodily processes. Both involve spatial thoughts, objects and actions, and, through this intersection, skateboarding and architecture can be seen to carry the presence of each other, a dialectic that institutes the supplemental realm of a super-architectural space. Three different kinds of territories of occupation are implicated in this production: the physical or natural space that is simply found, constructed space, and the space of representation.

FIRST TERRITORY: FOUND SPACE

Early skateboarders in the 1960s were commonly surfers, and used skateboards when the surf was flat. The suburban modernism of Los Angeles – skateboarding's historical

Garden of Eden – allowed frustrated surfers to re-enact the sense of being on the sea, rolling down tarmac as if it were an ocean wave. This is artificial, second nature[4] architecture, a kind of Californian decentralised version of the new town,[5] re-thought as natural space. These early skateboarders also found other terrains on which to skate, in particular the gentle banks found in many Californian school yards. Most famous was Kenter Canyon school in Brentwood, Los Angeles, where skaters transcribed surfing techniques even more directly. Skaters rode along the length of the bank, just as a surfer carves across the front of a wave, or emulated surfing in other ways, touching the surface of the bank as if trailing the hand in watery spray, or re-enacting surf tricks, like the 'Hang five' move where the rider hangs five toes over the front of the board.

Through such moves skaters provoked a recombination of body, board and terrain, producing something at once simulative and original; the skateboard enabled the skater to both simulate one activity – that of surfing – and to initiate a second – that of skateboarding. In spatial-architectural terms, the modernist space of suburbia was appropriated and re-conceived as another kind of space, as a concrete wave; second nature was returned to first nature. This combination and recombination of body, image, thought and action lies at the heart of skateboarding. It is an integral combination of the abstract and the concrete, to which I shall constantly return.

The emulation of surfing and the production of skateboarding space occurred from around the early 1960s up to the early 1970s. But apart from gentle banks of Kenter and other Los Angeles schools, skaters found other, more challenging terrains. Above all, this meant swimming pools. Los Angeles, particularly the Hollywood Hills and the other more moneyed districts of Santa Monica, Malibu and Pacific Palisades, has many substantial individual homes, many of which have swimming pools. It is this architectural resource which skaters exploited, following the mythologised discovery by Gary Swanson in his own backyard Santa Monica pool that, once drained of water, such pools offer a curved transition from base to wall up which the skateboarder could ride.[6] Pools known to skaters by such names as Dog Bowl, Egg Bowl, Fruit Bowl, Manhole, Canyon Pool, Gonzo's, Teardrop and the Soul Bowl[7] offered an extreme terrain on which surf-related skating could take place.

To begin with, this meant riding along the surface of the wall in a single sweeping movement known as a carve. This is one of the most basic of skateboard moves, in which the skater gradually learns to ride higher and higher, prevented from falling by the centrifugal force generated by their speed. It is also a move directly derived from surfing, duplicating the surfer's carve across the face of an ocean wave.

Skating in pools also means creating an empathy and engagement with the surface of the pool wall. This occurred in two ways. First, skaters encounter the *wallness* of the wall – when riding up a wall, they sense the change of the pool from

4 Lefebvre, *Production of Space*, p. 109. See also H. Lefebvre, *The Survival of Capitalism*, London, Allison and Busby, 1974, pp. 14–15.

5 H. Lefebvre, 'Notes on the New Town', in *Introduction to Modernity: Twelve Preludes September 1959 – May 1961*, London, Verso, 1995, pp. 116–31.

6 Lowboy, 'Truth and Screw the Consequences', *Thrasher*, June 1989, vol. 9, no. 6, p. 42.

7 *SkateBoarder, passim*, and Glen E. Friedman, e-mail, 23 March 1997. See also Glen E. Friedman, *Fuck You Heroes: Glen E. Friedman Photographs, 1976–1991*, New York, Burning Flags Press, 1994; and Glen E. Friedman, *Fuck You Two: the Extras + More Scrapbook*, Los Angeles, 2.13.61 Publications and Burning Flags Press, 1996.

Iain Borden

floor to wall, such that it presents itself to the skater as a surface which becomes a wall under their very feet. The skater's experience is that of an encounter with this transition, and that experience becomes heightened as they ride higher up the surface – the higher up they go, the more vertical, the more wall-like that surface becomes. This involves a double-movement – and *movement* is key – of body and architectural surface: initially, there is the sudden compression of the body hitting the bottom curve of the transition, in which the terrain is felt to press back on the skater, translating momentum into a forced acceleration of her/his trajectory up the wall; and at this point the second stage of the movement arrives, tense compression is released, and the skater feels the enclosed concave curvature of the transition give way to vertical flatness, and to a corresponding sense of speed and expansivity of space.

The second engagement with the pool wall is through its pure surface, and particularly the tactility or materiality of that surface: its smoothness as a texture, like a cloth, and its smoothness as a concave plane, like a mathematically complex curve. Here the micro-architecture of grain, asperity, cracks, ripple become evident, translated into body space through judder (from wheels, to deck, to feet and upward), slide/grip and – above all – noise. The skateboarder's traverse on the clear white wall creates a mono-tonal hum, so near silence yet so clearly audible that it creates a dramatic calm interlude to the shuddering, high-speed fire rasped out by hard wheels passing over blue ceramic tile and metal truck grinding along concrete coping. These aural salvos remind us that '[s]pace is listened for, in fact, as much as seen, and heard before it comes into view'[8] and that hearing mediates between the spatial body and the world outside it. This is a 'sensuous geography'[9] created by a phenomenal experience of architecture, a 'sensory space' constituted by 'an "unconsciously" dramatized interplay of relay points and obstacles, reflections, references, mirrors and echoes'.[10]

Pool skateboarding is not just about emulating surfing, and also involves an imaginative production in terms of the moves skaters conceive and enact. In particular, this involves thinking less about the pool wall as a concrete wave, and more as an element which, together with the skateboard and skater's own body, can be recombined into an excited body-centric space. In the pools, skaters explore both the boundaries of the surface on which they skate and the space beyond. They concentrate on the top of the pool wall, shuddering over the blue tile to grind the rear truck against the pool coping blocks before dropping back down. Here the edge condition is important, the skater addressing the very limits of the wall, and the precise micro-space of the skateboard wheel and truck in relation to that edge. More spectacularly, the skateboarder can perform an aerial: pass over the top of the wall, torque around in mid-air while holding onto the side of the skateboard hand and return to solid surface some four metres below. Moves like these – first enacted in the 1970s – initiated a

8 Lefebvre, *Production of Space*, pp. 199–200.

9 P. Rodaway, *Sensuous Geographies: Body, Sense and Place*, London, Routledge, 1994.

10 Lefebvre, *Production of Space*, p. 210.

Iain Borden

Figure 11.1 *Jay Adams,
'Adolph's', May 1977. © Glen E.
Friedman. Source: Glen E.
Friedman,* Fuck You Heroes: Glen
E. Friedman Photographs,
1976–1991, *New York, Burning
Flags Press, 1994.*

Iain Borden

Figure 11.2 *Tony Alva, 'Dog
Bowl', September 1977. © Glen
E. Friedman. Source: Glen E.
Friedman,* Fuck You Heroes: Glen
E. Friedman Photographs,
1976–1991, *New York, Burning
Flags Press, 1994.*

Iain Borden

unique airborne spatial experience, wherein space is produced centrifugally, a spiralling field of influence thrown out from the body, and then centripetally, pulling the terrain underfoot back into the realm of body space.

SECOND TERRITORY: CONSTRUCTED SPACE

By 1975 *SkateBoarder* magazine had a circulation of 165,000 and, according to *Time* magazine, Southern California had some two million skateboarders.[11] And by 1978, *Skateboarder* had one million readers.[12] Although other terrains besides pools and schoolyard banks could be found – notably large circular concrete drainage pipes at Mount Baldy, Palos Verdes and further out in the Arizona desert[13] – skateboarding was rapidly outstripping the available found terrains. The Los Angeles commercial sector responded with a number of purpose-built skateparks which extracted and exaggerated fragments of the city to create perfect skateboarding architecture. One of the first and best was 'Pipeline' skatepark in Upland, opened in May 1977. Featuring the first circular pipe and vertical walls intended for skateboarding, Pipeline emulated and improved upon the pipes, drainage ditches and pools found in the Los Angeles area. As competition from other skateparks increased and as skateboard moves became increasingly demanding, the 'Combi-Pool' was added to Pipeline, effectively a square pool with rounded corners and a circular pool joined together at a common entrance point.[14] From the start, Pipeline was a great success and was quickly emulated by others: in 1981 the Los Angeles region alone had at least eight other skateparks of a similar standard, including 'Concrete Wave' at Anaheim, 'Skateboard World' at Torrance, 'Skate City' at Whittier, 'Big O' at Orange and others at Colton, Lakewood, Marina Del Rey and Carlsbad.

This specialised architectural activity was repeated throughout America, Europe and Asia, all these skateparks mimicking backyard Californian swimming pools, Arizona pipeline projects and other features of American architecture and civil engineering. In the United Kingdom, for example, around twenty-five purpose-built skateparks were constructed by 1980, including 'The Rom' near Romford in Essex and another by the same constructors at Harrow, both of which continue to operate.

From the early 1980s onward, these skateparks were also increasingly complemented by the provision, often by skaters themselves, of ramps. Typically of free-standing, above-ground timber construction, the most common form of ramp is the half-pipe, referring to the U-section profile and two parallel side walls. A flat bottom between the two transitions allows greater time between moves. Overall height varies between two and five metres, the walls being topped off with a narrow platform

11 La Vada Weir, *Skateboards and Skateboarding: the Complete Beginner's Guide*, New York, Julian Messner, 1977, pp. 14–15.

12 Glen E. Friedman, e-mail, 16 February 1997.

13 D. Hunn, *Skateboarding*, London, Duckworth, 1977, p. 20; E. Dressen, interview, *Transworld Skateboarding*, June 1989, vol. 7, no. 3, pp. 97–103 and 160–72; and Chris Miller, interview, *Thrasher*, May 1989, vol. 9, n. 10, pp. 62–9.

14 'Upland Pipeline: Closing Comments', *Transworld Skateboarding*, April 1989, vol. 7, no. 2, pp. 64–72.

Iain Borden

allowing skateboarders to drop in at the beginning of their runs and providing easy observation. Smaller versions known as mini ramps are made for cramped sites, constructed rapidly and at minimal cost. At the other end of the spectrum, complicated multi-unit combinations are built for demonstrations and competitions, with half-pipes of varying size and shape placed in combination to enable skaters to transfer directly from one to another.

These various constructed architectures of skateboarding are not, however, despite their unique contribution to the specialist typologies of the differentiated built environment, the principal contribution of skateboarding to architectural space. This lies instead in the performative aspects of skateboarding. In particular, the terrains both replicated but also formally extrematised the terrains found within the modern city, and so enabled a new form of spatial engagement to occur. The Combi-Pool at Pipeline, for example, offered the same white walls, blue tiles and concrete coping as a typical backyard Los Angeles pool, but, benefiting from design advice from professional skateboarders, was also now deeper (and hence more dangerous) and with greater areas of vertical wall, faster transitions from base to wall, a flat bottom between walls, and a smoother surface optimised for skateboard wheels.[15] And of course skateparks also offered a controlled social space free of outraged pool owners and patrolling police.

15 National Safety Council, *Skateboarding*, Chicago, 1978, p. 3; and *Thrasher*, June 1989, vol. 9, no. 6, pp. 53–8 and 127.

Skateparks and ramps thus provided a theatre, an arena for the display of skateboarding in which skateboarding and its body moves became partly spectacularised. This is immediately evident from the new moves that skateboarders invented within skateparks. At first this took the form of more extreme versions of the same moves, with aerials becoming larger, rising some two metres or higher out of the top of the pool or ramp wall. Aerials were also adapted to other variants, the most bewildering being the 'ollie' air, in which the skater flies out into a normal aerial, but this time without holding onto the board; here the aerial manoeuvre is performed entirely by controlled flight and balance, with a very delicate friction–weight–force relation between the skater's body, feet, board, and terrain below. Other, even more complicated and technical moves were also rapidly developed at the end of the 1970s and early 1980s, including 'invert' aerials, in which the skater performs what is in effect a one-handed hand stand out of the top of the pool, a 'layback', stretching their body off the back of the board and across the pool wall, held up by an outstretched arm, and a 'rock 'n roll', in which the skateboard is laid over the top of the wall, rocking like a see-saw before the skater turns and descends.

At the first 'Framed' series of architecture and film shown at the London RIBA Architecture Centre in 1996, film-maker and architect Patrick Keiller showed a short by Len Lye.[16] *Particles in Space* was created without camera or lens but by

16 RIBA Architecture Centre, London, 20 March 1996.

Iain Borden

Figure 11.3 *Jay Smith, Marina Del Rey skatepark, September 1979.* © *Glen E. Friedman. Source: Glen E. Friedman,* Fuck You Heroes: Glen E. Friedman Photographs, 1976–1991, *New York, Burning Flags Press, 1994.*

17 *Particles in Space* was made over three decades and finally finished in 1979.

scratching directly on to the film, and depicts a swarm of dots and lines pulsing on a black ground.[17] The resulting depiction of compression and tension, eruption and repetition, pulse and stillness, humour and gravity, lead Keiller to describe it as the most architectural-spatial film ever made. Although devoid of any 'architectural' subject (there are no buildings, no drawings, no concepts – only the development of a sense of space), the Lye film does indeed manage to convey a sense of spatiality entirely missing from most other attempts at representing architecture's spatial character.

It is this exploration which lies within the skateboarder's complex spatial actions, using a series of front–back, left–right, up–down reversals and rotations, in combination with precise relations of board, hand/body and terrain, to generate an extraordinary movement and production of body-centric space.

18 Lefebvre, *Production of Space*, p. 170.

Before producing effects in the material realm (tools and objects), before producing itself by drawing nourishment from that realm, and before reproducing itself by generating other bodies, each living body is space and has its space.[18]

19 H. Weyl, *Symmetry*, Princeton, Princeton University Press, 1952; and Lefebvre, *Production of Space*, pp. 170–1.

20 Lefebvre, *Production of Space*, ch. 3 'Spatial Architectonics', pp. 169–228.

21 ibid., pp. 171–3.

As Lefebvre notes, following Hermann Weyl,[19] symmetries of all kinds exist in all manner of natural and non-natural phenomena, including – and especially – architecture and the body. In this context, the prepositional 'in' of Lye's title – *Particles in Space* – is wrong, for the space is entirely produced *by* that series of dots, in their movement and collective evolution. In the same way, the spatial architectonics of the skater, to use Lefebvre's body-centric terminology,[20] is a space produced *by* the skater, out of the dynamic intersection of body, board and terrain. This is the kind of space which Lefebvre describes as having 'properties' (dualities, symmetries, etc.) which come not from the mind or spirit, but from a particular occupation of space with particular 'genetic' production operations, in the same way that, for example, the relationship between nature and space in a shell or a spider's web is 'immediate' and independent from any external mediation of spirit, God or conscious design.[21]

22 Another relation of body-centric to architectural space concerns the traces and marks inscribed by the body in space, ibid., p. 174. This is dealt with in I. Borden, 'Another Pavement, Another Beach', in I. Borden, J. Kerr, J. Rendell and A. Pivaro (eds), *The Unknown City: Contesting Architecture and Social Space*, Wiley, forthcoming.

In this spatial production, space is produced outward from the body, centrifugally, then centripetally pulled back in. It is a gestural[22] and phenomenological space, a space of flow and action, of direct engagement with the terrain. In particular it involves the skater in an extremely precise engagement with the terrain underfoot, a temporal as well as spatial engagement simultaneously measured in the extensive run (the total range of moves and traverses made over a minute or so), and in micro-seconds and millimetres (the specific meeting of board, body and terrain). The skateboard itself becomes a tool-in-hand, mediating the body–terrain space. Indeed, within the act of skateboarding, the skateboard is less a piece of equipment and takes on more the character of a prosthetic device, an extension of the body as a kind of fifth limb, absorbed into and diffused inside the body–terrain encounter.

But the body is not the sole producer of space in a Leibnizian sense, in which 'absolute relative' space is waiting to be filled, and where a specific body is considered capable of defining space by gesture and movement.[23] Sensory-sensual space is, ultimately, simply a component in the construction of social spaces.[24] Body-centric productions of space are not purely sensorial; instead, the body produces its space dialectically with the production of architectural space.

> [T]here is an immediate relationship between the body and its space, between the body's deployment in space and its occupation of space [. . .] This is a truly remarkable relationship: the body with the energies at its disposal, the living body, creates or produces its own space; conversely, the laws of space, which is to say the laws of discrimination in space, also govern the living body and the deployment of its energies.[25]

What then is the nature of dialectical interaction with architecture? Given the body-centric nature of skateboarding space, it makes sense to consider this in relation to the operations of the skater's body, particularly their multi- and inter-sensory nature.

Architecture frequently operates as a kind of social mirror, forming a kind of Sartrean 'Other's look',[26] the user self-checking their identity and validity against a building or boundary.[27] For its part, modern architectural space in particular tends to ignore the space of the body.

> This modern space [is] the space of blank sheets of paper, drawing-boards, plans, sections, elevations, scale models, geometrical projections [. . .] It forgets that space does not consist in the projection of an intellectual representation, does not arise from the visible-readable realm, but that it is first of all heard (listened to) and enacted (through physical gestures and movements).[28]

In practices such as skateboarding, however, a process of resistance and re-creation occurs. The Sartrean look is not only returned, but architecture ceases to be purely the Other, and is instead absorbed into the body–board–terrain relation.

> Consciousness is being-towards-the-thing through the intermediary of the body.[29]

This process takes place through a very precise (although undoubtedly limited) questioning of architecture put forward by skateboarding. What is architectural form

23 Lefebvre, *Production of Space*, pp. 169–70.

24 ibid., p. 212.

25 ibid., p. 170.

26 J-P. Sartre, 'The Look', *Being and Nothingness: an Essay on Phenomenological Ontology*, London, Routledge, 1989, pp. 252–302. See also M. Jay, *Downcast Eyes: the Denigration of Vision in Twentieth-Century French Thought*, Berkeley, University of California Press, 1994, pp. 263–328.

27 M. Augé, *Non-Places: Introduction to an Anthropology of Supermodernity*, London, Verso, 1995, pp. 92 and 101–3; and I. Borden, 'Thick Edge: Architectural Boundaries and Spatial Flows', *Architectural Design*, special issue on 'Architecture and Anthropology', October 1996, pp. 84–7.

28 Lefebvre, *Production of Space*, p. 200.

29 M. Merleau-Ponty, 'The Spatiality of One's Own Body and Motility', *Phenomenology of Perception*, London, Routledge & Kegan Paul, 1962, pp. 138–9.

Iain Borden

for? To what purpose can it be put? What is the relation of ground, verticals, textures, surfaces? The skater's body and actions here interrogate architecture as another body in relation to its own demands and actions.

> Objects touch one another, feel, smell and hear one another. Then they contemplate one another with eye and gaze. One truly gets the impression that every shape in space, every spatial plane, constitutes a mirror and produces a mirage effect; that within each body the rest of the world is reflected, and referred back to, in an ever-renewed to-and-fro of reciprocal reflection, an interplay of shifting colours, lights and forms.[30]

30 Lefebvre, *Production of Space*, p. 183.

These questions are of course very phenomenal – unconcerned with historical or cultural purpose of architecture – but they are none the less single-minded and demanding in their line of attack. They also resist the intellectualisation[31] and 'logic of visualization'[32] implied by much architectural space, for skateboarding uses, beside intense vision, a highly developed responsivity of touch, sense, balance, hearing, posture, muscular control, strength, agility and fluidity by which to perform.

31 ibid., p. 200.

32 ibid., p. 98.

Much of this stems from the essentially dynamic nature of skateboarding. As both Maurice Merleau-Ponty and August Schmarsow noted, we tend, in particular, to express the relation of space to ourselves by imagining that we are in motion, using terms like 'extension', 'expanse' and 'direction', and measuring size by the movement of the body and the eye.

> [B]ecause movement is not limited to submitting passively to space and time, it actively assumes them.[33]

33 Merleau-Ponty, *Phenomenology of Perception*, p. 102.

> The spatial construct is a human creation and cannot confront the creative or appreciative subject as if it were a cold, crystallized form.[34]

34 A. Schmarsow, 'The Essence of Architectural Creation', *Empathy, Form and Space: Problems in German Aesthetics, 1873–1893*, Santa Monica, Getty Center for the History of Art and Humanities, 1994, p. 290.

Because skateboarding is both body-centric and motile, space is projected from the whole body (and not just the eye or the intellect); as well as being an engagement with the architecture, it does not ever assume that architecture is the dominant projector of space, but rather treats it as one projector of space that can be interpolated with another moving projection of space from the body.

> Architecture produces living bodies, each with its own distinctive traits. The animating principle of such a body, its presence, is neither visible nor legible as such, nor is it the object of any discourse, for it reproduces itself within those who use the space in

question, within their lived experience. Of that experience the tourist, the passive spectator, can grasp but a pale shadow.[35]

35 Lefebvre, *Production of Space*, p. 137.

In skateboarding, unlike the scopic-dependence of the tourist gaze, user and architecture are separate potential systems of projection, which then come together in the active performance of skateboarding to create a new spatial event, an *occupied* and *occupying* architecture. Architecture is at once erased and reborn in the phenomenal act of the skater's move.

But architecture is not the only space creatively destroyed in this process. The space of the body is equally reconstructed as a 'spatial body', subject to the various symmetries, interactions, planes, centres, peripheries and other determinants of space.[36] As Lefebvre clarifies from its ambiguous presence in Marx, the concept of appropriation – the modification of the natural to serve a group – comes to the fore in the context of space and this spatial body. We need to combine the pure mastery of dominated space with appropriated space, and to understand this recombination in relation to time, and to rhythms of time and life.[37] In particular this involves the body.

36 ibid., p. 195.

37 ibid., pp. 165–6.

38 ibid., pp. 166–7.

> *Dominated by overpowering forces, including a variety of brutal techniques and an extreme emphasis on visualization, the body fragments, abdicates responsibility for itself – in a word, disappropriates itself [. . .] Any revolutionary 'project' today, whether utopian or realistic, must, if it is to avoid hopeless banality, make the re-appropriation of the body, in association with the reappropriation of space, into a non-negotiable part of its agenda.*[38]

39 Kevin Thatcher, editor of *Thrasher* skateboard magazine, quoted in A. Keteyian, 'Chairman of the Board', *Sports Illustrated*, 24 November 1986, p. 48.

Skateboarding operates in this context, a partial glimpse in the society of the spectacle of a recovery of the body that resorts neither to the world-stage commercialism of professional sport (skateboarding is, perhaps, the only 'sports' activity whose practitioners actively campaigned for it *not* to be included in the Olympics),[39] the conscious artistic intellectualism of performance art,[40] nor the narcissistic 'mirroring body'[41] of such practices as body-building and consumer-shopping, obsessed with their surface and monadic, internalised world. In skateboarding, the body is treated neither as an image nor as commodifiable entity; more than anything, it is in the act of skating that the skater's body is constructed, born from the poetry of its intricate spatial distortions and from the rehearsal of its conflictual body–board–terrain events.

40 M. Carlson, *Performance: a Critical Introduction*, London, Routledge, 1996, pp. 101–3.

41 A. Frank, 'For a Sociology of the Body: an Analytical Review', in M. Featherstone, M. Hepworth and B. S. Turner (eds), *The Body: Social Process and Cultural Theory*, London, Sage, 1991, pp. 53–4 and 61–8. See also C. Shilling, *The Body and Social Theory*, London, Sage, 1993, pp. 95–7.

> *I am not in space and time, nor do I conceive space and time; I belong to them, my body combines with them and includes them.*[42]

42 Merleau-Ponty, *Phenomenology of Perception*, p. 140.

Iain Borden

43 ibid., p. 100. See also Lefebvre, *Production of Space*, pp. 42 and 363.

44 The terms and descriptions here are taken from Lefebvre, 'Twelfth Prelude: Towards a New Romanticism?', *Introduction to Modernity*, pp. 322–4.

45 H. Lefebvre, *Éléments de rythmanalyse. Introduction à la connaissance des rythmes*, Paris, Syllepse-Périscope, 1992; and Lefebvre, *Production of Space*, pp. 205–7. See also H. Lefebvre, *Writings on Cities*, Oxford, Blackwell, 1996, E. Kofman and E. Lebas (eds), pp. 217–40.

46 Lefebvre, *Everyday Life in the Modern World*, p. 20.

47 ibid., p. 4.

48 This, of course, is only part of the social and political character of skateboarding, which is considered in Borden, 'Another Pavement, Another Beach'.

The skater's body is an assertive act, constructed out of the activity of skateboarding performed in relation to architecture; as Merleau-Ponty describes it, the spatiality of the body is not an assemblage of points of stimuli, located in relation to other objects, a *spatiality of position*, but is presented to the self as an attitude directed towards a certain task, a *spatiality of situation*.[43]

In short, skateboarding is a destructive-absorptive-reproductive process of both body and architecture. Consequently its mode of spatial composition is very different to that of the dominant modes of discourse and production of architecture, replacing architecture's classicist mode with one of romanticism.[44] In place of the organised cosmos of architecture – classicism's cohesion, internalised hierarchies, imitation and balance – we have the waves, undulations, vibrations and oscillations of skateboarding's ludic procedures, suggesting conflict and contradiction, emotion, chaos and confusion, the internalisation of the external world within the self, spontaneity and the affective. Like Lefebvre's concept space of rhythmanalysis,[45] it is closer to the rhythms of music or the imagined spaces of poetry and literature than the sights of the visual arts, linking inner and outer life, body and architecture, action and meaning.[46] Like Joyce's 'festival of language, a delirium of words',[47] skateboarding is a festival of movement, a series of precise spatial-temporal actions rendered demented and deranged, and which ultimately destroys and recreates body and architecture together. This is super-architectural space.

THIRD TERRITORY: SPACES OF REPRESENTATION

So far consideration of skateboard performance has been mainly as a kind of pure activity, a spatial invention restricted to the confines of the skater's own body and the immediate terrain beneath. I turn here to focus on the problematic of the *integrated* nature of representations in skateboarding; through this process, the full performativity of the body, skateboard and architecture is played out.[48]

TECHNICAL IMAGES

Considering a skateboarder as an image or representation can be undertaken in two ways. First, and most obviously, this can be done through the technicity of the image as a published or projected medium. Originally, this took place in specialist skateboard magazines as photographs, using conventional still imagery. Particularly after the advent of skateparks in the late 1970s, skateboard photographers used new high-speed motor-drive technology to capture innovative moves. Photographers used wide-angle lenses to get close to the action, while also showing the skater in the context of the location (a side-effect was to often exaggerate the height and posture of skateboard moves). Images like these enabled skaters to both celebrate and to analyse what was going on.

Another technique, frequently used in low-light or indoor conditions, is the combination of flash photography with a slower shutter speed. This produces a sharp image of the skater overlaid onto their blurred movement across surrounding terrain. Although undoubtedly successful as dramatic composite images, they also expose the partial limitation of still photography with respect to time. As a technology which is based on the freezing of a singular moment, the photograph has a tendency to eradicate both the immediate time of movement of the event being captured, and also to dehistoricise the time of its location.[49] Although readily available in a large number of specialist magazines, such images are restricted by the limitations of the medium itself.

In response to this limitation, and to the inherently dynamic nature of skate-boarding, skateboarders commonly exploit the camcorder and video to capture and distribute skate moves. A large number of skate videos are now available, some as video magazines with skaters from all kinds of different locations, such as the American *411* or the English *Video-Log*, and some as elaborate manufacturer videos showcasing their own professional team skaters. The latter can also be very experimental and sophisticated in their forms of representation; for example, the *Ban This* video, made by Stacy Peralta for his Powell-Peralta company in 1989, manipulates such elaborate devices as tracked shots, skateboard-mounted cameras, special lighting, overlays, montage and high-design graphics.

The problem, however, for skateboarders is that the forms of distribution for these media – specialist magazines, commercial videos – are still very much closed access. Instead, it is increasingly the internet on which skaters are receiving and posting images. Over 130 sites range from commercial manufacturers and retail shops to professional 'digital magazines' like *Influx*[50] and *Heckler*,[51] to good college sites, like the *DansWORLD* site,[52] to skaters' own home pages, like the *B-Grrrl* site run by mostly female skaters in Melbourne,[53] or *Skate Geezer*, a site catering for older veteran skaters of the 1970s and early 1980s,[54] to the Usenet *alt.skateboard* site, with incessant conversation on a myriad of topics from how to perform tricks, equipment, phrases, the existence of god, general abuse, to (most popular of all) skate shoe design.[55] From these sites skaters obtain communication about skate moves ranging from the usual textual descriptions, representations using the ASCII character set, still photographs and movie clips. All these can be viewed on the screen or down-loaded. The internet also offers an easier chance for skaters to place their own material for

[49] For a more extended discussion of the problematic of photography, time and space in relation to architecture and the urban, see 'Strangely Familiar', special issue of *Scan*, Photographers' Gallery, London, 1996, vol. 1, no. 1.

[50] URL http://www.enternet.com/influx/, as accessed 7 February 1997.

[51] URL http://heckler.com/HomePage.html, as accessed 7 February 1997.

[52] URL http://web.cps.msu.edu/~dunhamda/dw/dansworld.html, as accessed 7 February 1997.

[53] URL http://netspace.net.au/~butta/butta1.htm, as accessed 7 February 1997.

[54] URL http://www.terraport.net/abrook/skategeezer.htm, as accessed 7 February 1997.

[55] A. Bender, *alt.skateboard* listing, as accessed 5 January 1997.

Iain Borden

global consumption. It is much simpler to post a photograph or movie clip onto an internet site than to publish in a commercial magazine or video; the internet allows skaters both to represent skateboarding, and to receive and distribute these representations worldwide.

LIVED REPRESENTATIONS

Describing these different kinds of imagery and distribution channels at some length discloses their emphatic presence within skateboarding. However, their importance does not lie in their quantity, for images *per se* are only an *apparent* stage of the representation process within the skateboarding production of space. Instead, we must introduce the second way of thinking about the image, realising that skateboarders use imagery less as pure image, and more as an integration and re-presentation of that imagery through skateboarding practice. The lived representation of skateboard images occurs when skaters undertake the moves themselves, reliving and re-producing photographs, video footage and the internet movie clips through the agency of their body. This needs to be taken apart in more detail.

Skaters perform moves. The predominant way in which a skateboarder perceives of their activity is as a set of moves performed within a sequence of such moves; on a ramp or in a skatepark pool, a skater might do say ten to thirty moves in a run lasting no more than a minute or so. The predominant self-identity for a skateboarder is then the number and kinds of moves they perform – the more difficult the moves a skater can do, the greater their achievement. It is not only a quantitative matter, however, and a number of factors also come in to play here, including the *style* in which the skater develops and performs. The refinement, elegance, fluidity, speed, apparent ease and, above all, *attitude* with which skaters perform moves is just as important as the fact that they can perform them at all, while, conversely, performing moves without style is frequently met with disdain.

56 M. Sinclair, interview, *SkateBoarder*, September 1979, vol. 2, no. 6, p. 32.

You can mix style and aggression together. A lot of people don't do it; they just mix aggression with tricks without the style.[56]

In purely quantitative terms, however, the move is the unit of exchange between skaters, and skaters spend much time poring over photographs in order to understand and acquire them.

57 J. Henderson, interview, *SkateBoarder*, September 1979, vol. 2, no. 6, p. 30.

We see a hot shot in the magazine, and we have to figure what went on before that.[57]

This process is analogous to the way consumers accumulate commodities and capitalists accumulate money, except that of course skateboard moves cannot be hoarded or invested – there is no bank for real moves, only the image bank of the photograph, film, video or internet – and to maintain ownership the skater must continually re-perform the move. Consequently, when skaters undertake a run, they are not so much performing an act of pure physical spontaneity, as reproducing through their body-actions the activity of skateboarding as it can be systematically codified, and understood, as a set of *produced* images.

This is a complex intersection of lived experience and mechanically reproduced imagery, in which the latter acts as a kind of mirror, not only reflecting the subject's image back to the subject but also extending a repetition/symmetry immanent to the body into space;[58] the mechanical image projects the skater both back to themselves, and to others. That both the image/reflection and the skater's own move are 'weightless' (in the case of image being the representation as pure image, and in the case of the skater being the momentary equilibrium of gravity and trajectory which the skate photograph frequently arrests) emphasises the fantastical nature of this projection in which the skater forever dreams – alongside the immediate phenomenal engagement with the terrain – their display to the eyes of other skaters. The 'reflection' is of course not coincident with the body of the skater, but merely *represents* it as something identical but at the same time 'radically other, radically different'.[59]

This is further complicated by the collective nature of skateboarding as a practice in which many skaters perform the same moves, and so act as mirrors both for themselves and others. Thus skaters' reproduction of themselves as images involves both the reproduction of themselves as a reflection of other skaters and, second, the reproduction and externalisation of that image as being exactly like others, but different again – they are the mirror for skate moves and other skaters; every time a skater performs a move, they are both reproducing themselves as themselves (seeing themselves do a move), themselves as other than themselves (seeing themselves in the role of others), and other skaters as themselves (they are the reflection of other skaters). The desire to enact the move and to have it reproduced is then the desire to be, at the same time, oneself, oneself as someone else, and all other skaters in oneself. And the process by which this occurs is the skate move as something simultaneously performed, mechanically-produced and imagined.

The skate move, like the mirror, does not then *constitute* the unity of the subject, but acts as means of disclosure of consciousness of the skater and their body.[60] The skateboard move is the projection of the self through the imaginary-and-real medium of the photograph; it is neither pure activity or image, but a lived image. The skateboard run (the combinatorial series of moves) is at once a communication,

58 Lefebvre, *Production of Space*, p. 182n14.

59 ibid., pp. 184–5.

60 ibid., p. 185.

Iain Borden

development and lived enactment of things such as the *Influx* digital journal, or Friedman photographs.

This has some interesting spatial effects, not least that, particularly in the context of internet imagery and communication, skaters continually oscillate between the very immediate physicality of their own bodies and a globally dispersed skate community. There are skateboarders today in just about every city around the world, such that when a skater from, say, London's Notting Hill talks about their immediate friends or community, they will frequently feel more in common, and have more contact or communication, with other skaters in Mexico City, Prague or Philadelphia than with other non-skaters in Notting Hill. And the way this community is knitted is through a continual exchange and re-experiencing of a lexicon of skate moves. The image becomes not only a locally lived but, simultaneously, a globally reproduced and exchanged phenomenon.

There are also two other, and somewhat different, roles of the image that should be considered. The first concerns the role of the photographer, for, as former skateboard editor and photographer Tim Leighton-Boyce points out, skateboard photography goes far beyond the technical exaggeration of space and temporality.[61] Skateboard photographers' employment of wide-angle lenses is near unique, having initially borrowed the technique from surf-photography where fish-eye lenses are often used by photographers in the water,[62] for in all other sports photography the main lens is the telephoto. In part skateboard photographers use wide-angles to emphasise locational context, but they also do so for a very different reason, to become a close participant in the scene; the optical characteristics of the wide-angle forces photographer and subject into a proximate spatial relationship, such that the photographer often leans over and projects the camera underneath or even within the orbit of the skater's body. At times this immediacy even becomes directly evidenced in the photograph itself: for example, one of Glen E. Friedman's earliest hardcore images of skateboarding – of Jay Adams in the Teardrop pool – shows his own foot at the base of the images, caught in the same frame as the explosive skater.[63] Friedman, the epitome of the involved reporter and artist, is not a distant observer, recording the action with an external gaze, but a participant, someone intimately – socially and spatially – connected to the activity in front of their lens.

The second concerns the image of the terrain in the particular context of the purpose-built skatepark. While everyday architecture is encountered as a natural given, the more spectacular forms of architecture, often those designed by named architects, are revered as much for their aura as for any particular encounter that we have had with them. The same may be applied to particular features of skateparks, which as given rather than found terrains are always invested with a conscious, representational

61 Conversation, 9 August 1996.

62 Glen E. Friedman, e-mail, 16 February 1997.

63 'Jay Adams, "Teardrop", West Los Angeles, California, October 1976', Friedman, *Fuck You Heroes*, first plate, unpaginated.

Figure 11.4 *Jay Adams,*
'Teardrop', October 1976. © Glen
E. Friedman. Source: Glen E.
Friedman, Fuck You Heroes: Glen
E. Friedman Photographs,
1976–1991, New York, Burning
Flags Press, 1994.

Iain Borden

quality; this is particularly the case with those special attraction features – often the centre-piece pool – with an (often deserved) reputation for difficulty and danger.

Particular elements of skateparks become invested with a spectacular life – the reputation of a facility such as Pipeline's Combi-Pool for example, invested it with an aura beyond the basic ground on which skaters skated. In undertaking a move in a place like the Combi-Pool, the skaters perceived themselves as much for their positioning within the image of the element as for the simple phenomenal interaction with a physical terrain. The move became perceived both individually and socially as not just, say, an ollie air, but as an ollie air in the Combi-Pool. This may in part explain the frequent territorialisation of skateparks, in which 'locals' claim and treat that skatepark, and in particular specific elements within it, as belonging to them, and consequently treating any strangers or outsiders with an attitude ranging from disdain to outright tribalised aggression. In such a process, locals see the element less as pure image, their intimate and repeated use of it having stripped it of its external aura (as known to outsiders, the image reproduced in magazines), and more as a known entity, re-invested with a character of their own construction. Through a long drawn-out and often painful intimacy built up over months and years with the element, they have an invested physical and emotional relationship with that element.

> *The deployment of the energy of living bodies in space is forever going beyond the life and death instincts and harmonizing them. Pain and pleasure, which are poorly distinguished in nature, become clearly discernible in (and thanks to) social space. Products, and a fortiori works, are destined to be enjoyed (once labour, a mixture of painful effort and the joy of creation, has been completed).[64]*

64 Lefebvre, *Production of Space*, p. 137.

Skaters give the element, and the element returns to them, a knowledge of each other. The incoming outsider, conversely, threatens to obstruct the intensive local use of the skatepark, getting in the way, and possibly even skating better. The arriving stranger is an interference and a potential rival.

The spectacular nature of skateparks creates the possibility for skaters to become dissatisfied with them, either becoming bored with skateparks as a whole, perhaps no longer providing the right kind of terrain, or rather because the element 'wins', creating a terrain that they cannot alternatively master or relate adequately to, either by themselves or in competition with others. Unlike the urban streets of the city itself, on which most skateboarding now takes place, the skatepark is always a *provided* terrain, a mental projection and representation of skateboard terrain, and so yields a peculiarly focused kind of terrain: its architecture is consciously and deliberately functional with regard to skateboarding.

This may be why some skaters prefer banks and more gentle skatepark terrains, partly because they do not represent the extreme challenge of the pool or half-pipe, and partly because they consequently appear to just be there, allowing skaters to reassume the position of creative adaptive user rather than compelled consumer. Here, like Lefebvre's description of speech and activity in the city, the play of the skater's adaptation of terrain comes to replace the legitimised, fashionable moves performed in skatepark pools and pipes.

> In the city speech will unify the scattered elements of social reality, functions and structures, disconnected space, compulsive time; the city will have its everyday life, but quotidianness will be banished [. . .] The city's uninhibited self-expression and creativity [. . .] will restore adaptation so that it prevails over compulsion and [. . .] so that play and games will be given their former significance.[65]

[65] Lefebvre, *Everyday Life in the Modern World*, pp. 190–1.

In this context, skateboarding is, despite the codification and routinisation of moves by name and repeated performance, a resistance to the reduction of the subject to alternatively either a purely mechanistic performer, mental entity or capitalist competitor. The dislike of skateparks by many skaters is also a resistance to the common practice in commercial skateparks of not only charging entrance fees but also imposing certain social standards, such as the requirement for safety equipment or a particular kind of behaviour. Such economic and social values run against the continual confrontational and anarchist tendency within skateboarding.

Instead of accepting codification and regulation, skaters enact a 'practical and fleshy body conceived of as a totality complete with spatial qualities (symmetries, asymmetries) and energetic properties (discharges, economies, waste)',[66] a 'practico-sensory totality'.[67] Skateboarding as a quantitative set of places and actions (moves, routes, routines, sites) is not only further invested with quantitative measures (size, height, distance, duration, speed) but also with qualitative measures (difficulty, complexity, innovation, surprise) and experiential conditions (noise, texture, sound, flow, touch, rhythm, space–time). Placed within the skater's imaginative absorption of the body–subject as an actively experienced and produced engagement with the terrain underfoot, already described above, this creates an inter-dependent relation of skater and terrain, each internalised within the other.

[66] Lefebvre, *Production of Space*, p. 61.

[67] ibid., p. 62.

> The 'other' is present, facing the ego: a body facing another body. The 'other' is impenetrable save through violence, or through love, as the object of expenditures of energy, of aggression or desire. Here external is also internal inasmuch as the 'other' is another body, a vulnerable flesh, an accessible symmetry.[68]

[68] ibid., p. 174.

Iain Borden

Architecture is both external and internal to skateboarding, its concrete presentness being at once the other and the accessible symmetry to the skateboarder's physical activity. Similarly, the architect as designer of built terrain is both the other to the skateboarder, and re-presented within the skateboarder, the creative act being transposed from the 'classicist' realm of balanced order into the 'romanticist' sphere of destabilised movements. Architecture is dissolved, recast, and re-materialised. Skateboarding is nothing less than a sensual, sensory, physical emotion and desire for one's own body in motion and engagement with the architectural and social other; a Ballardesque crash and rebirth of body and terrain.[69]

69 J. G. Ballard, *Crash*, London, Jonathan Cape, 1973.

Philip Tabor

striking home

THE TELEMATIC ASSAULT

ON IDENTITY

Certain ideas seem to crystallise with particular and lasting intensity in certain countries.[1] As far as the idea of home is concerned, the home of the home is the Netherlands. This idea's crystallisation might be dated to the first three-quarters of the seventeenth century, when the Dutch Netherlands amassed an unprecedented and unrivalled accumulation of capital, and emptied their purses into domestic space. Simon Schama, whose thesis on the psychology of the Dutch Golden Age I borrow to introduce this chapter, quotes a contemporary: 'in Amsterdam, and in some of the great cities of that small province . . . the generality of those that build there, lay out a greater proportion of their estates on the houses they dwell in than any people upon the earth'.[2]

HOME

A common post-Freudian speculation is that the infant is born unable to distinguish between itself and the world at large, and that its mental life is therefore non-spatial and decentred. But there comes a time, the so-called 'mirror stage', when the child develops the view that fundamentally the world is divided into two categories: he or she is Number One, the world out there is Number Two. Subject is distinguished from object, the self from the 'other'. Significantly, this self/other dualism is experienced as spatial – indeed, as the simplest geometric relationship, enclosure.

Recent research casts doubt on the theory that a newborn infant cannot distinguish between itself and the outside world, or that its inner life is non-spatial. After all, it has just had the greatest topological shock it will ever suffer, having burst from the fetal sac into the glare of exteriority. But, whether the self/other distinction happens before or after birth, the idea remains that the personal world has a basic spatiality, centred on the self, and that it comprises (a) an interior, where the self resides, and (b) an exterior.[3]

Separating the inside from the outside is a conceptual boundary, a picture-frame, an envelope, a skin. The primary metaphor is that the self's interior is the human body. This conceptual membrane is elastic. It can expand to enclose within the metaphorical interior: clothing, a car, a room of one's own, a house, a country, or perhaps some non-physical zone of personal operation. A house identified as the self is called 'home', a country identified as the self is called 'homeland'. Home is a surrogate for, and extension of, the self and the body. A sense of home, however you define it, is as important to self-identity as the persistence of personal memory.

The idea of the building as a body has recurred in architectural theory since Roman times. Burglary of a home often causes more distress than the objective loss deserves,

1 A version of this paper was given in November 1994 at the 'Doors of Perception: @ Home' conference, Amsterdam, organised by the Netherlands Design Institute and *Mediamatic* magazine.

2 Bernard de Mandeville, quoted in S. Schama, *The Embarrassment of Riches: An Interpretation of Dutch Culture in the Golden Age*, London, Fontana, 1988, p. 297, and in N. Bryson, *Looking at the Overlooked: Four Essays on Still Life Painting*, London, Reaktion, 1990, p. 103, in his discussion, to which I am indebted, of Dutch art and 'oversupply'.

3 C. Trevarthen, 'Infancy, Mind in', in Richard L. Gregory (ed.), *The Oxford Companion to the Mind*, Oxford and New York, Oxford University Press, 1987, p. 363: 'Recent research with infants [suggests that they] do not, at any stage, confuse themselves with objects "outside" nor do they fail to recognise that other persons are separate sources of motives and emotions.'

Philip Tabor

because it is experienced metaphorically as an assault on, a penetration of, the owner's body. A child draws his home: its windows are eyes, its door a mouth.

Unlike the house, in short, home is a subjective construct, a metaphor of the self and body. But its conceptual envelope is expandable to include any appropriated zone, geographical or mental. In the rest of this chapter the word 'home' always has this generic psychological meaning, although it may sometimes simultaneously refer also to the physical house or dwelling.

INTERIORS AND STILL-LIFES

The economic explanation for the seventeenth-century domestic spending spree is that the Netherlands had no collective economic sink, such as a royal court or princely church, to absorb their inflow of capital: faced with this 'embarrassment of riches', the Dutch poured their gold into their houses. But a familiar explanation in terms of national psychology also merits attention: the Netherlands, much of which lies below sea-level, have a perilously elastic envelope separating the homeland from sea, a condition which has impressed into the individual Dutch soul a paranoiac anxiety to defend an inhabited interior (the self) from a menacing exterior. If this conjecture has any truth, the literal house, as an emblem of inner personal tranquillity and security, would be well worth throwing money at.

This paranoia, if such it was, was distilled into cultural form by the stupendous pictures of domestic interiors of the time: one thinks especially of Pieter de Hooch and Johannes Vermeer. It is certainly astonishing how *interior* these interiors are. Much, perhaps most, previous painting had placed the action comfortably in the frame, leaving the viewer some distance outside the picture space, looking in. But these Dutch interiors extend to the frame like a photograph, drawing us into their intimacy and security.[4]

The generous windows depicted in these interiors, while admitting a light as clear and clean as the domestic space they wash, offer us oddly little glimpse, if any, of the world outside – almost as if the paintings on the wall had supplanted windows in their role as eyes looking out into the external world. These paintings on the walls might be interior scenes themselves, homely conversational groups, or still-lifes of earthenware pots and pewter platters. But some were very strange indeed: I refer to those extravagantly labour-intensive still-lifes by such as Pieter Claesz or Willem Kalf. These might show a vase of riotous flora, say, or the remnants of a feast – jugs, goblets half-full with wine, a creased tablecloth, a china plate of uneaten food, a spiral of lemon peel.[5]

4 M. Jay, *Downcast Eyes: The Denigration of Vision in Twentieth-Century French Thought*, Berkeley, Los Angeles and London, Univ. of California Press, 1994, pp. 60–2, discusses Svetlana Alpers' (*The Art of Describing: Dutch Art in the Seventeenth Century*, Chicago, University of Chicago Press, 1983) contrast between the interiority of Dutch painting and the perspectival 'distance' of 'southern' art; and notes (p. 132) the link made by Anne Hollander ('Moving pictures' in *Raritan*, 5: 3, Winter 1986, p. 100) between the increased interest in photography in the 1860s and the simultaneous revival of interest in Vermeer and his contemporaries.

5 Bryson, *Looking at the Overlooked*, pp. 108–9, discusses the contemporary cost of making and buying Dutch flower paintings, and (pp. 127–8) the disturbingly 'proximal', price-laden and exotic nature of the 'banquet-pieces'. R. Barthes, 'The world as object', in N. Bryson (ed.), *Calligram: Essays in New Art History from France*, Cambridge, Cambridge University Press, 1988, pp. 107–8, suggests that the 'sheen' of the still-lifes is 'to lubricate man's gaze amid his domain, to facilitate his daily business among objects whose riddle is dissolved'.

Philip Tabor

Figure 12.1 Johannes Vermeer,
Officer and Laughing Girl.
Copyright, The Frick Collection,
New York.

Philip Tabor

These give me the creeps. They have the gloss, the high production values, and the lascivious exposure of studio pornography. Their close-up gaze, their in-your-face intimacy, insists that we stroke the silk, taste the meat, smell the flowers – enjoy them bodily as possessions. They resemble television in their close-up intrusiveness, internal luminosity and shallow spatial depth. They also have an immersive vividness which electronic virtual reality only aspires to.

This simile is not too far-fetched. The still-life was then a new medium. It hung on the domestic wall like a screen and, as a phenomenon, related to previous, that is scenic, painting as television does to film. The type of glossy still-life I refer to was indeed literally *tele*-vision in that it depicted not home products but porcelain, glassware, fabrics and exotic botanical species newly imported from afar – from the Levant, say, the East Indies or China. Such still-lifes were also a sort of shopping channel, in that the cost of the things depicted, their exchange value, was an important part of the picture's message: the painting transformed objects into commodities.

INVASIONS

No actual home has all the attributes which define the ideal, the Platonic, Home. But home as an idea is the place of being, not doing – of ends, not the means to ends. It is a place of familial and moral value – not of monetary value. It is no place for the instrumental mentality, commerce or business (that is, masculine work). It is, moreover, a place of unmediated authenticity ('home truths' are truths bluntly and directly told) and therefore perhaps a country uncolonised by the 'empire of signs'. At home we can be true to ourselves: there is no need for show.[6]

So those glossy still-lifes represent a forced opening of a window, a puncturing of the skin protecting home from the outside world, an infection, a pollution of purity by danger, and an assault on homeliness by worldliness. Like the naval maps which also figure in the painted interiors, they represent an invasive penetration of a protected, largely feminine, domain by the external world of men and adventure. And, by representing monetary value and, by extension, the instrumental mentality, they symbolise the piping into the Faraday cage of home an untamed and threatening foreign energy. They are symptoms, in short, of the volatile imbalance, chronicled by Schama, in what he calls the seventeenth-century 'moral geography of the Dutch mind': a psychic unease, a blurring of self-identity, caused by a rocketing increase in available information and power.[7]

The parallel between the seventeenth-century experience and our own is obvious. The second half of our century has seen, in the advanced economies, a huge and quite

6 R. Barthes, *Empire of Signs*, London, Jonathan Cape, 1982, p. 107, claims that in Japan 'everything is habitat'. I (ab)use his title to describe the opposite condition.

7 Though not in these terms, Schama, *Embarrassment of Riches*, p. 389, discusses the Dutch tension between home and global commerce, and the allegorical virtues of housewifehood. The phrase 'moral geography . . .' is on p. 609.

Philip Tabor

221

Figure 12.2 *Richard Hamilton, Just What Is It That Makes Today's Homes So Different, So Appealing?, 1956. Copyright Richard Hamilton 1998. All rights reserved DACS.*

8 J. Meyrovitz, *No Sense of Place: The Impact of Electronic Media on Social Behavior*, New York and Oxford, Oxford University Press, 1986.

sudden enlargement of personal access to information and power. Starting with the phone, electronic media have cracked the dykes of home and admitted into it all that was traditionally excluded: impurity, worldiness, business, disrespect and instrumentality. Joshua Meyrowitz, for instance, has recorded in detail how the media, especially television, has changed American home life by breaching former barriers between community and privacy, subservience and authority, male and female, childhood and adulthood, leisure and work, and so on.[8]

Meyrovitz's study concentrated on the social effects. But quite as significant are the subjective inner responses, perhaps unconscious, to electronic media. Jean Baudrillard sees the media as an invasive virus, robbing life and meaning from the mental home constructed by humanity. '[T]his electronic encephalization,' he asserts,

Philip Tabor

'this miniaturization of circuits and of energy, this transistorization of the environment condemn to futility, to obsolescence and almost to obscenity, all that once constituted the stage of our lives. . . . [T]he presence of television', he continues, 'transforms our habitat into a kind of archaic, closed-off cell, into a vestige of human relations whose survival is highly questionable.'[9]

At the common sense level this apocalyptic rhetoric seems unjustified and hysterical: we should be able to take a few electronic gizmos into our homes without blubbing about it. Yet today, as in the seventeenth-century Netherlands, an informational wave beats against the hull and causes the cargo to shift uneasily below decks.

UNEASY DREAD

Although published in 1919, a much-studied essay by Freud throws light on our current situation. Its title, translated into English, is *The Uncanny*: the uneasy dread evoked by undefined and unlocated menace. In the original German it is *Das Unheimliche*, literally 'the unhomely'. One example of the uncanny/unhomely which Freud cites are 'doubts whether an apparently animate object is really alive; or conversely, whether a lifeless object [like an automaton] might not be in fact animate'.[10]

Machines threaten the home because, as I have suggested, the home is about ends themselves, not means to ends – whereas technology is by definition instrumental. In our electronic era, moreover, it is clear that the machines with which we crowd today's habitat are indeed lifeless but, growing ever more responsive and interactive, increasingly resemble pets – beasts which are domesticated (significant verb) into a category half-human, half-object.[11] And just as mechanical devices increasingly seem to be extensions of our body, so our mental attention seems increasingly monopolised and penetrated by media, particularly interactive media. Our collective imagination is haunted or exhilarated by the notion that in our home we copulate with machines, are becoming cyborgs, half-meat, half-metal: *Blade Runner*, *The Terminator*, *Robocop*.[12]

Freud also instances as typically uncanny the feeling that your self is divided, when you meet your double say – or, conversely, when two selves appear oddly unified, as in cases of apparent telepathy. The uncanny emerges, too, when statistical probability is violated, when for example everything repeatedly goes right for you so that the causal barrier, which normally divides the external world from inner thoughts and desires, threatens to disappear.[13] In our electronic era, again, those who spend a large proportion of their conscious life on the Net or navigating informatic space may be

9 J. Baudrillard, *The Ecstasy of Communication*, Brooklyn NY, Autonomedia Semiotext(e), 1988, pp. 17–18.

10 S. Freud, 'The uncanny', in J. Strachey and A. Dickson (eds), *The Penguin Freud Library, Vol. 14: Art and Literature*, Harmondsworth, Penguin, 1985, pp. 336–76; esp. p. 347 on automata. A. Vidler, *The Architectural Uncanny: Essays in the Modern Unhomely*, Cambridge Mass. and London, MIT Press, 1992, exposes the philosophically uncanny aspects of Modern and subsequent architecture and urbanism.

11 J. Baudrillard, *The Revenge of the Crystal: Selected Writings on the Modern Object and its Destiny, 1968–1983*, London and Concord Mass., Pluto, 1990, p. 46: 'Pets are a species intermediary between beings and objects.'

12 Films referred to in this chapter: Ridley Scott dir., *Blade Runner*, Warner, Ladd, Blade Runner Partnership, 1982; James Cameron dir., *The Terminator*, Orion, Hemdale, Western Pacific, 1984; Paul Verhoeven dir., *Robocop*, Rank, Orion, 1987; Steven Lisberger dir., *TRON*, Walt Disney, Lisberger-Kushner, 1982; Steven Spielberg dir., *Poltergeist*, MGM, SLM, 1982.

13 References in this and the next

Philip Tabor

paragraph are to Freud, 'The uncanny',
pp. 356, 358–60, 362.

prey, if only fleetingly and unconsciously, to feelings that barriers of identity are dissolving between selfhood and otherhood; that the mechanisms of resistance and causality, which had assured us we were separate from the outside world, no longer operate; that we float in a space outside the self.

According to Freud, then, some experiences (in our case, electronically-induced) evoke feelings of omniscience, omnipotence, disembodiment and decentredness which, at their most extreme, indicate clinical madness. Involuntarily and unconsciously they revive that infantile mental state before the inner and external worlds could be distinguished. What was long suppressed knocks like a risen corpse at the door of adult consciousness; the uncanny, the *Unheimliche*, erupts into our mental home and our self is sucked out through the breach to dissolve itself into the outside world.

Even if we discount the general Freudian thesis that the child is father to the man, and that suppression breeds disease, we can still recognise in this essay the syndrome of what might be called the 'telematic uncanny'. Electronic media have partly eroded not only social boundaries which previously divided individuals and families from society as a whole, but also some boundaries of the self which previously defined individual identity. Films are a good guide to collective angst, and several, *TRON* and *Poltergeist* for instance, depict people being sucked through a monitor or TV screen into a world in where they are no longer 'at home'.

COLLABORATION, RESISTANCE OR *ENTENTE*

How, then, do we respond to the telematic invasion of our literal or inner homes? Three possible strategies apply to all forms of invasion or attempted seduction. The first strategy is to lie back and enjoy it. The popular arts of recent times envision an entropic dystopia, an American homeland fouled by technological detritus, haunted by robots and cyborgs. Every interior is exposed to the exterior world, its commerce and its sign-system: spotlights from an airship advertising emigration to the Off-World pierce through the skylight of the Bradbury Building. There is no safe home: a replicant may suddenly smash his head through the wall at you: 'Time to die'.[14] That techno-despair and alienation exert such glamorous attraction confirms the view that the purpose of art is to reconcile us to the inevitable by accustoming us to the intolerable.

The second strategy against the home's invasion is to strengthen the walls, reinforce the dyke, and lock up your daughters; market researchers call it 'cocooning'. An extreme instance would be the Amish, the Pennsylvanian Anabaptists, who in 1909 banned the phone from the home – as they have since banned radio and TV, as well as

14 All references to Ridley Scott,
Blade Runner.

Philip Tabor

new technology like electricity and the internal combustion engine: this protects the home from external spiritual pollutants and reinforces the sacred separate identity of the community.[15] More usual, however, is to admit technology into the home but in familiar disguise: the electric lamp beneath its silken shade, for instance, or the dishwasher behind its oaken front panel. Software designers use similarly homely disguises (they prefer to call them 'metaphors'): the Magic-Cap (like the former eWorld) online system uses as its operating metaphor the geography of Hometown USA, for example, and the Hypercard manual reassures us that 'no matter what other cards and stacks you have, you always have home'.[16]

The problem with using a familiar metaphor to represent unfamiliar situations, as the Modern Movement designers and their nineteenth-century precursors realised, is that it is at least partly a lie. And the practical (rather than moral) defect of a lie is that, when situations change, new lies must be added to sustain the illusion. But the greater the number of lies, the more difficult it is to make them cohere. In a rapidly changing environment, then, the disguise or metaphor eventually collapses through incoherence.[17]

This justifies the third and strategic response to the invasion of the home: to let the walls fall, but build new ones further out, and learn to feel 'at home' in a broader world. Like Mother, early architectural Modernism argued that in the long run it is wiser to tell the truth. It believed that the twentieth-century home and city, the technology which builds them, and the lifestyles they accommodate, change constantly and irresistibly. So it is better to dump the old classical language of structural form, based on stone construction, as well as the hierarchical patterns of bourgeois living, and to devise a totally new and flexible language whose form neither conceals nor arbitrarily represents each new condition, but inherently reflects it.

A central element of this Modernist project seemed to be war against the home: Le Corbusier famously defined the house as a 'machine for living in'. The home was to be destroyed because collective lifestyles, being tested in revolutionary Russia, and the new technologies of electricity and glass, would together soon evict man from it. But home was not to be abolished, only replaced by a new 'home of Man' which would welcome the machine. Plate-glass architecture would not dissolve the dualisms which formerly separated private from public, inside from out, selfhood from otherhood. But it would redraw them more lightly, and further out. Humanity would inhabit a wider, windswept, more transparent home.[18]

This is echoed in the current dream of the universal networked community. The rhetoric of electronic utopianism is arcadian, and derives from Shakespeare filtered through Jefferson, Thoreau and Twain. It uses terms which glorify rootlessness: 'the informatic badlands', 'cybercowboys', 'telematic nomads' and so on. But settlement is

15 D. Zimmerman Umble, 'The Amish and the telephone: Resistance and reconstruction', in R. Silverstone and E. Hirsch (eds), *Consuming Technologies: Media and Information in Domestic Spaces*, London, New York, Routledge, 1994, pp. 193–4.

16 Online data services: Magic-Cap, General Magic Inc., Mountainview Calif., 1994; eWorld, Apple Computer Inc., Bridgeton MO, 1994. Apple Computer Inc., *Macintosh Hypercard User's Guide*, Cupertino CA, 1987, p. 48.

17 I caricature here the historical arguments for structural, constructional and functional 'honesty' in architecture. Fuller but ideologically contrasting accounts are: P. Collins, *Changing Ideals in Modern Architecture 1750–1950*, London, Faber, 1965, esp. chs 18–19; D. Watkin, *Morality in Architecture: The Development of a Theme in Architectural History and Theory from the Gothic Revival to the Modern Movement*, Oxford, Clarendon, 1977.

18 Le Corbusier, *Towards a New Architecture*, London, Rodker, 1927, p. 10. Le Corbusier and F. Pierrefeu, *The Home of Man*, London, Architectural Press, 1940.

Philip Tabor

19 L. Marx, *The Machine in the Garden: Technology and the Pastoral Ideal in America*, New York, Oxford University Press, 1964, traces the arcadian theme through American literary history. S. Bukatman, *Terminal Identity: The Virtual Subject in Postmodern Science Fiction*, Durham NC and London, Duke University Press, 1993, p. 145, briefly reports its link with 'hyper-technologized space'. H. Rheingold, *The Virtual Community: Homesteading on the Electronic Frontier*, Reading Mass., Addison-Wesley, 1993.

20 W. Gibson, *Neuromancer*, London, Grafton, 1986, p. 67.

21 M. Pawley, *Theory and Design in the Second Machine Age*, Oxford and Cambridge Mass., Blackwell, 1990, pp. 114–15.

never far behind: Howard Rheingold's book, *The Virtual Community*, is subtitled *Homesteading on the Electronic Frontier*.[19]

REVELATIONS

What shall we see when we look through the open windows of our electronic homestead? Most predictions are that we shall see luminous representations of data – however sophisticated and complex. This view even informs imaginative fiction: William Gibson's *Neuromancer* famously defines cyberspace as 'a consensual hallucination. . . . A graphic *representation of data* abstracted from the banks of every computer in the human system' [my italics].[20] This definition reflects a widespread view that mental activity is primarily about the reception, decoding, evaluation, transformation and output of information, and that the main purpose of new electronic technologies is to make information-handling more powerful, efficient, vivid, sexy, and so on.

An episode of architectural history may indicate why this view is mistaken. The architecture critic Martin Pawley recently described the Gothic cathedral as an archetype of 'information architecture'. Its structural system relieves the building's external skin of load-bearing duties, which allows the walls to take on an informational function: most of the cathedral's skin can comprise vast (and vastly expensive) backlit glass screens. The screens – mosaics of coloured glass pixels – display images, icons and alphabetic strings, which together the user 'reads' to learn the complex codes and narratives of Christian cosmology. Pawley calls Gothic cathedrals the 'predecessors of the paperless office and the electronic dealing room', implying that the windows communicate data – albeit of an elevated, spiritual kind. His thesis is thus an update of the traditional view that the Gothic cathedral is 'the poor man's bible'.[21]

This ingenious thesis, though true, tells the least important part of the story. For we know from contemporary writings that Gothic ecclesiastical architecture was explicitly invented and designed to carry into built form the vigorous blend of theology and philosophy, Scholasticism, particularly associated with St Bonaventure and St Thomas Aquinas. Scholastic metaphysics classified light as a substance, an 'embodied spirit', which distributes divinity to all God's creation. God is present in all things, argued Bonaventure, because light emanates from even the humblest material: glass is made from sand and ashes, fire comes from coal, you rub a stone and it shines. Scholasticism was far from philistine or iconoclastic, but it had a strong subjective aspect which valued communion more highly than the reading of words and images: revelation more highly than information. And light was the main vehicle of revelation: St

Philip Tabor

Bernard of Clairvaux described union with God as 'immersion in the infinite ocean of eternal light and luminous eternity'.[22]

Such luminous revelation was no vague psychedelic dazzle. For medieval thinkers agreed with modern psychologists that the senses are not just passive receptors of stimuli but have an active and immediate rationality of their own. Light could communicate directly to the intellect. The sanctuary door at the abbey of St Denis, for example, shone in gilded bronze, and its inscription urged the pilgrim 'to let its luminous brightness illuminate the mind so that it might ascend "to the true light to which Christ is the door"'. So the Gothic cathedral was designed to be literally divine, as immaterial and as luminous as possible. Architecture was to be as ethereal as electronic phenomena. Through the stained-glass windows Divinity radiated more through light as essence than through the images depicted on the windows. Light's primary role was performative. The medium was the message.[23]

Marshall McLuhan claimed of course that electronic media are returning us to a medieval, pre-Gutenberg mentality. Much recent art, design, movies and fiction, certainly, has the poetic and abstract qualities associated with medieval culture: sublimeness, grotesqueness, and artificiality. Like the medieval mind we are fascinated by fragmentation, complexity, translucency, layering – and things which, jewel-like, glitter and glow. We are all Gothic now.[24]

WINDOWS

Every home needs windows, perhaps electronic windows, into the world. But we look through those windows or screens neither just to take in or give out information, nor just for instrumental motives. Everybody needs to keep an eye, a window, on the world to reassure the self that it differs from the world and thus to reinforce the self's identity. Prisoners or patients permanently confined indoors want to know what the weather's doing, though this knowledge is of no practical use at all. Similarly, the amount of hard data broadcast by TV news programmes is remarkably small, and what little there is seldom affects our actions, but we seem to need at least twice-daily fixes of it.

Modern culture has for a long time believed that information is best communicated through words and numerals. Lately have we accepted, rather grudgingly, that visual images might transmit data equally powerfully. But if a large part of what is transmitted and absorbed is not information at all, but light as an essence, triggering some mental alteration, those working in computer media may need to downgrade the importance they have only recently conferred on images and icons. Perhaps, for example, the search for virtual reality overemphasises the need for figurativeness, indeed for reality

[22] My quick sketch, in this and the next two paragraphs, of the varied, complex philosophical foundations of the Gothic style derives from: O. von Simson, *The Gothic Cathedral: Origins of Gothic Architecture and the Medieval Concept of Order*, Princeton, Princeton University Press, 1984, pp. 51–2, 114, 123; and E. Panofsky, *Gothic Architecture and Scholasticism*, Latrobe PA, Archabbey, 1951, pp. 12–15, 37–8. M. McLuhan, *The Gutenberg Galaxy: The Making of Typographic Man*, London, Routledge & Kegan Paul, 1962, pp. 105–7, quotes Panofsky and Von Simson to assert the non-textual, revelatory aspects of pre-typographic 'light through, not light on'.

[23] The title of ch. 1 of M. McLuhan, *Understanding Media: The Extensions of Man*, New York, New American Library, pp. 23–35.

[24] A minor but striking example is the pictorial similarity between the medieval illuminated manuscript – combining text and jewel-like, many-scaled images and icons – and the multi-media screen.

Philip Tabor

at all. To become so fixated on image-borne data as a vehicle for purposive communication might lead us to forget the potential of the computing media for direct revelation through abstract light, colour and sensory immersion generally.

This abstractly immersive mode can be traced back in painting at least to J. M. W. Turner or, say, Frederick Church, the American Luminist. They responded differently to emergent technology: Turner enhaloed steam engines and smokestacks in hazy glory, while the Luminists radiantly memorialised a virgin nature threatened by industrialisation and modern transportation. But all invited their viewers, through the blessing of light, to transcend their fragmented modernity and thus regain a unified, panoramic and sublime world-view. Continuing this transcendentalist tradition, Mark Rothko's paintings, ambiguously defined blocks of colour which appear to glow and shimmer, allude explicitly to the meditative potential of abstract luminosity. So does an artist much influenced by Rothko, James Turrell, who describes his work thus: 'It's not about light or a record of it, but it is light. Light is not so much something that reveals, as it is itself the revelation.'[25]

25 J. Turrell, *Mapping Spaces*, New York, Peter Blum Editions, 1987.

Significantly, to achieve their transcendentalist aims, the work of both Rothko and Turrell tends towards the condition of the electronic screen and of architecture. Both deal in fictions, indeed illusions: Rothko aims to make immobile paint seem to shimmer, Turrell to make light appear as solid plane or volume. And both enclose the spectators' bodies to control the limits of their vision: Rothko by arranging sets of paintings around them, Turrell by constructing darkened interiors or artificial horizons to the sky.

This suggests an alternative response to the electronic invasion of domestic space: to welcome it in but radically change its character. In their current 'informational' role, the telematic media are sleepless, fidgety, and demanding. They are, in a precise sense, 'uncanny' in that they threaten the frontiers of selfhood. And they discourage that mental state of still coherence – achieved when we stare into a flame, gaze idly from a window, or watch shadows lengthen – which rebuilds the self.

Here, then, is a role for the architects of space and of software. To make that mental state easier to achieve, architecture (too long obsessed with its iconography) could borrow the luminous, vaporous splendour of the electronic screen. The electronic screen, in exchange, could borrow from architectural space its revelatory abstraction, its ability to register the flow of daily and seasonal time, and its capacity to cup light, like liquid, in its hand. Then, when the screen pours light over us like the pearly glow of Vermeer's interiors or the jewelled radiance of the Gothic cathedrals, we would not be reading but communing with it. We would be looking without needing to see.

Philip Tabor

doing it, (un)doing it, (over)doing it yourself

RHETORICS OF ARCHITECTURAL

ABUSE

In a love affair most seek an eternal homeland. Others, but very few, eternal voyaging.
These latter are melancholics, for whom contact with mother earth is to be shunned.
They seek the person who will keep far from them the homeland's sadness. To that
person they remain faithful.[1]

1 W. Benjamin, *One Way Street*, London,
Verso, 1992, p. 75.

DOING IT

I was taught the right way to do architecture. I was taught how to make things stand up. I was also told the amazing story of architecture, of how architects did architecture all on their own. As if by magic, they imagined architecture, and then, with minimal fuss, and certainly no mess, they made it, whole and perfect pieces of it – just like in their dreams. After they had made it, there was nothing to do, but dream some more and make some more.

2 Le Corbusier, *Towards a New Architecture*, London, The Architectural Press, 1985, p. 17.

The Architect, by his arrangement of forms, realizes an order which is a pure creation of his spirit.[2]

I was also told that architects were important people, very important people, the most important people in the building trade. For architects, the building trade can be used metaphorically – to refer to the world.

(UN)DOING IT

For a while I swallowed this simple and straightforward story. But then I started to get suspicious, and thought there might be a twist to the tale. I thought the twist most likely involved those busy architects, dreaming and making, dreaming and making, dreaming and making . . . those busy architects who did not bother about the architecture once it was made, unless other people started doing things with it. These other people, the 'non-architects', were not to be trusted. They were involved in subversive activities which resulted in hideous and frightening things – they were attempting to (un)make architecture, to (un)do it completely, making it almost as silly as themselves. There was only one way to deal with this threat to architecture – ridicule. I went along with this – poking fun at their monstrous (un)doings worked a treat. Although occasionally I could have sworn that I had been involved in some (un)doings myself.

But then one day, in Moscow, something strange happened. I visited Mr Melnikov's house – a symphony of great architectural geometry. A safe haven I thought – no silliness here. But, in the marital bedroom, the very place which Mr Melnikov shared with his wife and two children, Mrs Melnikov had gathered together all kinds of decorative trappings, ornaments and lace, funny old beds and chairs, and, with complete disregard to her esteemed husband's dreamings and makings, she had made a mess. This was architecture (un)done.

Jane Rendell

If you dig beneath the surface then you discover the unexpected. This process can reintroduce the city to the urban dweller, offering an opportunity to discover something new, and through their own agendas and perspectives find a new mapping and a new way of thinking about cities. The strange becomes familiar and the familiar becomes strange.[3]

3 I. Borden, J. Kerr, A. Pivaro and J. Rendell (eds), *Strangely Familiar: Narratives of Architecture in the City,* London, Routledge, 1995, p. 9.

(Un)doing architecture made sweet disorder.

(OVER)DOING IT

My interest in Mrs Melnikov's Soviet bric-à-brac resulted in an architectural awakening, of sorts. My own architectural undoing did not pass unnoticed. But no-one thought it clever, least of all me. As an architect looking for work, celebrating the charmed and charming places created by non-architects was not clever.

Through telling new stories, the unknown, undiscovered city can be laid open to critical scrutiny, to new urban practices, new urban subversions. . . . The agenda is radical in its intent, but I would like to suggest that the unknown is not so easily known – indeed, it may be all too visible, right in front of our eyes, buried into the infrastructures of everyday lives, so intrinsic we hardly even feel their presence anymore. And when we do, do we really want to know?[4]

4 S. Pile, 'The Un(known) City . . . or, an urban geography of what lies beneath the surface', in I. Borden, J. Kerr, A. Pivaro and J. Rendell (eds), *The Unknown City: Contesting Architecture and Social Space,* Chichester, John Wiley, forthcoming.

OCCUPIED TERRITORIES

But I've been (over)doing it. Let's start again. The architectural profession – the institution which protects the role of architects – encourages us to think of architecture in a certain way. The architectural profession insists that the real stuff of architecture consists of the bits which architects do. (Some of these bits are real enough to touch – walls, roofs, floors, bricks, timbers, tiles.) As architects, it is essential that we remain true to this ideal real structure, and ensure that we, and only we, do things our way. For architectural practice to sustain itself, doing architecture must be a privileged activity, carried out by certain people, at certain times and in certain ways – architecture is an occupied territory, occupied by architecture.

Jane Rendell

5 T. T. Minh-Ha, *When the Moon Waxes Red: Representation, Gender and Cultural Politics*, London, Routledge, 1991, p. 227.

The waning of the hegemonic professional ethos is a necessary condition for the emergence of new relationships and complex forms of repressed subjectivities.[5]

But we all know that architects are not the only doers of architecture. Most obviously, architecture is physically made by builders, and long after the building has been made the non-architects continuously do architecture. When we, as non-architects occupy a space, when we start to use it, we start to 'do-it-ourselves'. But we do this in an already occupied territory, where the activity of doing architecture has been classified and claimed by architects. The rules have already been established; rules about site and space; about permanence, structure and stability; about the relation of form and function, the design of details, the installation of services, the arrangement of furniture and the application of decoration. Other people cannot do architecture, their activities can only be categorised as (un)doing or (over)doing it. We also find that there are people occupying the territory as both users and architects – the territory is starting to get over-occupied.

OVER-OCCUPIED TERRITORIES

The (un)doing of architecture though use, and the (over)doing of architecture through critically attending to such abuse, creates rather dense territories of occupation. We need to think critically:

6 ibid., p. 229.

Critical work is made to fare on interstitial ground . . . critical strategies must be developed within a range of diversely occupied territories where the temptation to grant any single territory transcendent status is continually resisted.[6]

Thinking about time can help to redefine the territorial occupations of doing and using. The design and production of the building up to so-called 'completion', constitutes only a small part of architectural time. But instead we should consider architectural time as encompassing the use, re-use, destruction and decay of spaces and building components. New temporalities, ones which go beyond the construction of a set of pre-designed drawings, can also be created through consumption. Through consumption, the traditional logic of need, which requires the architect to design for perceived use, can be upset. Through the purchase of commodified buildings and fittings by the user, one set of territorial occupations can be undone. Consumption can be taken to be a simple economic act of buying and selling, but it can also be looked

Jane Rendell

at from a symbolic point of view. Goods represent social values. Consuming, acquiring goods, is a means of gaining a certain social status and constructing a corresponding social identity. The occupation and consumption of architecture reinforces who we think we are and who we would like to be.

> *What am I going to do with my theories, all so pretty, so agile, and so theoretical. . . . All my more and more perfect theories, my shuttles and my rockets, my machines rivalling in precision, wit, and temerity the toughest research brains, all the champion theories I have so carefully shaped, with such satisfaction, all of them.*[7]

7 H. Cixous, *The Book of Promethea*, Lincoln, University of Nebraska Press, 1991, p. 6.

Houses are by far the most expensive commodities which we buy. The houses we choose to live in, and the way we choose to live in them, distinguishes us from others by emphasising difference and/or by maximising similarity. Our choices are limited by all sorts of factors – by our gender, class, race, age, mobility, but not least by our internal desires. Nowhere do these desires resonate more spatially than in the place we call 'home'.

> *Home is that place which enables and promotes varied and everchanging perspectives, a place where one discovers new ways of seeing reality, frontiers of difference.*[8]

8 b. hooks, *Yearnings: Race, Gender, and Cultural Politics*, London, Turnaround Press, 1989, p. 148.

OVER-OCCUPIED TERRITORIES, OR, HOMELANDS

On a leafy street in Clapham, minutes from the common, is a terraced house which was my home for two years. Scattered all over London, all over England, all over the world, are other homes, houses where I once lived. In some still standing, I return and revisit past lives and loves. Others have been destroyed, physically crushed in military coups, or erased from conscious memory only to be revisited in dreams.

> *Of course places can be home, but they do not have to be thought of in that way, nor do they have to be places of nostalgia. You may, indeed, have many of them.*[9]

9 D. Massey, *Space, Place and Gender*, Cambridge, Polity Press, 1994, p. 172.

In all the places I have lived I recognise parts of myself, my body in parts, but this particular house represents something very special to me. It was, and still is, a spiritual home. Its spaces echo my attempts to resist the domination of social systems, like patriarchy and capitalism. The ever changing, neglected and decaying fabric of my home and its strangely disparate and changing occupants challenged stultifying

10 I. Eberhardt, *The Passionate Nomad: The Diary of Isabelle Eberhardt*, Boston, Beacon Press, 1988, p. 36.

domestic ideologies, offering a way of living which had nothing to do with comfort, security, safety and permanence.

> *Perhaps the strange side of my nature can be summed up in a single trait: the need to keep searching, come what may, for new events, and flee inertia and stagnation.*[10]

Through its fragile structure this house physically embraced my need for transiency, and it was perhaps this unhomeliness, which made it feel more like home to me than any other. This home, and the friend I shared it with, showed me, what I can only call 'the rhetorics of architectural abuse' (a term borrowed from Pierre Bourdieu, and abused).

THE RHETORICS OF USE

11 P. Bourdieu, *Distinction: A Social Critique of the Judgement of Taste*, Cambridge, Harvard University Press, 1984.

According to Bourdieu, the social construction of identity and patterns of lifestyles and consumption can be explained through the 'social dynamics of negative distinction'.[11] The display of status symbols is as important as their possession. Distinctions are created not just through buying more goods, but by creating ever more subtle distinctions, by playing with an existing 'vocabulary' of material signs through the development of a 'rhetoric' of use. Distinct social identities of resistance and difference can be represented through the use (and re-use) of space and materials. Particular kinds of occupational activities develop different rhetorics of architectural use, some reinforce dominant modes of spatial behaviour, others choose to resist them. One of the causes, but also the consequences, of social comparison through distinction, is desire. Desiring creatures transgress the boundaries of natural needs. 'Desiring Practices'[12] resist conventional ways of thinking about architecture, a 'desiring practice' undoes architecture: it is a form of architectural abuse.

12 D. McCorquodale, K. Ruedi and Sarah Wigglesworth (eds), *Desiring Practices: Architecture, Gender and the Interdisciplinary*, London, Black Dog Publishing Limited, 1996.

THE RHETORICS OF ARCHITECTURAL ABUSE

The doing, (un)doing, (over)doing of 'home', transgress architectural and social definitions of domestic space and time, implying blissful and dangerous notions of disorder and impermanence. These spatial and temporal rhetorics of use are strategies of resistance. They stem from a desire to challenge ideas, within architectural practice and integral to patriarchal and capitalist society, about the ways we occupy and inhabit space. Paralleling feminist and socialist critiques, the spatial

Jane Rendell

rhetorics of use in this house in which I once lived, challenged, through alternative forms of occupying territory, the ways architects do architecture. Here making space meant taking it apart, doing-it-yourself meant both undoing it and overdoing it. These are rhetorics of architectural abuse.

> Spaces can be real and imagined. Spaces can tell stories and unfold histories. Spaces can be interrupted, appropriated, and transformed through literary and artistic practices. As Pratibha Parma notes, 'The appropriation and use of space are political acts'.[13]

13 hooks, op. cit., p. 152.

BORROWING NOT BUYING

Squatting is an activity which resists property ownership and chooses to occupy without buying. It involves the use of premises without permission, without wishing, or being able, to pay rent. Squatting questions issues of purchase, property and occupation. Squatters may use places in ways that may differ from the original design intention. The occupation of places through squatting is more transitory than other forms of residence. Connections are easy to make with moving homes, barges and boats, buses and vans, but here, although the home may not be tied to one specific place, the relationship of occupier and place is often one of ownership.

London has not had many urban squatters. The attitude of English property owners towards squatters is very different, for example, to the regime of 'repressive tolerance'[14] Edward Soja has described in encounters between the authorities and the squatting communities of Amsterdam. David Carr-Smith gives an intense account of the 'architecture of psycho-physical effects'[15] in the squats of Amsterdam's dockland community, Edel Weiss, KNSM and Silo, conjuring up spaces of real physical danger but also of real physical community. In London empty buildings stay empty, the homeless remain on the street. It is in other cities that these places are inhabited, in other cities where there are communities of squatters. But other cities are strange to us and so hold more utopian appeal.

> Cities new to us are full of promise. Unlike promises we make to each other, the promise of the city can never be broken. But like the promise we hold for each other, neither can it be fulfilled.[16]

In Amsterdam, Silo is to be converted to luxury apartments. The squats, ad hoc bars and cafés in east Berlin which I spent time in just after the wall had come down are

14 Edward Soja, 'The Stimulus of a Little Confusion: On Spiustraat, Amsterdam', in I. Borden, J. Kerr, A. Pivaro and J. Rendell (eds), *Strangely Familiar: Narratives of Architecture in the City*, London, Routledge, 1995, p. 30.

15 D. Carr-Smith, *Silo: An Architecture of Psycho-Physical Effects* (unpublished paper).

16 V. Burgin, *Some Cities*, London, Reaktion Books, 1996, p. 7.

Jane Rendell

now permanent fixtures. Squatters may occupy marginal spaces through social circumstance or political aspiration, but it is important not to over romanticise. Squatters are not always lovely people. My mother's family home was squatted, they ripped tiles from the floors, plants from the garden, timbers from the floor to make fires. Some of the squatters I have known did not live an easy co-existence with each other, let alone the wider community. In north London, the occupation of abandoned houses scheduled for demolition due to road building plans, resulted in rising tensions. Rival gangs, who protected and controlled the rights to certain properties, emerged, resolving disputes over territory through violence. Problems of exclusion, of poverty, and the physical hardship of living without decent heating, lighting and sanitation cannot be overlooked.

17 Massey, op. cit., p. 169.

The identity of a place does not derive from some internalized history. It derives, in large part, precisely from the specificity of its interactions with 'the outside'.[17]

REFUSING RENT

Many of the houses on the street where I lived had, up until the time I came to be there, been squatted. Gradually they were bought by respectable families, repaired and restored. The woman who owned the house where I lived, refused to accept rent. Although her house (my home) was quite large, five stories including the space directly under the roof, she preferred to live frugally off her pension, in two first floor rooms. She had shared these rooms with her sister, for a short while with her sister's dead body, but most recently she was alone. Although her presence filled the house in a physical way, her occupation was predominantly psychic. She lived in a world just beyond the everyday, where spirits controlled the use of space.

18 C. Clément, *The Weary Sons of Freud*, London, Verso, 1987, p. 58.

To regress, that is, to step out of daily life, to be recognised as mentally ill – pure paradise.[18]

These spirits, which she called, 'the powers that be', decided on home improvement plans and DIY. The 'powers' were not very adept in the material world, their decisions were made at random and often for no apparent reason. The plans they made concerning the rearrangement of large pieces of furniture occurred nightly, and they could order unwanted objects out at any time. Plumbing, electrical installation and general household maintenance followed their erratic management systems. The 'powers' refused offers of council money for repairs – this would only have disturbed

Jane Rendell

the natural karma of decay. Following this schema, rent money was also rejected – after all what could you do with money?

> *The gift has no goal. No for. And no object. The gift – is given. Before any division into donor and recipient. Before any separate identities of giver and receiver. Even before that gift.*[19]

19 L. Irigaray, *Elemental Passions*, London, The Athlone Press, 1992, p. 73.

SHARED SPACE

My home challenged conventional ideas about property ownership and renting, and also shed some light on the problem of shared spaces in domestic life. This house was home to quite a number – friends and strangers – all people who, in their own ways, set themselves outside conventional codes of living. Two young children, with their mother, then their father, and finally joined by the mother's lover, lived in the basement. Nearby they ran a ramshackle restaurant selling pulse and rice dishes and some obscure, mainly south American, beers. Once a year, the kids plus the restaurant were moved to Glastonbury. Two young women, to whom I smiled but rarely spoke, lived on the ground floor, and most recently two homeless young Polish men moved in. Most of the time, we lived in a pleasant, though remote, harmony. But there have also been conflicts, and a number of vicious attempts to wrest control of the property.

I lived on the top floor with my friend. He was the one who originally discovered the house, derelict with a pigeons' graveyard in the roof. *He* was the one who did and (un)did it, who made it home for *me*.

> *She entered the book. She entered the pages of the book as a vagrant steals into an empty house, or a deserted garden.*[20]

20 S. Germain, *The Weeping Woman on the Streets of Prague*, Sawtree, Cambridgeshire, Dedalus, 1993, p. 27.

There was a garden, not so much deserted as intermittently habited. It changed according to season and in relation to the attentiveness of the occupants. Sometimes vegetable stripes cut through the tangle of lengthening grass, rotting armchairs, rusting bicycles, abandoned 'Fisher Price' toys and sad old Mexican hammocks pining for the Caribbean. There were other shared spaces, in between places. Coming in off the street you entered the hallway.

> *Doors*
> *banged.*
> *He entered,*
> *sprayed by the street's gaiety.*[21]

21 V. Mayakovsky, *The Bedbug and Selected Poetry*, London, Weidenfeld and Nicolson, 1961, p. 129.

Jane Rendell

The hallway was sad and shabby, as any other communal hallway. Naively generous in their financial decisions, the 'powers' were strict about hygiene. Daily, they demanded that the staircase was cleaned with a powerful detergent. Any dirt or dust on the steps, the handrail, the intermittent patches of orange and brown lino was to be stripped away. Despite this intense domestic labour, the hallway was an interstitial space which to me, still smells of neglect.

22 P. MacNaghten and J. Urry, Contested Natures, London, Sage, 1997, p. 14.

What thus needs investigation are the diverse 'smellscapes' which organise and mobilise our feelings about particular places (including what one might also call 'tastescapes'). The concept of smellscape effectively brings out how smells are spatially ordered and place-related. In particular, the olfactory sense seems particularly important in evoking memories of very specific places.[22]

Everything flapped, the front door on its broken hinges, the letter box until its flap got lost, the streamers of dark white wallpaper and me. I flapped when the lock, which always needed fixing, bothered me. I'm not good with locks, nor with tools. I found it best to watch and wait and see what happened. Unclaimed papers piled up (fast). Dust accumulated (incredibly fast). Wood rotted (slowly). No-one broke in (as far as I noticed).

'LIVING ON THE EDGE'

Squatting can say things about the construction of identity, the display of a distinct social status in relation to conventional lifestyles. Architecture too can speak of the desire to be different. Desiring difference means doing architecture differently, intentionally (un)doing and (over)doing it. Often it is those trained as architects, but who feel they do not fit in, who challenge most purposefully, through their everyday inhabitation of the occupied territories of architecture, traditional ways of designing and making spaces. In search of their own identity, through their desire to do it differently, they refuse standardised rules, the principles of structure, services, construction and detailing, and resist ideologies concerning functionalism, space division and decoration.

Spaces evolve through more amorphous living arrangements, the placing of boundaries which re-negotiate the conventional divisions of public and private domesticity – privacy and secrecy are rethought with reference to bodily wastes and pleasures – *secretive display*. Standard details and materials are questioned. Services are installed in a way which challenges institutional codes and ideals of low maintenance and instead opts for a high degree of strenuous user involvement – *form follows*. . . . Structural elements, such as timber members and walls, are taken as superfluous extras, whilst decorative features fulfil the roles of construction – *de-stabilising structures*. Collection, scavenging, recycling and bricolage, bizarre hybrids of junk shops and designer pieces, replace buying goods for the sake of it and buying goods only to be used in specific ways – *wandering objects*. Temporality is redefined, subjects and objects are linked through non-specific uses and random juxtapositioning, as fluid spatial processes – *wandering subjects*.

Distinction is constructed through a self-conscious and eccentric relationship with architectural principles and components. Designs are never fit for the purposes they were intended, form never follows function. This means living and using space in often contradictory and difficult ways, ways which follow the trajectory of the artist as bohemian, outsider or tortured soul. Notions of architecture as the other who completes the self are rejected.

The loss of the other here too brings the implosion of the self. The other has been necessary as text, lover and life-blood. The performance of identity has been dependent on a partner who acts both as accomplice and audience. In his/her absence, the mask falls and the self is no longer clothed in her identity and his desire.[23]

23 E. Wilson (ed.), *Sexuality and Masquerade: the Dedalus Book of Sexual Ambiguity*, Sawtree, Cambridgeshire, Dedalus, 1996, p. 25.

The simple pleasures of commodity consumption are ripe for elaboration. 'Texas Homecare' and other (sub)urban sheds (on circular roads around towns) offer a satisfying Sunday afternoon solution to the malaise of house proud home-owners. These week-end picnic spots are veritable bazaars, jammed full of purpose-made tools and a glittering array of easy-fit, ready-to-fit, components which slip soporifically into domestic bliss. The bricoleur is a home-maker who finds new uses for found objects and, with defunct tools, collages them randomly into space. The bricoleur does DIY differently. Doing it differently desires the (un)doing of the commercialisation and commodification of traditional DIY. It is a spatial practice which signifies an act of resistance, which attempts to establish identity by celebrating difference.

SECRETIVE DISPLAY

Living space is usually divided up according to a number of social conventions about domestic life, where sleeping is divided from playing, playing from living, living from eating, eating from cooking, cooking from shitting, shitting from sleeping, and so on. Every activity has its compartment, mapping and defining social relations very precisely

Jane Rendell

in space. In my home the boundaries which control and contain public and private activities were intentionally blurred and transgressed.

24 D. Levy, *Swallowing Geography*, London, Jonathan Cape Ltd, 1993, p. 73.

A border is an undefined margin between two things, sanity and insanity, for example. It is an edge. To be marginal is to be not fully defined.[24]

The bath sat in the centre of the roof space. The roof space was bedroom, workroom and living room, and many other places all at once. From the bath you could look up into the sky, and down into the toilet, or directly onto the stove, beyond it to those eating at the table, and further through the window into the street. The beauty of lying in the bath and being able to talk to the person lying in bed next to you, or downstairs to the person preparing food in the kitchen, showed to me the importance of rethinking the kinds of divisions of spaces which we so readily accept.

25 L. Aragon, *Paris Peasant*, Boston, Exact Change, 1994, p. 53.

At the baths, a very different kind of temperament tends towards dangerous daydreams: a twofold mythical feeling that is quite inexpressible comes to the surface. First, there is the sense of intimacy in the very centre of a very public place, a powerful contrast that remains effective for any one who has once experienced it; secondly, there is this taste for confusion which is a characteristic of the sense, and which leads them to divert every object from its accepted usage, to pervert it as the saying goes.[25]

Some New York and more recent London 'loft style' developments completely miss the point – the excitement of living in huge places is about using them differently. Why else would you want to sleep in a foundry? In new loft living everything is re-compartmentalised for you, but in my home, walls were removed rather than built. This was not to enable the free flow of pure space as in the modernist open plan, but rather to intensify the occupation of space by overlaying one kind of living over another – the way the place should have been used, with its (un)doing. We might call this a new mapping of domestic space, a questioning of the boundaries of bodies and places. Architecture is soft like a body if you (un)do it.

26 Charles Baudelaire quoted in E. K. Kaplan, *Baudelaire's Prose Poems*, Athens, University of Georgia Press, 1990, p. 27.

A room that resembles a reverie, a truly spiritual room, where the stagnant atmosphere is lightly tinged with pink and blue. Here the soul takes a bath of laziness, perfumed with regret and desire. – Something like twilight, bluish and pinkish; a dream of voluptuous pleasure during an eclipse.[26]

Sitting on the toilet is probably the most private activity that takes place at home, the one place where we do expect a degree of privacy from prying eyes, ears, noses. All these expectations were contradicted. The door was spliced like a swing door in a saloon bar. This tiny deep blue room had no ceiling, it opened directly to the roof space. To flush the toilet, you placed your hand through a smooth circular hole in the wall out into the stairwell, where you grabbed a wooden spoon hanging from the ceiling on a rope. Bare bottomed in an intimate and private space, your arm was extended into a public void, as if raised in greeting to a visitor. Coming up the stairs to the front door, searching for the door knob, your hands would meet fingers wrapped around a spoon.

> . . . space is broad, teeming with possibilities, positions, intersections, passages, detours, U-turns, dead ends, one-way streets. Too many possibilities indeed.[27]

27 W. Benjamin, *One Way Street*, London, Verso, 1992.

FORM FOLLOWS . . .

To do architecture we play by certain institutionalised codes – planning and building regulations, for example. To use architecture we follow these rules – we attach appliances in the right way, we sort out the plumbing as we are told we should. The most immediate work carried out by my friend, which made the spaces inhabitable, involved installing toilets, gas appliances, electricity, and so on. This it seemed had been done in a straightforward way. But I soon learnt that everything was of a quirky nature, sometimes following rules of simplicity rather than those of artifice. The soil pipe gushed diagonally through the stairwell and out of the rear wall of the house. In other homes it would have been hidden; but here it was proud feature of the hallway.

> However difficult, I must live out my theory of limiting one's needs.[28]

28 I. Eberhardt, *The Passionate Nomad: The Diary of Isabelle Eberhardt*, Boston, Beacon Press, 1988, p. 14.

In other cases, rules had been grasped in order to be undone. In the same way that ideas about danger and safety were challenged, so too were ideas about structure and decoration, purpose and utility. Treating structural fabric as surface, as malleable and mouldable, meant the place was decorated by the cracking of the brickwork, and the revealing of rubble over a hundred years old contained between the splintering timber battens and studs of the partition walls. On the ceiling, jagged metal rivets worked to hold the old and decrepit plaster together, at night they shone like stars.

Jane Rendell

DE-STABILISING STRUCTURES

To occupy the roof as a habitable space, a truss had been removed. There were only three and this was the central one. To connect the two floor levels, the second floor and the roof space, a huge hole was cut out of the ceiling. There were structural implications, not least the fact that the roof space had not been designed for occupation, nor for bathing.

But danger was a driving force. The removal of structural members from the roof and the ceiling, the stripping back of partition walls to reveal the studwork – all decreased the stability of the house but allowed a myriad of potential interconnections.

> *She may go anywhere and everywhere, gaining entrance wherever she chooses; she sails through walls as easily as through tree-trunks or the piers of bridges. No material is an obstacle for her, neither stones, nor iron, nor wood, nor steel can impede her progress or hold back her step. For her, all matter has the fluidity of water.*[29]

29 Germain, op. cit., p. 27.

Asserting the fabric of the building as a living component of the space meant interacting closely with materials, existing in a state of close symbiosis with inanimate objects. It meant existing in the time of decay. Architecture, normally solid and dependable, here was transient, lacking in permanence, incapable of providing us with reliable shelter – architecture as fragile as we were. We existed in the time of a house whose walls were falling out. We survived on trust.

30 R. M. Rilke, *Letters to a Young Poet*, New York, Vintage Books, 1986, p. 92.

> *And only if we arrange our life in accordance with the principle which tells us that we must always trust in the difficult, then what now appears to us as the most alien will become our most intimate and trusted experience.*[30]

Challenging the propriety of structure questions the ordered comforts of domestic routine, but also starts to tip the balance of safety and danger. Life lived with unstable physical materials becomes fraught with physical danger. Compared to the terrifyingly dangerous environments of the Silo homes described by Carr-Smith this was child's play. Compared to the risks some people have to take daily this was a farce. But this life was still a challenge, a challenge to the way we occupy space and to the social relationships we take for granted. It was a rejection of comfort and laziness. There was no room for complacency. You felt your own body in every moment of occupation. Using architecture felt like an *écriture feminine* – a writing from, and on, the body. The ladder to the upper floor was far too short, it had missing rungs, and in one place a

Jane Rendell

thick piece of sharp cold iron. Vertical movement, especially at night, took place as a series of jolts and slipped footings.

> Admitting that writing is precisely working (in) the in-between, examining the process of the same and the other without which nothing lives, undoing the work of death, is first of all wanting two and both, one and the other together; not frozen in sequences of struggle and expulsion or other forms of killing, but made infinitely dynamic by a ceaseless exchanging between one and the other different subject, getting acquainted and beginning only from the living border of the other; a many-sided and inexhaustible course with thousands of meetings and transformations of the same in the other and in the in-between, from which a woman takes her forms.[31]

31 H. Cixous, *The Laugh of the Medusa*, London, Harvester, 1981, p. 46.

One morning I awoke to a horrible crash and scream; a friend unfamiliar with the intricacies of the household, had missed her step and fallen three metres to the kitchen floor below. Her head narrowly missed the cast iron stove. She spent months in hospital.

> Most people have (with the help of conventions) turned their solutions toward what is easy and toward the easiest side of the easy; but it is clear that we must trust in what is difficult; everything alive trusts in it.[32]

32 R. M. Rilke, *Letters to a Young Poet*, New York, Vintage Books, 1986, pp. 68–9.

Trusting in the difficult, was proving emotionally too difficult. I moved on shortly afterwards.

WANDERING OBJECTS

Chopping into timber joists with no respect for structural forces challenges laws of physics, laws which go beyond the definition of the relationship of architect and user. Sometimes doing things in non-conventional ways is madness. But there are other rules which we follow for no good reason. As users we adhere to all kinds of codes in architectural territory just because we are told to do so. We buy and use spaces, we buy and use objects, in the ways they were designed, for certain purposes, with no intention of using them for anything else.

The house was heated by open fires. But terrified of the rusting circular-saw lying in its wood pile lair (an assortment of deck chairs) in the garden, improvisation was called for. Nightly, I carried the fire from one room to another in a large baking tray, puzzling over myths of the campfire as the original organising feature of social space.

Jane Rendell

33 Levy, op. cit., p. 72.

*Each new journey is a mourning for what has been left behind. The wanderer some-
times tries to recreate what has been left behind, in a new place.*[33]

Servicing elements, usually fixed, certainly in function, often in space, were given
flexibility. The spaces themselves functioned flexibly. Using the attic as a bathroom is
not perhaps a radical mis-use of space, but coming home to a kitchen performing as a
public café was more surprising. A limited number of possessions provided a catalyst
to achieve this degree of flexibility through transformation. In a matter of days, a
table had gone from being the crowded focus of a lively drunken evening, to being
rearranged as a number of smaller tables as in a restaurant, to framing candle-lit icons
to be sold in a Saturday street market. At last it was left to blaze in the grate on a
particularly cold night. This shifting relation between spaces and their potential
utilities produced a continuous sense of doubt and uncertainty. You could never be sure
exactly what something was and what it was not. This heightened my awareness of the
ever-changing nature of static objects. Settled things can be wanderers too.

34 ibid., p. 69.

*She is the wanderer, bum, émigré, refugee, deportee, rambler, strolling player.
Sometimes she would like to be a settler, but curiosity, grief and disaffection
forbid it.*[34]

Deciding just how and when to use an object in a certain way provokes interesting
questions. At what point does a piece of furniture become firewood? The same
questions apply to the (re)use of other people's waste. Re-using products can be a
matter of economics – it can save money. The roof was lined with newspaper; this was
cheaper, less of a pollutant, but less effective and rather more of a fire hazard than
standard insulation. Re-using objects for traditional purposes involved finding specific
items. Only in an area like Clapham where there were pockets of wealthy inhabitants
could fine furnishings be found abandoned in the street; rugs, three piece suites, four
poster beds, washing machines, tables, duvets. My friend had a detailed knowledge of
the geography of the local skips. Re-using waste relied on availability but also on
plentiful scavenging time and the fertile imagination required to create the new uses.
But when objects had no fixed relation to their potential use, then the task of the finder
was more demanding. The finder, my companion, had a remarkable gift for this kind of
search.

35 A. Breton, *Mad Love*, Lincoln,
University of Nebraska Press, 1987,
p. 15.

*You only have to know how to get along in the labyrinth. Interpretive delirium begins
when man, ill-prepared, is taken by a sudden fear in the forest of symbols.*[35]

Combining objects derived from many sources compares to postmodern inter-
textuality, the weaving of quotations. Placing found objects in new contexts encourages
us to make connections we would not normally make. Everyday items become
lively, animate and communicate in new ways. In his account of the Silo, Carr-Smith
describes in great detail this, the 'psychic' life of objects. Designer condoms in brown
paper jackets rested comfortably on the mantle piece, next to an Italian gelatine mix
and three steel tart cutters. The imagination creates these fluid relationships, rejecting
the constraints imposed by rules of domestic order where 'everything has its place'.
The dividing line between messiness and tidiness is blurred. Inside is outside. The
seams are the decor.

> In any case, what is delightful here is the dissimilarity itself between the object wished
> for and the object found. Thus trouvaille, whether it be artistic, scientific, philosophic,
> or as useless as anything, is enough to undo the beauty of everything beside it. In it
> alone we recognize the marvellous precipitate of desire.[36]

36 ibid., pp. 14–15.

Placing things and bodies in unusual combinations, positions us in new uncharted
territory. Lost in space, our cognitive mapping devices de-stabilised, we imagine a new
poetics of space and time. We understand anew the world we occupy, the relations
between dreams and realities, between mental life and social relations, between
objects and subjects. This space–time is unlimited, it is not stagnant with the
inscriptions of specific and expected responses. Such potentiality opposes the auto-
cratic architect's pompous regimes of mono-functionality and also rejects the banality
of highly flexible multi-purpose spaces designed for anything (but nothing) to happen in.
The accidental and continually shifting juxtaposition of apparently unconnected things
produces a density of interpretation. The layering of different daily patterns of
understanding and using invoke architectural time as transient. There is no moment of
completion, rather you are aware everyday of the continually widening cracks, the
disintegration of the building fabric, the shifting spaces and roles of the furniture
contained within them. Links are made between real objects, real and imagined
objects, and real and imagined subjects – dreams are lived, lives are dreamt.

> It is only by making evident the intimate relation linking the two terms real and imagi-
> nary that I hope to break down the distinction, which seems to me less and less well
> founded, between the subjective and the objective.[37]

37 ibid., p. 55.

Jane Rendell

WANDERING SUBJECTS

Although economics determines much of the recycling of waste, so too does a desire to subvert the system of consumption and to transgress the logics of economics. A decision to cut a number of roof lights for starlit baths meant waiting. We waited through a few winters, finely tuning the exact design details and spending the money we saved to buy the expensive components.

> *The separation of art and life, so peculiar to the West, has been violently denounced since the beginning of the century in all artistic domains. To live and not to imitate – this necessity which has become a keyword in all intellectual circles, seems nevertheless to have suffered the unchanging destiny of ideas which remain at the level of a concept.*[38]

38 Minh-Ha, op. cit., p. 135.

We stapled and re-stapled blue plastic sheets over the twin holes, but the wind blew in and rain water dripped onto the edge of my bed. Still, the sky was a blissful *fantasy blue*. Finally, glass sheets were laid to rest directly on slim timber linings rising just proud of the roof slates and the sky was revealed un-obscured and *incredibly blue*. Elegant steel yachting hooks and rope delicately attached the glass to the frame, carrying through in the details the transparency from inside to outside. But alas too delicately for bathing *en plein air*. Lifted to allow in balmy air on a sunny morning, one pane shattered directly into the soapy water narrowly missing a tender skinned bather. We had many disagreements about the unsuitability of nautical details for domestic requirements. Finally I threatened to (re)do it, to buy a 'Velux' roof light, possibly from 'Texas Homecare'.

39 ibid., p. 137.

> *Undoing, doing, and redoing interact mutually in their dispersion and continuity.*[39]

For my friend, his living patterns were formulated through his habitual re-occupation of architecture. His rhetorics of architectural abuse were strategies of resistance. By performing DIY through the undoing of architecture his home expressed a desire to be different. But a point had been reached where the forms created followed anything but function – had we been overdoing it? Doing it, then (un)doing it and finally (over)doing it . . .

Jane Rendell

INDEX

Note: Page numbers in *italic* type refer to illustrations.